THE PAST AS PRESENT

THE INDIA LIST

THE PAST AS PRESENT

Forging Contemporary Identities Through History

ROMILA THAPAR

Seagull Books

This book is for the youngest ones I know—Hamir, Safik, Amrit and Sujan—in the hope that when on becoming adults they read it, it may help them to decide on what is worth protecting in their heritage.

Seagull Books, 2019

Printed in arrangement with Aleph Book Company

First published in India by Aleph Book Company, 2014

This edition is not for sale in the Indian subcontinent (India, Pakistan, Sri Lanka, Bangladesh, Bhutan, Myanmar and the Maldives).

ISBN 978 0 8574 2 644 4

British Library Cataloguing-in-Publication Data
A catalogue record for this book is available from the British Library

Printed and bound by Hyam Enterprises, Calcutta, India

CONTENTS

A NOTE ON TERMS USED IN THIS TEXT

Hindus

The word Hindu as the name of a religion does not occur in Indian sources until quite late in about the fourteenth century AD. The term 'dharma' was used in an ethical sense and not as the name of a religion. The edicts of the Mauryan Emperor Ashoka (third century BC) refer to various religious sects and mention the two broad groups as bamanashramanam—brahmanas and shramanas (from Buddhist and Jaina monks). This form is also given by the Greek Megasthenes who writes about Mauryan India, and refers to those associated with religion as consisting of two groups, the Brachmanes and the Sarmanes. The mention of these continues into later times as for example in the grammar of Patanjali who mentions the two and their opposition to each other. Al-Biruni writing in the eleventh century refers again to the brahmans and the shamaniyyas. Possibly by now the latter category may have included a variety of other heterodox sects. The two were not rigid religious identities but covered a range of sects in varying degrees of agreement and disagreement.

What is of interest in the history of the term Hindu, is that its origin lies in its being a geographical name. It goes back to references to Sindhu, the Indo-Aryan/Vedic Sanskrit name for the Indus river. When the Indus region and the north-western borderlands became part of the Achaemenid Empire of Iran in the mid-first millennium BC, this area was referred to in Achaemenid inscriptions as Gandara and Hin[d] ush, the Indo-Aryan 's' changing to 'h' in Old Persian. The Indo-Greeks referred to the river as Indos. Subsequent to this the Arabs referred to this area and that beyond the Indus, as al-Hind, and the people came to be called Hindu.

The geographical identity of the term Hindu remained current until about the fourteenth century when gradually the name came to be applied to all those who lived in al-Hind but were not Muslims. The entire range of non-Muslims came to be termed Hindus. The distinction between brahmanas and shramanas begins to fade.

The colonial view of religion in India differentiated between Islam which they were familiar with from the Crusades and as the religion of west Asia, and the Hindus that were more diverse and less familiar. So the sects of the Hindus were brought under a single umbrella and this was labeled Hinduism.

Some scholars of the history of Hinduism would trace it back to the Indus Civilization but little is known for sure about this. Suggestions have been made some of which link it to the later religion and some do not. Once the pictograms are deciphered then there might be more knowledge about the religion of this civilization and whether it forms a prior history of the later religion.

The known history of the Hindu religion begins with Vedic Brahmanism from the late second millennium BC and winds its way through a variety of sects, belief systems and ritual practices to the present. It is therefore not possible to date it precisely. Jainism, Buddhism, Christianity and Islam, were all founded at a particular point in time, by a historical person. This makes them different from Hinduism.

Vedic Age

Historians regard the Vedic age as the age when the *Vedas* were composed and recorded. The generally accepted time bracket ranges from about 1500 BC to 600 BC. The *Rigveda* was composed in the period from 1500 to 1000 BC and was compiled and edited thereafter. The other three *Vedas*—the *Sama*, *Yajur* and *Atharva*—date to the period after 1000 BC. This was also the period when technical works on grammar, etymology and phonetics were composed.

Indus Civilization

Cultures of the Indus plain and the north-western borderlands of the sub-continent, that evolved from agro-pastoralism and agrarian settlements gave rise to city cultures such as those of Harappa and Mohenjo-daro, in both these areas in the early third millennium BC. The early stages are traced to sites in Baluchistan such as Pirak and Mehrgarh and to Kot Diji and Mundigak in the borderlands. There is in this area an archaeological record of a gradual evolution towards urbanism. Attempts have been made to suggest that there was an earlier evolution of cities in the Cholistan area of southern Punjab in Pakistan, on the now extinct Hakra river which some have identified with the extinct Sarasvati. Hence the occasional use of the label Indus-Sarasvati Civilization. However the evidence for this suggested earlier beginning is not generally accepted. The Hakra disappeared in the early second millennium BC and the identity of the Sarasvati with the present-day Ghaggar is uncertain. There is also the problem that the Haraxvati in the Helmand area of Seistan in Afghanistan, neighbouring Baluchistan and northeastern Iran, could as well have been the river referred to in the early *Rigveda*. Given the interchange of the 's' sound with the 'h' sound, the Old Iranian Haraxvati would have been rendered as Sarasvati in Indo-Aryan.

Harappa Culture

Archaeological cultures are sometimes named after the first site discovered of a particular culture. In the case of the city-based Indus Civilization, excavations at Harappa were among the earliest. Therefore the cities are sometimes referred to as those of the Harappa Culture.

Vedic People

This label is sometimes used when referring to the people who are thought to have created the culture encapsulated in the Vedic texts or Vedic Corpus. It is not the most precise term as the span of the Corpus covers a millennium. With the discovery of various archaeological cultures in northern India during the period from 1500-500 BC, the mapping of the different cultures is becoming a little clearer. This discourages the use of a blanket term that does not differentiate between the cultures.

Ancient Aryans

The term Aryan is often used casually to mean many things. Initially it referred to people who spoke and used a particular language, namely, Indo-Aryan. By extension it sometimes included those who observed a recognizable cultural pattern in their social relations—the caste system, and who in their belief systems were generally in agreement with views propounded in the Vedic Corpus. Aryan is not a race. However the application of the label underwent changes in the course of history and came to refer to various other categories and groups.

PREFACE

On 15 August 1947 I was in the last year of school in Pune. The entire school, the parents of the students and other well-wishers were invited for the celebration. The principal had told me that I would have to lower the Union Jack, raise the Indian flag in its place, plant a sapling, and make a short speech. I had spent sleepless nights wondering what I should say in my short speech and was terrified of addressing a public audience—a discomfort that I have always had. Planting the sapling was fun. Raising the Indian flag was an intensely emotional moment, given that so much political drama had been played out in Pune during the 1940s and some of us had made it a point to rush from school in the late afternoon to attend Gandhiji's prayer meetings during periods when he was out of prison. But the toughest was the speech and the more I consulted my friends, teachers and parents, the more confused I became. Finally I decided that I would only address the question of what I was anticipating as a young Indian after independence.

And that was something fairly simple, reflecting the thoughts of most Indians at that time. It revolved around two intertwined themes: one was that now that we were getting the opportunity of constructing a free society what form should such a society take, and tied into this was the need to know what our identity as a people was. Now that I think back on it I feel that these two themes have hovered in my mind throughout my life. Researching one's own culture and society as I have done implies enquiring into social and cultural identities in the past and such enquiry is inevitably an interface with the present. I have over the years of my research been struck by the frequency with which the present makes use of the past either in a detrimental manner where it becomes a part of various political ploys, or alternatively in a positive manner to claim an enviable legitimacy and inheritance.

The essays in this book encapsulate my thoughts on certain themes that I have written and spoken about for half a century. The themes pertain largely to the way history has been used in contemporary times, particularly in what has become the debate on Indian identity. The interpretations of Indian history have changed, especially in the late twentieth century. The earlier focus on political and dynastic history has been vastly broadened to include many facets of social, economic and cultural history. These have led to new questions particularly pertinent to the issue of how a nation formulates its identity. My endorsement of this identity has been an insistence that it be the identity of the Indian citizen, over and above religious community and caste. This has of course met with opposition from those for whom the identity politics of religion and caste are primary.

I have explained in some of the essays why the communal interpretation of Indian history where Hindu and Muslim communities are seen only as religious groups—invariably antagonistic—has been replaced by a more analytical way of investigating the relations between communities, going back to pre-Islamic times. Those who argue that the earliest inhabitants of the subcontinent were Aryans and that Vedic culture is the foundational culture of India, have problems in accepting the new analyses of early history where the role of other cultures has been registered. The controversies have extended to much more than this. They have included the modern readings of the epics, and the need to accept variant forms of the *Ramayana* that have existed since at least two thousand years. Another theme that has become significant in recent decades is that of the status of women in the past and how that relates to attitudes towards women in the present. The existing mindset that claims to draw from the past needs to be understood in more than historical terms. But if at least the history could be explained without being blurred, it would help change the mindset.

It seems to me that what makes the essays especially pertinent is that the ideas contained in many of them were first formulated at a time when not only the discipline of history but the broader structure of education was changing from a colonial foundation to a system associated with a liberal and secular democratic society and intellectual explorations of various kinds. Changes in educational structures seem often to have fallen by the wayside, but the change in the discipline of history has been effective, and has illumined many new areas of the past. Such change is of course never completed since this exploration is a continuous process of ideas evolving from the past and conditioned by the present. This in part accounts for the hesitancy of some to recognize the changes in virtually every discipline.

My ideas today are not substantially different from what they were a few decades ago although the emphasis on nuances may differ. I must confess that in re-reading the essays in order to revise them, I was saddened that the issues remain contentious and our movement towards a solution seems distant. But perhaps this may be just my impatience. The noticeable decline in liberal values is disturbing, especially as fewer and fewer persons appear concerned about this decline. My generation grew up on the cusp of independence, with confidence in the new society that was to come soon after. But what has come is not the society we had anticipated. The substratum message of these essays is that despite the events of the last quarter century, hopefully, one day that society can emerge. My intention in publishing these essays however, is that the reading public will be acquainted with some of the ideas and controversies that we work with as historians, and to familiarize a larger readership with the kinds of questions and investigations that we are pursuing. However, the essays are all based on research that I have done on various themes. For those interested in following up on this research, I have included a bibliography of my writing.

Some of the essays in the book examine how a particular issue was dealt with over a period of time—this is the reason the reader will sometimes find more than one essay on a subject. I have arranged and introduced the essays thematically. These essays were addressed to the general reader and in their revised versions continue to do so.

The essays are largely, but not altogether, in response to debates that have surfaced in the public arena on questions concerning historical interpretation. As a historian I have felt it necessary that there be responses from those of us who are concerned about the future of our discipline, and about a rational understanding of our past, even if allowing a hint of romanticism. I have confined myself largely to the early period since that is the history that I am most familiar with and is also the one perhaps most often debated in the public arena. However, my implied comments on some ways of viewing early history would also apply to the history of later times, although the evidence dealt with would differ.

Much of the debate stems from the question of national identity and most people assume that history provides the answer. What is not realized is that if the history is mangled then the identity or identities can be hopelessly off course. If the past is to be called upon to legitimize the present, as it so frequently is, then the veracity of such a past has to be continuously vetted. In speaking of the relationship of past and present we seldom stop to think of how much of our present hangs on what we assume to be the actual past.

Romila Thapar
New Delhi
January 2014

I

HISTORY AND THE PUBLIC

Most of the essays in this book are about how the present draws on the past not necessarily always to better understand the past but to use the past to legitimize the present. E.H. Carr's often repeated statement that history is a dialogue between the past and the present is true, but perhaps with a caveat. A historian of medieval Europe, for instance, maintains that the past does not literally speak to the present, but when it is being used for legitimation we insist that it is saying what we want to hear, even if we are imputing thoughts to the past that may have been alien to it. In a sense this may partially explain some historical controversies, where not every historian agrees with what the past is said to be stating. But this is also where a systematic historical method of enquiry can assist in evaluating the validity of diverse views.

The understanding of history has changed radically in our times from what it was a century ago. In the past it was enough to discover the evidence, look for further clues, and like Hercule Poirot or Sherlock Holmes, find the solution. So, in the early days of my teaching I used to suggest to my students that they read Agatha Christie. But soon this became redundant with the shift towards evidence having to be not just read but analyzed, the author's intentions having to be clarified, the reasons for addressing particular audiences having to be explained, and only subsequent to all this could there be a possible historical statement. I have attempted to provide a few examples of this. The nature of this change can perhaps be encapsulated in the formula of questioning existing knowledge through a critical inquiry into evidence and its reading. This obviously extends to all forms of knowledge and not just history. Not that this necessarily makes the explanation of past events foolproof; but it widens the range of what we take to be the causes of events and consequently of our exploration of these. More questions can be asked and more answers suggested provided they draw on reliable evidence, conform to a rational analysis and provide logical generalizations. This, up to a point, perhaps takes away from the romance of history. But it does help to differentiate between the historian and the author of historical novels. Both draw on the past but in entirely different ways.

Our perception of the past has obviously to change as and when the evidence increases and the methodology becomes more precise. Since the existence of the past is not entirely tangible, the presence of artifacts and monuments from the past being few, the past is constructed by putting together a variety of evidence. All societies over the centuries have constructed their past, often in accordance with contemporary theories about the meaning of the past. The past therefore is represented in various ways: in the oral traditions of mythology, folktales, ballads—some of which were incorporated into literary forms as epics, narratives, drama and chronicles. This becomes the data of what we call 'traditions'. But as Eric Hobsbawm and Terence Ranger have shown, 'traditions' can also be invented in later periods, although purporting to have emerged in early times. This is one reason why ascertaining the chronology of the evidence used is crucial. Dates are not just an obsession with historians (even if occasionally they become so); they do have a vital role in authenticating evidence.

In contemporary times we not only reconstruct the past but we also use it to give legitimacy to the way in which we order our own society. Given that with the advance of knowledge, we have more ways of discovering new evidence and of asking fresh questions of the evidence, we can therefore construct a past that is more credible and precise. This becomes a past that is better assessed by those who are trained to do so, such as historians. The more technical the training required, especially where the evidence goes beyond texts to artifacts, the greater the gulf between the professional historian and the lay reader. Controversies, however, often involve historians with those who gather rumoured information and who are not trained to assess the evidence.

A few decades ago the study of history was geared primarily to listing the activity of those in power, largely rulers of various kinds, and placing them in chronological order, the order being as accurate as the sources of study would allow. In the three decades of the 1960s, 70s and 80s, the interest in the past came to be re-oriented in a significant way. It was no longer limited to political and dynastic history. It introduced the interface of these aspects with others such as social and economic history and the flow of what was called culture/civilization that largely addressed religion, language, literature, the arts and philosophy. This change can be illustrated in various ways in the themes that younger historians started researching that were concerned with trying to construct a larger picture of society. The change was associated partly with history becoming a social science, partly with its being written from a Marxist perspective on the history of society, or on specific aspects of religion and on concepts of legitimation from a Weberian perspective, and partly with new directions suggested by different sources and new questions arising from dialogue with other disciplines. Some examples of the latter were the function of technology in changing society, a more realistic gender history than had been written before, and the investigation of environmental factors affecting history.

Early History

In the writing of early Indian history, both Archaeology and Historical Linguistics have provided new evidence and new ways of interpreting existing evidence. Archaeology received enhanced attention after independence because interest in it was fuelled by the need to ascertain whether there were sites of Harappan urbanization on the Indian side of the border, the major sites of Harappa and Mohenjo-daro being located in Pakistan after 1947. Archaeological investigation resulted in the spectacular discovery of Harappan cities in Gujarat, Rajasthan and Punjab. This gave much encouragement to exploring other archaeological cultures as well in order to see the flow from less complex societies to more complex ones, culminating occasionally in urban centres. And this interest in turn grew with research into regional history.

Methods of Historical Linguistics provided less dramatic but equally significant evidence. There was the recognition that seemingly similar words had meanings that were not identical. The reference to 'pur' in the *Rigveda* was not to city but to something like a stockade. This makes it very different from the term 'pura' meaning a town that was used in later texts. Therefore, the argument that the *Rigveda* was familiar with urban living, on the basis of pur, was questioned—it was also necessary to keep in mind the fact that the process of urbanization was not just one settlement evolving into a town, but a substantial social change accompanied by different social and economic structures now supporting urban centres as compared to the previous ones.

Historical linguistics when applied to crucial words in a text can provide historical clues to their meaning and to the language to which they belong. The occurrence of Dravidian linguistic elements in the text of the Vedic corpus, inevitably leads historians to asking different questions from those they asked before these elements were recognized. The origins of words are historically significant. For example, langala, a plough, in the *Rigveda* opens up a new set of questions, as it is not of Indo-Aryan origin. Where texts show evidence of the use of more than a single language, there the historian has to ask whether there might have been some bi-lingualism involving earlier settlers and later, newcomers. This might suggest interesting cultural possibilities of the interface between speakers of different languages. For instance, were there some forms of culture such as customary law or religious beliefs that were exchanged? What was inducted from one society into the other?

The other use of linguistics to history has been in sorting out the different stylistic forms that occur in a text. These indicate the chronology of the segments that went into the making of a long text, allowing the separation of the earlier portions from the later. This technique has been used for instance by T.R. Trautmann in the analysis of the *Arthashastra* of Kautilya, suggesting a period of composition that stretched from the fourth century BC to the third century AD. Similarly, A.L. Basham has also suggested that the *Bhagvad Gita* may not have been composed at a single point in time.

Evidence, no matter how reliable, and irrespective of whether it is an abstract fact from a text or a tangible object from an excavation, has to be interpreted. Interpretations can differ, and do differ, and such differences account for what goes into the making of different approaches to history. But this is precisely where it is necessary to go through the procedure of applying the method of analysis that we have come to associate with new forms of research. This involves assessing, through various means, the reliability of the evidence used as the basis of the argument, and the links between cause-and-effect that are drawn in a logical way from the evidence.

In the study of ancient history for example, the historian would have to know how to follow reports of archaeological excavations that now have become quite technical. Archaeology draws increasingly on scientific disciplines for analyses, making it necessary to consult the specialist in the particular science. Few excavators would have the expertise to differentiate between the bones of an onager and a horse, the identification of which might tell us when the horse was introduced into India. A specialist working on faunal bones would have to be consulted. Such specialist consultation is even more necessary now that DNA analyses have been introduced into determining the identity of social groups from both the past and the present. Here the shoe is often on the other foot: the DNA specialists need to know more about the sociology and history of caste and ethnic groups and how they acquire an identity, before they trace them back to antiquity or pronounce on their continuity.

Reading inscriptions requires some familiarity with paleography and the evolution of the script. Making sense of coins improves if one knows how to differentiate between the properties of metals, or alloys, and techniques of casting and even statistical methods, not to mention the basic information on economies that used money. In the same way when reading a text, knowing the language is necessary but not sufficient in itself, since a number of further questions have to be asked concerning the author, the audience for whom the text is intended, and above all, the agenda of the text since all texts have an agenda. Such an analysis cannot be based on guesswork.

New sources and new methods of analyses can lead to historical readings different from previous ones. A comment frequently made is that since historical facts do not change, how can history change? This reflects a lack of awareness of the sources and methods currently being used in historical interpretation. The facts may not change, although sometimes they do as a result of fresh information or new ways of analyzing old information, but the interpretation of these facts can change. History is not just a directory of information; it also involves analyzing and interpreting this information.

Having been through a rigorous training process and later having demanded it of my students, I am always surprised at the popular assumption that historical writing requires no training. The world and his wife can write history, and can take umbrage if criticized by historians for writing junk. It is ironic that the historian today can be confronted by non-historians insisting on their version of the past being correct and accusing the historian of prejudice! The non-specialist does not, in a similar manner, question the views of other social scientists or of natural scientists, because these disciplines do not go into the making of social and political identities to the extent that history does. A rationally argued cause-and-effect connection within the limits of the evidence is required, as it is in all investigation. This procedure will necessarily question the fantasy pasts being palmed off as history. And while it can be fun for historians to analyze such fantasies, the best thing that could be said about such texts is that they reveal more about the authors than about the past. This does not preclude the rare leaps of historical imagination that are not written as history but are knowledgeable and sensitive about the past.

Early History as a Social Science

History in the last fifty years has become a part of the social sciences. I tend to agree with those who prefer to combine the social sciences and the humanities and refer to them as 'the human sciences' in contradistinction to 'the natural sciences'. With history moving towards the social sciences, there was a spurt in the dialogue between historians and economists, social anthropologists, geographers and even specialists in literature. This encouraged historians to look for new kinds of evidence, much of which had an impact on their interpretations of the past. I remember, for example, a long discussion that I had in the 1960s with a demographer on how to estimate the population of ancient cities, and why this had significance for the study of the nature of early urbanization. These were not the kinds of questions that we had been trained to ask in our student days. A new slew of questions are now being posed, changing the focus on the past.

Explanations of how societies and economies functioned in the past are often based on what have been called 'grand theories'. The last two centuries have seen attempts to formulate patterns of historical change that may have universal application. There is now a turn to retaining some broad contours but seeing change at localized levels and analyzing why there are variations. Grand theory may well persist but its effectiveness requires recognizing and understanding the diversities within it. The ill-informed assumptions that Marxism, for instance, advocates economic determinism or that Weber gives priority to religious forms, need correction. Explanations of how a society functions, by their very intention have to consider the interface between various facets. Although priority may be given to some, these are not deterministic features.

The effective change came with asking new questions of the sources. For instance, inscriptions of the period from the seventh to the twelfth centuries AD had been deciphered in the nineteenth century and were read as sources for a hundred years. They were mainly studied for information on rulers and their chronology. Most of such inscriptions had to do with grants of land, so when questions pertaining to society and the economy of that time came to be asked from this inscriptional evidence, new dimensions of the history of those times opened up, relating to the agrarian economy, caste and religious sects.

1

INTERPRETATIONS OF EARLY INDIAN HISTORY

Research in any field generally involves two stages: collecting the data and checking its reliability, and then interpreting it. The reliability of the data is crucial as is also the consulting of all the available evidence pertinent to the research. The same holds for the writing of history. I am assuming that the first stage is familiar to most people and shall therefore focus on the second. In this, one of the more interesting aspects is how the historical evidence of early Indian society has been interpreted in the last two centuries and how these readings have been and are still changing in recent decades. I shall be looking into the broad trends that have shaped the interpretation of Indian history of the period from about 1000 BC to AD 1300.

The modern study of early Indian history begins with history as constructed by colonial scholars. Although there were views on the past in ancient Indian sources these were set aside as not being historical. The history of India was constructed in accordance with nineteenth century European views on what history should be and what was thought to be Indian history. This colonial view also influenced Indian nationalist perspectives on the past, with some agreements and some disagreements.

At the time of Indian independence, in 1947, we had inherited a history of the subcontinent that incorporated two substantial views of the past: the colonial and the nationalist. Both claimed to be based on contemporary techniques of historical research. They were primarily concerned with chronology and sequential narratives about ruling powers, a concern that has been basic to much historical writing.

Three arguments were foundational to the colonial view of Indian history. The first was periodization. James Mill in *The History of British India* published in 1818-1823, almost two hundred years ago, argued for three periods: Hindu civilization, Muslim civilization and the British period. These labels were taken from the religions of the ruling dynasties—first the Hindu and then the Muslim. The divisions were endorsed by the assumption that the units of Indian society have always been monolithic religious communities—primarily the Hindu and the Muslim—which were mutually hostile. Religion was believed to have superseded all other authority. On the basis of their numbers in the Census of 1872 and subsequently, the Hindus came to be called the majority community, and the Muslims and others were the minority communities. It was argued that there was an absence of historical change in India, therefore all institutions were static until the coming of the colonial power. The only thing that changed was the religion of the ruling dynasties. This periodization became axiomatic to the interpretation of Indian history. It also had a major political fallout effect in the twentieth century when the subcontinent was partitioned on the basis of the supposed two nations defined by religion.

The second assertion was that the pre-colonial political economy conformed to the model of what was called Oriental Despotism. This again assumed a static society, characterized by an absence of private property in land, despotic and oppressive rulers and therefore, endemic poverty. This pattern, commonly applied to Asian societies, did not envisage any marked economic change. A static society also meant that it lacked a sense of history and it was asserted that pre-modern India suffered from an absence of historical writing.

The third aspect was that Hindu society has always been divided into four main castes—the varnas. This division it was argued was based on Indian society being a collection of segregated races, with caste as the mechanism of segregation. Therefore it remained unchanging through history. Racial identity was to the forefront with the prevalence of what was called 'race science' in Europe. This notion of caste was derived by colonial scholars largely from what they saw as the Aryan foundations of Indian civilization, both as a race and a language. The earlier people were labelled as Dravidian because of its being another ancient language with a distinct geographical location and substantial numbers of speakers. Dravidian became the counter-point to the Aryan. Sanskrit was viewed as the dominant language of the Aryan civilization and the hegemonic religion was Vedic Brahmanism. In all three descriptions India was projected as the alien, the 'Other' of Europe. Europe had to be proved to be unique and Asia as lacking in the characteristics of European civilization.

However, the interest in history was also expressed in some less negative attempts to 'discover' the past of the colony. Much effort was made to collect data: archaeological excavations were begun by A. Cunningham, linguistic surveys carried out by G. Grierson, and a massive programme of collecting and reading texts was initiated. The oral traditions of bardic compositions, collected by L.P. Tessitori and J. Tod, were also part of this effort. Ancient scripts, such as brahmi, were deciphered by J. Prinsep and others, so that inscriptions which could be now read provided extensive, fresh information. All this data had to be organized and interpreted. The organization was efficient but the interpretation did not help in questioning colonial theories. Unfortunately nineteenth-century European notions of ancient history provided little understanding of the Indian material. Nevertheless, as Lord Curzon, the Viceroy of India stated, all this was the necessary furniture of Empire.

Colonial interpretations claimed to be applying the criteria of Enlightenment rationality in their interpretation of the history of the colony. But in effect they were imposing a history that was not divorced from justifying colonial dominance. These preconceptions, together with a focus on chronology and the narrative of dynasties, governed routine history. Colonial historians drew on texts encapsulating the upper-caste perspectives of Indian society and extended it to the whole of society. Indian historians writing on ancient India came from the newly emerged middle-class, and were of the upper castes and therefore familiar with these texts. There may have been some hesitation in analyzing their contents critically in the historical manner, as among the texts were those often regarded as sacred. The colonial routine continued. Nevertheless, a debate did emerge especially among historians influenced by nationalist ideas and opposed to some colonial preconceptions. The colonial periodization was generally accepted. A few changed the nomenclature to Ancient, Medieval and Modern, borrowed from Europe and thought to be more secular, although the markers remained the same and there was no effective change.

The theory of Oriental Despotism was, naturally, rejected by the more nationalist Indian historians. Curiously, however, there was little interest at this point in providing alternative hypotheses on the early Indian political economy and society. This would have meant critiquing the normative texts and giving greater credence to non-religious texts. Social history in standard works largely reiterated the description of the four castes as given in the normative texts—the codes of caste society known as the dharma-shastras—registering little recognition of deviations, leave alone explaining them. That the system need not have worked as described in theory was not generally investigated. Other ways of looking at the past were not admitted to the forefront of historical writing.

The predominant form of nationalism, described as anti-colonial and secular, was beginning to be imprinted on Indian historical writing. But parallel to this and initially less apparent in historical writing, were the two extreme religious 'nationalisms', Hindu and Muslim, both emerging in the early twentieth century, much encouraged by the colonial version of the Indian past. These were not essentially anti-colonial since their agenda lay elsewhere and they were tied to the political ambition of establishing separate nation-states. They were less interested in researching alternate paradigms and explanations of history, and more in seeking to use history to legitimize their political ideology and the mobilization that they sought. There was an even greater insistence that a religious identity had always been the seminal identity in the past and continues to be so in the present. They argued that this identity of Hindu and Muslim would define the character of the nation-states in contemporary times, even if it meant establishing two separate nations. From these two perspectives history was directed towards justifying what was to be the outcome of independence—the partition of India into two states, one upholding Islam and the other encapsulating the struggle between those wanting a secular democracy and those proposing a Hindu state. The colonial view of Indian history was being echoed in these ideas.

The last few decades have seen a protracted battle between religious organizations insisting on their version of history and professional historians with a more secular understanding of history. The battle came to a head over the writing of state-sponsored textbooks. And while history, as viewed by various religious organizations and political parties supportive of them, has been put on hold for the moment, and more meaningful history has come to the fore, our experience of the last two decades shows that ancient Indian history walks a tightrope. The political ideologues of the Hindu Right endorse a history rooted in colonial interpretations and are anxious to make that period of history a Hindu utopia.

The need to examine history in terms of a different set of parameters was beginning to be suggested by other writing. For example, the prehistory of the social sciences in India had begun in discussions around the nature of Indian society and the cause of poverty. The economist and nationalist Dadabhai Naoroji had maintained that the real source of Indian poverty was not Oriental Despotism but the colonial economy that had drained the wealth of India. This raised heated controversies over the colonial economy, but also led to some interest in the economies of the pre-colonial period.

The teasing out of the strands of the caste structure and its social implications was evident in the writings of some sociologists, such as N.K. Bose, who were juxtaposing social realities with the descriptions in the normative texts of the early past and thereby unfreezing the theoretical pattern. Describing the ground reality of caste underlined what differentiated it from theoretical norms, and new research on caste was initiated. But the point was not easily taken by most historians. The normative view was implicit to the then vision of Indian civilization where caste tied to the conventional reading of religion was seen as the enduring feature. The writings of the Dalit lawyer B.R. Ambedkar on the history of the lower caste shudras and Dalits challenged what had been depicted by normative texts of the upper castes. He emphasized the view that caste was not just a social hierarchy but was linked to the reality of domination and subordination. The recognition of social inequality is not sufficient and one has to ask who labours and who has access to resources.

Among the more influential colonial representations of the world at that time was its division into discrete and separate civilizations. Each was demarcated territorially and associated with a single language and religion. I might add as an aside that even now, although questioned by many, Arnold Toynbee's twenty-six civilizations have nevertheless merely been replaced by Samuel Huntington's eight, in the general perception of civilizations. The implicit counterpart to the civilized was the presence of the non-civilized—the 'lesser' breeds without the law. On a universal scale the civilized were the colonizers and the uncivilized were the colonized. But the more limited colonial definition identified caste Hindus as the civilized and the others less so, and labelled some of the latter as primitive, a label that persists at the popular level. Civilization was demarcated geographically and treated as self-sufficient without recognizing that civilizations are porous and interwoven. Indian civilization was located within the boundaries of British India, and was said to be defined by the one language, Sanskrit, and the one religion, Hinduism. This was further grist to the mill of what came to be called 'cultural nationalism', but which essentially reflected a religious identity.

Religious nationalism tied to the identity of a single religious community often claimed that it represented the broader culture of the community and tried thereby to define culture by religion. Added to this was the claim of the majority community as enunciated by V.D. Savarkar and M.S. Golwalkar that the Hindus were the primary citizens of India since both their ancestry and their religion were indigenous to India. This kind of nationalism was influenced by colonial readings of Indian civilization, and the Indian response to these. Few attempted to incorporate the complexities and multiple variations of pre-colonial culture that was in effect the reality prior to the colonial. The powerful intellectual controversies of earlier times, authored by the orthodox and the heterodox alike, tended to be treated as religious sectarian discourse. That these earlier discussions had drawn on a spectrum ranging across belief, mysticism, rational and logical reasoning—some approaching seemingly dialectical ways—and had recorded fundamental differences and dissent, was rarely explored. There was a preference for viewing them as minor disagreements within a centrally agreed philosophy often labelled as Hinduism. Early systems of what is now called proto-science by some, such as ideas on mathematics, astronomy and medicine, were described, but their intellectual implications were seldom part of the historical image of a period. It was not thought necessary to locate ideas in a historical background.

Cultural nationalism therefore stayed close to the contours dictated by colonial preconceptions. The claims frequently made by groups today to authentic, indigenous identities, unchanging and eternal, pose immense problems for historians. Identities are neither timeless and unchanging, nor homogenous, nor singular as maintained in the nineteenth century notion of civilization. Cultural nationalism is a constituent of every nationalism.

It now resonates in many parts of the world wherever societies have experienced nationalism. Cultural nationalism draws on ancient history. Understanding the construction of this nationalism requires familiarity with the pre-modern history on which it claims to draw, although those that claim it frequently lack expertise in its study.

The questioning of existing theories about the past began to be more distinctly formulated in the 1950s and 1960s. Gradually, it altered the criteria of analyses among historians. This widened the range of questions. It led to some distancing from both the colonial and the nationalist interpretations of Indian history. There was an appreciation of earlier scholarship but since knowledge is not chronos-free, it has to be related to a specific situation and time. This is more so where a shift in paradigm is involved, where the frame of reference is being re-aligned. In part, this shift had to do with questions related to the broader issues concerning the Indian nation-state in the 1950s. This was not an attempt at imposing the present on the past but seeing the link between the two through more insightful explanations of the past. History had ceased to be part of Indology—the study of anything Indian, and had become one of the more focused social sciences.

Emerging from a colonial situation, the initial question was how the new nation was to be shaped. It was thought that a better understanding of the past could provide the right context for any discussion on current concerns including debates about economic growth, the establishing of a greater degree of social equality and comprehending the potential of a multiple cultural heritage. Inevitably, this also led to questioning the view of history that had been constructed in the last two hundred years, which in turn introduced information about aspects of the past that had not been researched earlier. The questions were not limited to politics and the economy but extended to social forms, cultural and religious expression and the formulation of identities and traditions in earlier times. Historiography, that is, seeing the historian's worldview as part of the historical process, began to surface in a significant way.

In the questioning of existing explanations the validity of periodizing Indian history as Hindu, Muslim and British was increasingly doubted. It had projected two thousand years of a golden age for the first, eight hundred years of despotic tyranny for the second, and a supposed modernization under the British. Such divisions set aside the relevance of significant changes within these periods. That any age, stretching over a long period, can be described as consistently glorious or tyrannical was questioned, as also the characterization of an entire age merely by the religion of rulers. There was no space in this periodization for observing social, economic or even religious change that was clear from the evidence within each period. These doubts were encouraged when history became more than just the study of dynasties. There was also the realization that communities and religions are not monolithic, but are segmented and that segments have had their own varying relationships with each other, sometimes cordial and sometimes confrontational.

Alternate notions of periodization were in part a reaction to the opening up of a dialogue between history and other disciplines. Conventional history juxtaposed the succession of dynasties—one more glorious than the next—with the bare bones of an economic history, social history, the history of religion and of the arts. These were all included within the same chronological brackets but were not integrated, as is illustrated in the series entitled *The History and Culture of the Indian People* published by the Bharatiya Vidya Bhawan in the 1950s and 1960s. However, by relating them more closely to each other and to a common historical context they formed a network of inter-connected features. This gave greater depth to historical understanding.

In looking more analytically at the long stretches of many centuries, historians began to discern smaller periods with more recognizable characteristics. The Indus Civilization or Harappan urbanization dating to the third millennium BC, declined in the early second millennium BC. This was followed by widespread agro-pastoral chiefships, as evident from both archaeology and the Vedic texts. The second urbanization or what is called the Early Historical period began in the middle Ganga plain in the mid-first millennium BC. The Mauryan Empire and the post-Mauryan changes are part of this period that continues to Gupta times. The centuries from after the Guptas to about AD 1200, underwent considerable social and economic change. This lead to the debate on whether or not this change constituted feudalism. It is referred to as the Early Medieval period to differentiate it from the Medieval period that followed and introduced other changes.

Even if the Harappan cities are excluded, having been discovered subsequent to Mill, there was considerable change within what he calls the Hindu civilization. This involved more than just the propagation of Hindu belief and culture. The same was true of the second millennium AD prior to the coming of the British. The Bhakti and Sufi teaching had far more significance than the Islam of the Sultans and mullahs, or even the more creative Islam of the Mughals.

The interface between the past and the present encouraged the notion that earlier historical experience could provide insights into some contemporary phenomena. Historians also began to look at the way in which other disciplines studied aspects of society. This was particularly useful for instance, in trying to reconstruct societies from archaeological data which was now no longer limited to just listing artifacts. It also led to new ways of relating these readings to other sources, as for example in noticing the differences between hunter-gatherers, shifting cultivators, pastoralists, peasants, artisans and so on. More than merely noticing the difference was the requirement to explain historically how and why societies change.

History as a social science developed some new orientations different from its earlier concerns as a part of Indology. There was the growing recognition that the past had to be explained, understood, re-interpreted on the basis of what historians were now referring to as a historical method involving a critical enquiry. Early history became a more professional and technical discipline where one had to know how to read excavation reports, analyze inscriptions in archaic scripts, assess the linguistic basis of texts, and more recently use statistical methods and computer applications to investigate textual data or even numismatic data. The computer has been used in statistical analyses and in compiling concordances of the Harappan pictograms in attempts to decipher the signs. Even more recently a blatantly fraudulent attempt at manipulating evidence on the computer was made to try and prove the depiction of a unicorn as a horse on a Harappan seal, but the fraud was exposed in some detail and published in *Frontline* (30.10.2000). The hind parts of an animal from a broken Harappan seal was scanned on the computer to suggest a horse. The intention was to state that the Harappans were familiar with the horse and therefore were actually Aryans. And soon historians working on demography and migrations will also have to know how to read and assess DNA analyses now being claimed as identities of race and caste. It would help if molecular biologists consulted social historians and sociologists before identifying Aryans, Dravidians, and varna castes.

This it not to suggest that the earlier work of historians has been set aside. On the contrary the centrality that they gave to the reliability of the evidence and the logic of the argument, continues to remain central to the framework of reconstruction, but now there is a wider explanation of the historical context. Such explanations could also help in understanding the present in more focused ways than before.

Let me turn to the important exploration of knowledge that brought about a paradigm shift in the historical writing of early India. It involved not only the use of new methods of analyses that were in any case under discussion in many of the social sciences, but it also came about precisely through discussions between those working in these various disciplines. These related to society, the economy, culture and religion, and triggered off new directions in research. Some explanations of the past arose from hitherto unnoticed evidence or fresh discoveries, but more generally they arose from new enquiries into existing evidence. There were also many more dialogues between Indian historians and those from other parts of the world in which the common concern was to move towards new ways of explaining the past. I would like to consider some examples of the kind of historical themes that attracted historians of early India.

One of the themes that drew from comparative studies was that of the state in early times. The concept of the nation had run into confusion with the two-nation theory and the insistence on religious identities being primary historical identities. The clarification did not lie in taking the concept of the nation-state back to ancient times as some were suggesting, but in differentiating between nation and state, with the state having been the political entity in the early past. Related to this were questions such as when does a state emerge, and what is its form as discussed in early texts. A centrally administered kingdom had been assumed to be common to all states in early times. The break-up of these was equated with political decline and seen as the fragmentation of a polity accompanied by an absence of consolidated power. This was viewed as disastrous since empires were the order of the day. The British saw their empire as a later edition of the Roman.

The likelihood of variation in patterns of power gradually led to the demarcation between forms of political organization. Clan-based societies with chiefs, generally agro-pastoral, can be thought of as being the precursor to the existence of a state. The state often coincided with kingdoms and these demonstrated greater complexity of organization. The transition from clan-based societies to kingdoms is seen as seminal to the societies described in the early texts such as the *Vedas*, the *Mahabharata* and the *Ramayana*, as well as the early Pali Buddhist Canon. These studies will hopefully also shift the obsessive discussion on the origin and identity of 'the Aryans' and the Aryan foundations of Indian civilization, to broader questions of how early societies functioned. The questions being currently debated relate to the nature of social change, to the interface between multiple cultures, and to mechanisms of legitimizing power. All these are questions germane to enquiries into the early Indian past. Historical analyses are of course complicated by the fact that these variant forms do not necessarily move in a linear pattern. They have co-existed as they still do, and this complexity is reflected in historical sources. Suggested answers to such questions require detailed knowledge of both archaeological and literary sources and a healthy degree of inter-disciplinary information. This also involves looking at similarly structured societies of present times to see if their study might help us in understanding earlier social forms. This has been referred to as 'living prehistory' and the idea is not to simply take the present as the imprint of the past but to examine the present forms to see if such examination can help us ask more pertinent questions about the past, questions that might enable us to see how early societies function. These studies form a welcome change from maintaining that everyone in the ancient past of India was an Aryan, and conformed to a monolithic culture and identity.

When the structure of the state began to be discussed it led to a focus on the typology of state systems. How a state comes into existence at different times has now become a focused study in which the state is not something distinct from society. The nature of the formation of states suggested variables that were different from earlier to later times. The Mauryan state of the fourth century BC was not identical with that of the Guptas who ruled in the fourth century AD or that of the Cholas a few centuries later. The discussion on varied forms had implications for the definition of empire as well, as is evident in the study of what have been called imperial administrations. Thus it can be asked whether the Mauryan Empire was a highly centralized bureaucratic system as most of us had argued in our earlier writing, or whether it should be seen administratively as a more diversified system as some of us began arguing in our later writings. The tension between control from the centre and assertion of local autonomy has been a recurring feature and is now being commented upon. The regular use of the term 'empire' for most large kingdoms has come in for questioning with kingdom being differentiated from empire. Religion was an unlikely primary factor in the initial emergence of the state that required more utilitarian resources. But in the welding of segments into empire, as in the policies of Ashoka, the Mauryan ruler, and Akbar the Mughal, there was recourse to certain facets of religion.

The confrontation between the gana-sanghas—the oligarchies or chiefdoms, and the rajyas—kingdoms, earlier referred to in passing, is now eliciting greater interest. Their divergent ideologies are being recognized. Arguments and counter-arguments among intellectuals of those times were part of the urban experience. Earlier studies had noted that orthodox views were challenged by the heterodox, who the brahmanas referred to as the nastika (the unbelievers), and the pashanda (the frauds). The so-called heretics, the Buddhists and Jainas in the main—used the same epithets for the brahmanas when the debate on occasion became fierce. Such discussions, as for example, the divergent views on social ethics, are now being recognized as significant.

From the colonial perspective, the agrarian economy of India was primary and comparatively less interest was shown in the many dimensions of urban cultures and economies based on exchange. The latter have received considerable attention in recent historical studies. Urbanization in the Ganga plain in the sixth-fifth centuries BC was linked to the emergence of state systems. The investigation of the city focused on location in terms of environment, resources and demography, the use of new technology as well as its potential as a centre for the exchange of goods and of administration and not least as a centre where ideas were debated. Spaces on the outskirts of the town, generally parks, were called kutuhala-shalas, literally places conducive to excitement or curiosity or recreation. These were the venue of debates ranging from mundane matters to philosophy. The Greek groves where philosophers held forth suggest parallels. The study of urban characteristics was partially influenced by the focused research on the much earlier cities of the Indus Civilization, both in tracing their emergence as urban centres and in assessing the causes of their decline.

Exchange in varying forms, from barter to commerce, for which there is a spurt of evidence from the post-Mauryan period, provided an additional economic dimension. The study of coins was not limited to honing the chronology of rulers. It introduced the preliminaries of discussion on money and markets at exchange centres. Closeness to other parts of Asia was known through overland routes. Maritime connections have now come to the forefront, underlining new cultural and intellectual intersections. The maritime economy of western India has become relevant to trade in the eastern Mediterranean. The perspective on the Indian past earlier viewed largely from the Himalayas and the Hindu Kush mountains of the north, is now being extended to include the very different perspective from the Indian Ocean to the south. Potentialities of bilingualism in some regions—Prakrit and Greek in Afghanistan and the borderlands, or Sanskrit and Javanese in Indonesia—suggests a re-examining of the cross-currents in many cultures. Increasing evidence of maritime connections has also raised questions linked to complex commercial arrangements as described in the recently discovered Muziris papyrus referring to the Roman trade with India, and the Geniza records from a site near Cairo referring to the Arab-Jewish trade with western India in later centuries. The commercial orbit of a largely maritime trade ran across Afro-Eurasia, from Tunis in North Africa to Canton in south China, in the period prior to European expansion. The commerce crossed state boundaries and involved elements of what we would today call 'international trade and investments'. The known world was far more connected that we realize. Half-serious comments are being made on globalization before globalization. Serious observation questions the validity of discrete, self-sufficient civilizations.

What is of course a major lacuna is that until a half-century ago we had scholars trained in the sources of the cultures with whom India had contacts in the past. We no longer have them. Arab and Jewish traders came from Egypt and the Red Sea ports, and Persian merchants were part of the Gulf trade from the first millennium AD. Indians went to South-East Asia where their settlements gave rise to a mixed culture of substantial proportions. Both traders and Buddhist missions spread over Central Asia and into China. But where are the scholars in India researching these aspects of the Indian past? We are told that there are neither finances to train such scholars nor jobs that they can be given after being trained. So these aspects of history, significant to the understanding of the Indian mercantile economy and the ensuing culture as well as the export of Indian forms to other lands, no longer exist in the syllabus. The impoverishment is ours alone.

From the mid-twentieth century, in many parts of the world, ever since historical research directed its attention to explaining the past and not just collecting evidence about it, theories explaining the historical past were widely discussed. These focused on the writings of Karl Marx, Max Weber, and the French sociologists and historians of the Annales School, all of whom had commented on the Indian past. Their comments drew on colonial scholarship although in some instances on Orientalist thinking that was a shade different. Various historians researching India have debated these explanations of Indian society. The debates although not definitive have nevertheless introduced historians to aspects of the past that had earlier seemed closed, and brought the peripheral into the mainstream and in a meaningful way.

The centrality of social and economic history was evident in all these theories. Methods of analysis influenced by historical materialism were adapted by some but with the caveat that the Indian data was likely to suggest variant patterns. Marxist historical writing introduced the idea of Modes of Production that further altered periodization. The emphasis here was on access and appropriation of resources by some groups, control over the labour provided by others to work the resources, and explaining why societies change and what the change implies. Marx's notion of an Asiatic Mode of Production, a variant of Oriental Despotism, was his attempt to provide an alternate model for Asia. It was debated but rejected by most Indian Marxists. Together with this came other significant questions, such as, whether the state was collecting tax or rent from the intermediaries which had a bearing on their relationship with the occasions when there was ambiguity about this as in the discussion on the description of the Mauryan state as given by the Greek, Megasthenes. The possibility of a Feudal Mode of Production and the debate on the transition to capitalism captured historical interest in India. The notion of feudalism had drawn on European parallels but more recently the discussion centred on the Marxist model. Significantly, the critique of the Feudal Mode, initiated by Marxist historians, when joined by others including non-Marxists, became an even more vigorous debate.

The argument was based on changes in land relations in the latter half of the first millennium AD. The transition to feudalism lay in the system of granting land or villages, primarily to brahmanas, to temples, to Buddhist monasteries and to a few who had served the state. Since the granting of land became a focal point of the political economy, it brought about a tangible change. This became central after about the eighth century AD and was therefore a time-marker for a new periodization. The discussion for and against the feudal mode opened up new perceptions about the state, the economy and society, religious activities and other potential areas of investigation.

Grants of land to religious beneficiaries—Buddhists, Jainas and brahmanas—led predictably to innovations in their activities and beliefs. The grants to the Shramana institutions of the Buddhist and Jainas were generally not to individuals but to the Sangha or Order, whereas those to brahmanas were more frequently to individuals. The grants helped institutions such as monasteries and temples to become powerful property holders. Grants to individuals converted them and their families into landowners, often of a feudatory nature, or at least established them as samantas, intermediaries between the political authority and the producer. There are many hundreds of such inscriptions recording grants—they are a telling example of how a historical record is used only minimally until a new set of questions are asked. As we have seen earlier, these inscriptions had been read since the nineteenth century but largely for data on chronology and dynastic succession. Only in the last fifty years have they begun to be examined in depth for data on agrarian history and for assessing elite patronage to religious groups. More recently some sections on dynastic history are being read as historiographical perceptions.

Some religious cults became a network of support for particular dynasties, a process that was to be common but more visible at the local level. The Yadava dynasty, for instance, ruling in the Indian peninsula in about the twelfth century AD, were both devotees and patrons of the emerging cult of Vitthala, a form of Vishnu, widely worshipped in Maharashtra and parts of Karnataka with its centre at Pandarpur. It has been suggested that the iconography of the image points to its origins lying in the hero-cult of local pastoralists, a case of a local hero evolving over time into a mainstream Puranic deity. Royal patronage of a popular religious cult meant that the geographical distribution of the cult could become the area of support for the patron.

Sifting the activities covered by the all-inclusive label of 'religion', and attempting to unravel their social functions, helps to clarify the links between social roles and religious beliefs. Monastic establishments, quite apart from their role in fostering formal religion, were also agencies of intervention often in association with rulers. At the same time popular religious movements, some known to deviate from or even contradict the orthodox, occupied a prominent place on the historical canvas. An interesting argument concerns the relationship between the worshipper and his deity in the Bhakti tradition of popular devotional worship. This has been seen as parallel to the relationship of the peasant to his feudal lord. Although it remains a continuing argument, the discussion it has provoked throws light on the intricacies of relationships, both the religious and the political.

Max Weber's theories on Indian religion and the absence of economic rationality have been only marginally productive of further research. However, his discussion on the notion of legitimacy as a factor in establishing power, has been widely discussed in the context of kingdoms and dynasties in the centuries AD. Even the very limited work on the Indian historical tradition indicates that the need for legitimation was one reason among others for creating such a tradition.

This also relates to some studies of the Annales School on ritual as a source of power, particularly in societies governed by notions of reciprocal exchange. These are often characterized by an elaborate practice of gift-exchange that has implications both for the economy of such societies as well as the registering of status as suggested by the seminal work of Marcel Mauss. They are also the kind of societies where genealogies are central. Varying forms of kinship are helping to trace diverse genealogical patterns in the lengthy ancestral lists of heroes and anti-heroes, as in the *Mahabharata* and the *Ramayana,* and in the lists of descent of the lineages maintained in the *Puranas*. The earlier presumed uniformity is being replaced by seeing these lists as mechanisms of incorporating a variety of socially diverse groups into mainstream society.

What was earlier thought to be the immobile character of caste gave way to realizing that degrees of social mobility were not only possible but recognizable. The sociological theory of what was called 'sanskritization'—that lower castes sometimes sought upward mobility by imitating the patterns of life of upper castes, if they could, was applicable to a limited extent to certain historical situations. It was more appropriate to assertions of status among upper castes who were in effect sometimes of obscure origin. Elaborate origin myths involving deities and sages and eloquent claims to aristocratic castes, often indicate more humble beginnings.

Ritual specialists of various kinds could end up as temple priests when cult shrines mutated into the temples of the elite. Politics was an open arena and claims to kshatriya or aristocratic identities as part of legitimation, were required only to legitimize the family currently in power. The process was not always one of osmosis. Imitating lifestyles or being incorporated into them can sometimes be the cause of friction if not confrontation. This kind of upward movement was not restricted to the political sphere. When local cult shrines mutated into Hindu temples, ritual specialists attached to the cult could sometimes be inducted as priests. This category can be recognized by the local version of their names and their faulty use of Sanskrit especially in inscriptions.

If the adventurer controlling a principality managed to establish himself as king, he would have to adopt some high status symbols, doubtless explained to him by the brahmanas from the Ganga plain whom he invited to settle in his kingdom. Out of loyalty to the earlier deities and his continuing belief in his original gods and their priests, these too would be elevated into the Puranic pattern via various myths, and their priests inducted into performing brahmanical rituals for those of high status. A case in point is the continued worship of the aniconic rock referred to as Maniya Deo (Devi) by the Chandella rulers and much later its conversion into the goddess Sharada.

▪

The history of women in India is now eliciting far more interest than it has done before. Gender history is no longer just the accumulation of more data on the history of women. It now includes revised views on social relationships. Earlier, popular belief held that Gargi, who is said in the *Upanishads* to have asked complex philosophical questions, was proof enough that women were held in high esteem in ancient India. But such references, as has been pointed out by Uma Chakravati and others, sit uncomfortably alongside the evidence of a distinctly subordinate status of women, particularly that of the dasis, or women slaves, who were given away as chattel and part of wealth, recorded in the *Rigveda* and the *Mahabharata* (2.47-48). In the list of accepted forms of marriage in the dharma-shastras, the insistence on controlling women and through this controlling caste, is an unmistakable pointer to patriarchy. The most appropriate form of marriage we are told is the kanya-dana—when the father gifts his daughter. Included in the list is the rakshasha—the abduction of the young woman, which is regarded as legal and is resorted to by the best of heroes, Arjuna in the *Mahabharata*. In each form the woman is either gifted, or exchanged for wealth or abducted. The Buddhists and Jainas at least gave women the option of becoming nuns. Women were as central to the creation of communities and identities as were men, but their roles were diverse and their status varied according to differing situations. This variation requires historical explanations and such explanations are forthcoming in recent historical writing.

New modalities in the history of social change were hinted at where clans inhabiting the forests were changed to peasant communities with the clearing of forests and the cultivation of the cleared land. Recruitment was still by birth as was the right to inheritance, and marriage circles were socially determined. But the tendency of a relatively more egalitarian status in clan societies was slowly giving way to the sharper hierarchy that governed caste functioning. The hierarchy was particularly marked in relations between upper and lower castes.

A vignette of this process can be glimpsed in the *Harshacharita* of Banabhatta, a seventh century biography of the king Harshavardhana of Kanauj. The text describes the transition of the Shabaras, a forest tribe, who establish a village for exchanging produce with other people. It would seem that gradually the area was brought under peasant agriculture and converted to caste society. The mutation required the converting of a forested area into fields, and an erstwhile more egalitarian society accepting the hierarchies essential to caste. A permanent supply of labour was ensured by other means such as declaring that some ethnic groups and some occupations were so low and polluting as to make those people associated with them untouchable. They became a permanently ghettoized segment of society. Explaining how this came about and persisted through the centuries, provides another dimension of social history that is currently recognized as significant.

Connections between geographical regions, the environment and history are now beginning to be made. Environmental changes have begun to be studied. Changing river courses in the Punjab may have led to the shifting of settlements and possible migrations of the Late Harappans eastwards into the western Ganga plain in the early second millennium BC. The silting up of the Indus and Ganga deltas at the turn of the Christian era required the relocation of ports, as was observed by ancient Greek navigators, and this brought about a reshuffling of trade centres and routes; or deforestation altering the landscape and climate, would also have caused substantial change in settled areas. Investigations of environmental factors are hopefully encouraging a more focused study of the history of regions, drawing on archaeology and the use of sources in regional languages, apart from sources already being used.

The interest in regional history grew by degrees, assisted to some extent by the creation of linguistic states from the late 1950s, superseding the more arbitrary boundaries of the erstwhile provinces of British India. The newly created states came to be treated by historians as sub-national territorial units, but present-day boundaries do not necessarily hold for earlier times. Boundaries are an unstable index in historical studies. Ecologically defined frontier zones are more stable. The perspective of sub-continental history, conventionally viewed from the Ganga plain, has had to change with the evidence now coming from regional history. For example, the history of south India is much more prominent in histories of the subcontinent than it was fifty years ago. Regional histories form patterns that sometimes differ from each other and the variations have a historical base. Differences are not just diversities in regional styles. They are expressions of multiple cultural norms that cut across monolithic, uniform identities. This requires a reassessment of what went into making the identities that existed in the past.

Varying regional forms are reflected in the way resources are used—varying crop patterns would differentiate settlement patterns as for instance in wheat growing areas and in areas under wet rice cultivation; or in the hierarchy of castes where in one region the brahmana is dominant and in another the trading caste; or in the evolution of belief systems and worship and the degree to which local deities define the religious idiom. The most visual manifestation of difference is of course in architecture and in styles of art. To view it as a uniformity called civilization, as described in the nineteenth century, becomes problematic.

This often also means that the historian has to juxtapose a diversity of sources even if the sources are largely textual. Earlier Indological studies of texts were extensive with valuable investigations into the structure of the languages, the dating of texts and the reconstruction of a narrative of events. But this was not enough. It is now being extended by placing a text more firmly in its context, and by scrutinizing its author, audience and agenda, thus widening the possible range of meanings and intentions. Even in the official versions of the history of a dynasty there are differences that become crucial to understanding the intention of the text. It is necessary to keep in mind that the texts that have survived from the early period are generally of elite groups. Less has survived from those that were marginalized in past society—women, Dalits, forest dwellers, lower castes. A re-reading of sources is needed to search for the perspectives of such groups.

Let me conclude by saying that I have attempted to provide a glimpse of a few of the changes that underlie the study and interpretation of early Indian history. To look at the early past as a historical process rather than in isolated fragments, is a response to our curiosity about the past and our attempt to understand and explain it. But it also illumines our own times. The past is not static. We believe that because we have created it we can also give it shape. The shape we give it is generally in response to our current requirements one of which is the need for legitimacy from the past. And it then becomes contested. But the sources we use have already captured the pasts that preceded them. The past therefore is inherently layered and has a genealogy. When we speak to the past in the sources we use, we are tapping into points of time that have experienced their own pasts and have moved into their own futures, before we have even reached out to them. And when we invoke the past, we need to ask: What are we invoking? And why?

2

HISTORICAL PERSPECTIVES OF NATION-BUILDING

Historical perspectives are frequently perceived from the standpoint of the present. A society has many pasts from which it chooses those that go into the creation of its history. The choice is made by those in authority—the authority being of various kinds—although occasionally the voice of others may be heard. Today these voices are being heard in louder tones with an insistence that their histories be included. Perspectives on the Indian past have earlier tended to be given monolithic forms: an unchanging caste society; an economy totally conditioned by whether or not the state was owner of the land, and a religion—Hinduism, the modern understanding of which has run parallel to that of the Semitic religions. Some of these perceptions have to be reconsidered.

The concept of a nation and the coming into being of the nation-state is a development of modern times. The concept had its roots in medieval European communities and grew to importance only from the late eighteenth century, accompanied as it was by an expansion of economic opportunities, by the notion of liberal institutions, by an emphasis on legal forms, and by the growth of a culture of nationalism reflecting the emergence of a middle-class. The idea of the nation-state was itself a product of a particular historical moment. There is, therefore, a historical lag between the condition prior to the nation-state and its emergence. In part our present problems arise from our inability to comprehend the nature of this lag. It could be suggested that the coming of a renaissance might act as a bridge.

If we are to use the analogy of the European Renaissance then it is questionable whether in fact there was a renaissance in India in the nineteenth century. Quite apart from the fact that the catalyst came from outside and not from within Indian society, the major ideological contribution of the European Renaissance, the notion of Humanism which pervaded the approach to every aspect of life, drew from a rejection of the dominance of the Church even though this rejection sought legitimacy by going back to what were interpreted as the institutions of Greco-Roman civilization, prior to and antithetical to, the Christian Church. In India we are now seeking legitimacy from the past in attempts to build institutions that would be conducive to the powers of a Church should there have been a Church in India. For instance, by insisting on the historical existence of communities defined solely by an overarching religious identity, we endorse the potential of an ecclesiastical infrastructure even where it did not exist before. The idea that the religious community was a basic identity of Indian society was fostered in the nineteenth century. By accepting it we have moved a long distance away from the presuppositions of a renaissance.

The nineteenth century Indian 'renaissance' broadly accepted the European Orientalist view of the early Indian past which was derived largely from Brahmanical textual sources, and which conceded to a large extent the correctness of the colonial comprehension of our past. Even nationalist historians made only a few attempts to replace the paradigm constructed by European Orientalist scholarship, a paradigm conditioned by paucity of evidence but equally by European intellectual preconceptions within a colonial framework. A radically new understanding of our past demands not only the questioning of these preconceptions and this framework, but also the inclusion of perspectives of Indian sources other than the Brahmanical and those of the elite. This juxtaposition will also place all the sources in a more realistic historical context. Such changes are evident at some levels of focused scholarship but have perhaps not percolated to the perceptions of the past by the general intelligentsia.

The European Renaissance was also a rebirth of learning, where the established modes, methodologies and content of learning were scrutinized and reconsidered. Many were discarded. Our educational system in the nineteenth century was based on colonial modes that have been continued since. Indian society, in its broad context, has also become somewhat suspicious of the freedom of intellectual analyses, which the conservative establishment prefers to disown in order to cover up its disagreement or even at times its ignorance. In some circles of radical populist opinion it is described as the activity of the 'elite'. Yet there have been, in a quiet way, many attempts on the part of Indian scholars since the 1960s to change the paradigms. But individual activity cannot generate a movement and ideas do not get disseminated sufficiently enough to act as catalysts. If a respect for analytical intellectual activity is an urgent need, so too is the clearing of institutional obstructions to new ideas. This would require a frontal opposition to the bureaucratic structure of many institutions, a confrontation that becomes complicated by the fact that the state that is the patron of these institutions would prefer to maintain the obstructions as a form of control. If we are to create conditions which could lead to a Renaissance we have to open up learning in the true sense: the ability to maintain a sustained, questioning dialogue on all issues, irrespective of the heavy hand of stultifying patrons. Judging by the institutions established so far, the change to corporates financing educational institutions, will not result in a substantial difference, since the trajectory remains the same.

What needs probing is why this diversity of religious expression coloured with both Islamic and Hindu ideas and practices is now in many instances giving way to a recognizably fundamentalist way of thinking and acting. In the case of Islamic fundamentalism, the ideology that propels this has been traced back to the eighteenth century Wahhabi movement in Saudi Arabia that worked towards codifying the diversity of Islam into a single system. While suggesting that it was distancing itself from orthodoxy, it was in fact moulding fundamentalism. Some Sufis were disapproved of as part of the generally anti-Persian and pro-Arab religious stance, and women were back to being confined. There was as in all such movements the constant refrain of returning to the Golden Age, in this case of the Caliphate.

The offspring of this movement in India are a number of groups competing in being the most orthodox, among which are the Lashkar-e-Taiba, the Ahl-i-Hadith and the Tablighi Jammat. Their visible presence and popularity is recent and parallels that of Hindutva, as does much of their activity in organizing religious fundamentalism. They started to be visible and demanding, with events related to the Babri Masjid and the subsequent riots. They have a perch in political parties geared to using Islam for political demands and mobilization. The narrative echoes that of Hindutva—of 'hurt sentiments', attempts to reactivate places of worship that have been declared protected monuments—in this case mosques, refusing to consider changing the Muslim Personal

Law in favour of a revised and uniform civil code with better gender justice, banning films and books, making sure that the history taught in madrassahs is largely the glorification of Islam, and where possible controlling prime property whether directly or indirectly.

The Renaissance was also associated with a social crisis involving the identity of new social groups becoming dominant. In Europe it was the centrality of an urban society. In nineteenth century India the emergence of the middle class required new forms of expression, but was partially thwarted by its ties to upper caste origins. Today's middle class is drawn from a wider spectrum, consequently the effects of a social change are greater. The alienation implicit in modernization is sought to be assuaged by the creation of a past and of ideologies that legitimize the present. There has been, for example, too great a weightage on emphasizing the process of civilization in Indian society as a one-way process of aspiring towards Brahmanical culture. That Brahmanism itself has often had to accommodate itself to non-Brahmanical culture, in its extensive public role, and that even the constituents of what we know of some Hindu practice and ritual today incorporate elements from non-caste groups, is evident in various religious sects; and that there is some internalization of influences from other religions such as Islam and Christianity, are all features that are evident but are downplayed. Yet the very label 'Hindu' for the religion is of Greco-Iranian Islamic origin and European usage. Parallel to this, those who seek to define Islamic culture see only its Arab and Persian roots, and fail to incorporate the reality of the Indianness of Islam in India. Islam borrowed a past from the Judaeo-Christian tradition to which it added its own past, and this combination in turn had an interface with a Puranic past. An example of this is Shah Muni's Sanskrit text, the *Siddhanta-Bodh*, which discusses the possible closeness in concept of terms such as nabi and avatara, Narayana and Allah, the Shastras and the Qur'an. This is not so evident in the practice of Islam among upper-caste Muslims, but is prevalent among the larger population of those labelled Muslim in the subcontinent who belong to a variety of castes and sects. The Khojas, Bohras, Meos, Navayats, Mapillas and many others have their origins in this kind of Indian Islam no matter what the degree of Islamization may be in the present. The history of every religion in India requires a shift of paradigm if its origins and evolution are to be understood with accuracy and sensitivity.

Given the projection in recent times of religious identities as central to social and political action, there is now a greater turning to religiosity and ritual. Rituals are resurrected or invented, insisting that they go back to the past. Such resurrections are seldom motivated by reasons of religious sensibility and where rituals are concerned they can be equally a demonstration of affluence as they have frequently been in the past. Public demonstrations of ritual convey many messages: they lay claim to tradition and therefore to culture, their performers claim piety, and the wealth implicit in the more dramatic among the rituals underlines economic status.

Societies in the course of their history negotiate relations with what they perceive as the supernatural which they occasionally convert into deities. These take the form of religious beliefs. The religions of Indian civilization are no exception. Social alienation and crises at various points of historical change lead to the invention of new rituals that are nevertheless said to be traditional. The over-emphasis on ritual is also an attempt to compensate for the social change that often creates a distance from rituals practiced in earlier times. But the situation in India is further compounded by the pressure of political negotiation that is conducted in tandem with religious identities as in the argument supporting the existence of majority and minority communities defined by religious identities. To then maintain that every aspect of religion is sacrosanct and that nothing can be said or written about it, virtually amounts to a form of political blackmail. If religion is to play a political role as it does in the concept of religious majority and minority communities, then it must be subjected to the same analyses as all political ideologies and behaviour.

Religion as an ideology needs to be analyzed in all its dimensions, for, unless its political, social and economic dimensions are openly discussed, even if it is claimed that such discussion hurts sensibilities, there can be no real move away from dogma to humanism. Any renaissance or rebirth assumes a critical assessment of the past and such an assessment is still small and of a recent vintage in our society. In this connection it could well be asked whether there is really a tyranny of a bygone age or whether we are deliberately cultivating this idea as an excuse to avoid thinking through to their logical conclusion, the implications of the kinds of change envisaged in what we regard today as our ideals, such as secularism and democracy.

If the roots of a nation lie in its earlier communities then the nature of these communities has to be examined. A continuous historical process in India tied to that of social function was the creation of castes. Caste as the dominant organizational structure of Indian society was not the rigid, frozen system that we have been made to believe at least at the upper levels. It evolved over time, changed with reference to historical changes and adjusted to these. What was constant was the theoretical and ideological framework which it carried and which enabled the upper strata to control the rest. The structure of this social organization was closely related to a variety of factors: adaptation to the environment, control over technology, access to economic resources, patterns of kinship and marriage, and validation through ideology. The primacy of each of these could vary in specific situations. To stop at moral judgement on whether caste was good or evil is insufficient, as the assessment has to go much further and examine why this form of discrimination/organization was chosen. Early societies generally thought of human inequality as normal. Our problem is that we coupled social and economic inequality with birth and the notion of pollution, and thus segregated a section of our people into being treated as unable ever to change their place in society.

The problem then is one of integrating groups that have been part of history but have been excluded from history. The enormous ideological emphasis on hierarchy presupposes a tension with those further down the scale probably because there had to be vigilance over who was recruited to higher levels, as well as the continuing subservience of the lower ones. There was also tension with those outside the caste organization some of whom constituted what we today call 'the tribal peoples'. These were non-caste clans who, through being conquered or through induction, were either excluded as untouchables or else were slotted into the caste hierarchy at the lowest level or more often, were treated as beyond the social pale. Those reduced to untouchability joined others also designated as such, for reasons, it is said, of occupational practice. The intention was to have a permanent supply of labour, unable to change its status, given the universal practice among all formal religions in India to regard them as polluting.

The taking on of a caste identity by a non-caste group was a way of denying their past and their own identity. Today the insistence is not on a caste identity but on the acceptance of what I have called Syndicated Hinduism, defined through new forms and beliefs by various Hindu organizations of recent times. The ritual of conversion was invented for Hinduism in the nineteenth century, in imitation of religions that allowed converting. It was convenient for converting tribals—as it still is—who as non-caste groups could be inducted into caste society and could thus swell the numbers of those counted as 'Hindus'. The conversion to neo-Buddhism as an alternative strategy has not been of much help, for neo-Buddhists like neo-Hindus, lose out on the swings what they gain on the roundabouts; consequently many prefer to call themselves Scheduled Caste Buddhists. A policy of reservation, although it may seem to suggest a temporary solution, in fact reinforces distinctions. It might eventually have to be discarded for more effective solutions involving a restructuring of the distribution of wealth, of the accessibility to welfare needs such as education and health, and of enforcing social justice, all of which might expunge caste regulations.

Irrespective of changing dynasties and activities at the elite levels of society, this confrontation between caste and non-caste and the process of caste formation was historically a constant factor. Even religions that recruited across caste, such as Buddhism, Islam, Sikhism and Christianity, tended to conform to jati regulations in marriage and retain caste identities of occupation. Some new religious sects ended up becoming castes, such as the Lingayats. The pull of social organization was greater than ideological expression. Identity by religion, cutting across caste, region and language, has become something of a fantasy for pre-modern times.

These communities were defined by geographical location, by language, by clusters of religious sects that tended to follow the contours of jati groupings. Networks of jatis were meshed into customary law and local practice. Caste and the communities that it fostered was therefore one of the systems that conditioned our civilization. A uniform, homogenous, monolithic religious community was alien to this ethos. The attempt to break away from caste perhaps encouraged the notion of a religious identity as a larger unit of organization. This has left us today with the continuing inequity of caste and social hierarchies as well as the growing obsession with varieties of religious 'sensitivities'.

To replace caste by religion does not help the process of nation-building. But since we have entered this latter condition, possibly an opposition to both as essential identities might help in attempting a new system of social organization. In such a system the existing association of rights or an absence of rights, relating either to caste or to religious community, will have to be addressed in the context of entitlements and obligations of citizenship. The reality of caste, therefore, has to be seen in terms of the factors responsible for its continuance in a specific area. Why should it still be necessary that Dalits, low castes and tribals, provide the labour? The measure of change in a caste-based society should be gauged by these realities and not by the occasional Dalit minister. In the case of what have been called Scheduled Tribes, such a change could be introduced with greater facility if there is a will to do so.

▪

Since history is an essential component of nation-building, the question often discussed in recent times is whether a nation can have many versions of history. How an event is seen can vary according to the perspective of the viewer and the purpose for which it is being viewed. But historians do hold that every claim to history has to be vetted according to the methods now used to test the veracity of historical information. What this implies is that there could be a difference between the claims to historicity and the reason why they are being made, and that the historian therefore, in the course of assessing the claims, should explain why they are being made.

Anti-colonial nationalism produced a history that largely referred to the past of groups that had been active in the national movement and were therefore thought to constitute the nation. But since then other social groups of lesser status have been demanding that their history be written and incorporated into national history. The demand is held to be legitimate by the fact that such groups now have status and a voice. A different argument is also made that these groups have higher claims to being indigenous than the many elite groups that make these claims but are known to be migrants from elsewhere. Even if the migration may date back some centuries, they are still viewed as alien in an effort to exclude them.

The demand and the writing of the history of those whose status has improved is of course not a new phenomenon. It has been known from the time when records began to be kept. Aspirations to a higher caste status and the benefit it brought led to attempts to legitimize a higher status. One of the ways of doing so was to get a history written claiming the changed status as going back to respected origins. The frequency of claims to kshatriya status in Indian history is a case in point.

If today Dalits are demanding that Dalit history be written, the demand is legitimate along with those asking for the histories of other castes and sects. These histories however have to be integrated into the context of the larger society so that the relationships between groups can be represented since their identity is hinged to the context. The history of any social group cannot be a stand-alone history as this would be unnatural. The major problem with such historical reconstruction is the paucity of sources from such groups for early periods of history. Texts composed by Dalit authors are quite late. So for the early periods we have to draw out information from texts that refer to such groups only marginally or indirectly. Even oral history can only be used for the modern period or just before when oral traditions were composed and remembered.

What leads to problems is when the mythology associated with the history is claimed as history. The mythology has also to be subjected to the same critical analysis as the narrative of all else that is claimed as history—as is the case now with the history of any group whether elite or non-elite. The mythology cannot be taken as history but it can be analyzed to indicate the social assumptions on which it is based and why it is incorporated into what is described as history. When in earlier times a dynasty traced its origin back to the Moon-god as ancestor, earlier historians merely dismissed it; but today we ask the question as to why this claim is being made. Was it a way to ensure that the family would be thereby regarded as belonging to the prestigious Chandravamsha or Lunar Lineage? (Such claims would in any case have to be proved by other sources of information.)

Claims to history, irrespective of who they come from have to be critically assessed and the real reason for the claim has to be ascertained. Frequently, these are not so much attempts at writing history as of asserting mobility and status by inventing a history to support it. It meets with the same fate as all such attempts from the past, that if it is to be taken as history it has to be carefully evaluated both to test its veracity and perhaps more so to understand why it was composed. The historian no longer claims to be discovering 'the Truth'. The most we can do is suggest a plausible reconstruction of what happened in the past in order to understand an event and thereby provide an explanation.

Claims to status also imply that notions of identity go into the making of history. Identities have to be created, as they are not inborn. Here the historian has to trace the history of the creation of an identity and then see how the created concept plays a historical role. This is in some ways parallel to the role of memory in history. Memory is also constituted, and more so, collective memory, that is so often introduced into historical thinking. The memory of victimization, for example, has to be passed on from generation to generation for it to become a memory and obviously it changes in the process of being passed on. Alternatively, a memory is deliberately constructed, often around an event or around the ideas propagated by a person, as for example in chronicles or in biographies. The historian examines the construction, the point at which it is put together, and why and how it has been continued, used at various times for purposes that may even be different from the original construction. The historian therefore cannot deny that these constructions of a believed history will be constantly made but the historian has to demonstrate that they are invented and has to explain how and why they have been so constructed.

Social hierarchy was not divorced from economic stratification as it still is not. Changing economic patterns were tied into the degree to which economic resources were exploited. Land has generally been taken as a measure of the sources of income. But the intensity of its utilization varied according to times and regions. This can be judged in part by the change in policy, where earlier governments skimmed off the revenue in many areas, to later administrations that intensified the source of revenue from land to support a larger number of kingdoms with an increasing pressure on those who were the producers of revenue. Interestingly, the forms of peasant protest also change from references to peasant migrations being the main form in earlier times, to what have been described as peasant revolts, or peasants supporting rebellious samantas (intermediaries), being recorded from the early second millennium

AD. An increase in revenue also came from bringing forested areas or waste land under cultivation, often encroaching on the territories of 'tribal groups' living in the forests. The nexus of revenue collection involved not only the state and the cultivator but an increasing range of intermediaries as well. The politics of the latter was often the immediate reason for the need to increase revenue. Control over land as exercised by the intermediaries became the crux of the agrarian economy and the dominant factor of caste in rural areas, a situation that has not altered as much as it should have by now.

Agriculture was not the sole or main resource in all areas. Networks of exchange became more permanent in settled areas and in many regions trade was significant to the economy. Periods of intensive urbanization accompanied the wider networks of trade and in some areas the urban economy was a constant feature. Historically the Indian trader has played the role of middleman par excellence in various channels of Asian trade. It would seem that Indian traders were not necessarily the initiators of commerce on a large scale, but having entered a system of exchange, soon began to play a controlling role. The aggressive thrust of the Indian middleman has been a recognized aspect of the Indian presence in many places.

The mercantile community was a social area where the theoretical hierarchies of caste as envisaged in Brahmanical ideology were often upset, for trade was regarded as low in Brahmanical reckoning, whereas traders were frequently wealthy. They tended in early times to patronize non-Brahmanical religions that accorded them a high status, irrespective of Brahmanical hierarchies. It is not for nothing that the traders and financiers in Buddhist texts are referred to as setthis, from the Sanskrit, sreshthin, meaning 'the best'. Urban centres and trading activities had a parallel hierarchy in terms of the control and production of raw material and manufactured items. Economic activities had a lateral spread in that over time larger areas came under cultivation or were included in networks of production and exchange. The pace of development varied from region to region as it did in the context of changing technologies. This variation had political implications. Equally significant was the impact of economic change on caste hierarchy and organization, not to mention financial underpinnings of political activity. Economic categories in the maneuvering of social status would therefore not be alien to the historical experience of Indian society.

Politics was relatively an open field in early India. Despite the injunctions of the shastras that kingship should belong to the kshatriya caste, the status of even some major dynasties has been controversial. The Mauryas are shudras in the brahmanical *Puranas* but kshatriyas in the Buddhist and Jaina texts. The Mauryan kings having patronized the heterodox sects had to be downgraded in brahmanical reckoning and possibly for the same reason were upgraded in Buddhist texts. In later times, others who were of obscure origin, went to suspiciously elaborate and obvious lengths to have themselves proclaimed kshatriyas. The fact that politics was relatively open, gave access to the possibilities of participation in power to larger numbers than is generally assumed. Latching onto power therefore is not a new phenomenon. But the entry of people of obscure origin did not change the political system, since their claims conformed to the continuance of the system. In theory it remained the same, but in practice there were discrepancies. Nevertheless politics did not have absolute primacy. What is new in our times is the primacy given to politicians and to political activities and the latitude to abuse power. This latter was cautioned against no doubt not entirely successfully and methods were suggested to contain it.

There were at least two groups that could freely comment on the abuse of power and were only occasionally forbidden to do so. These were groups other than factions among the elite, participants in power and the usual contenders for power. One group was that of the bards (the sutas), the caste that legitimized the authority of the king by maintaining his genealogy—crucial to claims of appropriate origins. They had the right to accuse the king of having misused his power and could either do a dharna at the threshold of his court, or commit ritual suicide to force home the point. As they had given legitimacy to the people in power they also had the right to oppose them should they think that power had been wrongly used. We may well ask as to who are the actual legitimizers of power today and whether they exercise their function as critics of the abuse of power?

The other group was the much larger and more amorphous one drawn from many castes and who followed any among a range of ideologies and belief-systems, namely, the renouncers. These were the mendicants, monks, sadhus, faqirs, Sufis and such like. Some were pillars of the establishment and their centres were the foci of loyalty to political power and social authority. Others having opted out of social obligations, and opposed to religious orthodoxy, were the quintessential dissenters. Those in political authority often feared them for they commanded immense respect, and their criticism was heard and was believed to be impartial. They were respected by society because they had renounced power (although there probably were, as there are today, some, who used this as a front to be close to those in power and thereby wield it), and this enabled them to activate opposition where they thought it necessary. Such opposition was not revolutionary in context and was frequently not even confrontational. Sometimes it was neutralized by being appropriated by those against whom it was directed. Nevertheless it nurtured the yeast of dissent. The existence of autonomous individuals free to criticize was once a landmark of our civilization. Today they are becoming an endangered species. And autonomous individuals are crucial to the stabilizing of a society.

A nation cannot be built on a single identity nor is it feasible to collate diverse identities of religion, caste, language and so on, and hope for something to emerge. A nation as a state is a new historical experience and therefore requires a new identity. Ideally, this would be the identity of the Indian citizen constructed on the assumption that all citizens are equal before the law with the same rights and obligations. The theoretical basis for this exists in our Constitution, but it has to be put into effect.

3

OF HISTORIES AND IDENTITIES

The mid-twentieth century was a dramatic turning point in the histories of the countries of South Asia. It was the time of liberation from colonial rule that in many ways had unravelled the earlier past and left us somewhat bewildered about the future. There was the intoxication of freedom—the release from being a colony—but there was also the apprehension of having to define the nation-state that subsequently emerged.

All of us in South Asia, not to mention other ex-colonies, have faced the same questions of how to define ourselves as citizens of a new nation and of course, the question of identity or identities. We in India thought the answer was simple—it was the single identity of being Indian. But the reality on the ground has turned it into a complex question without a simple answer because even a single identity can subsume others. The utopias that we wished for have retreated in the face of identities in conflict.

Let me clarify that I am not using the word 'identity' with reference to the individual self, but rather as it is used currently to refer to how a collective of people or a community labels itself. And further, I am concerned with those identities where the label claims to have an accepted historical and cultural origin. I would like to assess the validity of this connection by re-examining these historical claims. An identity has a genealogy and knowing it would help us understand why it came into existence.

History, as we were taught in school and even later, was a representation of the past based on information that had been put together by colonial scholarship. But when identities relevant to the present claimed roots in the past it became necessary for us historians to unpack the past. In this process of unpacking one realized that the past registers changes that could alter its representation. The past does not remain static.

In examining the construction of the past that we had inherited from colonial scholarship it was further seen that aspects of nationalist thinking had borrowed from this colonial legacy. Nationalism, also born from a historical condition, builds itself of necessity on a single, focused identity that aspires to be inclusive of the entire society. But it can sometimes be more limited when it represents elite or majoritarian groups seeking dominance. Inclusiveness is problematic since every society since early times has overlooked the need for equality and has registered the dominance of some and the subordination of others. Inequality is thus predictable and results in multiple identities competing for visibility. Yet the wish for an egalitarian society or one relatively so has been an essential feature in envisioning future utopias.

In our present post-colonial times in South Asia, the multiple identities of the period before nationalism begin to surface but do so in a changed historical context. Each demands priority for its single identity, treated as exclusive, and this becomes an agency for mobilization. The multiplicity and inclusiveness of earlier times is set aside. In claiming legitimacy from the past that past itself is converted into an assemblage of what is most desired in the present.

Among our current identities in South Asia the more prominent ones go back to colonial times and were usually constructed with links to pre-modern history. Examples of this are identities of race, language, caste, tribe, and religion. Economic poverty and inequality was aggravated as part of the colonial heritage of large segments of the population. Interestingly these were issues widely discussed in Europe in the nineteenth century. They became the prisms through which Europe viewed the past of South Asia. The history of the colony was of prime concern in order to understand its alien culture, to govern its strange peoples and to exploit its wealth. Some of this concern resulted in path-breaking work on deciphering scripts, revealing tangible history through excavations and investigating language through philology—analyzing its linguistic components.

But at the same time it was argued that there was an absence of historical writing in South Asian cultures. Therefore, a history had to be constructed for the region by colonial scholars and this they proceeded to do. The subsequent nationalist historians tended to accept the positive assessments in this construction but rejected the negative. However, what were missing were alternate explanations where there was disagreement with the colonial construction.

Let me turn to some identities that emerged from these studies and are now being questioned in current historical work. Among the more prevalent identities has been that of being Aryan. The notion of an Aryan race has held the stage for almost two centuries. It was rooted in philology and in the Indian context it focused on Sanskrit, thereby discovering its affinity with Old Iranian and some early European languages. An ancestral language was reconstructed and called Indo-European, its South Asian component being Indo-Aryan.

As far as language analysis went this was a useful initial exercise. But it did not rest there. It was then argued that all those who spoke the same language belonged to the same race. What was started as a statement about language, came to be applied to race as well, resulting in the virtual equation of race and language. This simplified classification since languages were easily differentiated. It is obvious to us now that the equation of language with race has no validity. Race, if at all it exists, is a biological entity entailing birth within a specified group, whereas language is a cultural entity and can be used by anyone belonging to any group. The late nineteenth century in Europe was the high point of the new 'race science' as it was called. Its generalizations were adopted without adequate verification.

Insisting on a hierarchy among races predictably placed the speakers of Indo-European languages at the top. It was ancestral to the European languages. The Aryan or Indo-Aryan language was named after those who called themselves aryas in the *Vedas*. They were described as speaking Sanskrit and belonging to the Aryan race, although no mention is made of race in the texts. As such they were differentiated from the non-Sanskrit speaking dasas and mlecchas, but we are not told what languages they spoke.

These were not racial identities but were language labels and cultural identities. However, the confusion once introduced, continued. Even Max Mueller who warned against mixing language with race contributed to the confusion. For example, he described the eminent intellectual, Ram Mohun Roy, as belonging to the Bengali race. Soon every language group of the subcontinent became a race—Dravidian, Austro-Asiatic, Tibeto-Burman, and so on. Among these, importance was given to the speakers of Dravidian.

The notion of two separate Aryan and Dravidian racial identities had no basis in history but became axiomatic wherever local populations were believed to have descended from one of the two. There was talk then—and it hasn't stopped even today—of India as the homeland of the pristine Aryan, an idea supported by movements like the Theosophists eulogizing Vedic culture and prescribing a return to it, and by some leading members of the Arya Samaj with whom the Theosophists were closely associated for a while. The homeland was located by some in Tibet and by others in the borderlands to the west of the Indus in what is today northern Pakistan.

The origins of the Dravidian race were traced back imaginatively to the mythical continent of Lemuria where Tamil culture was said to have had its locus. Among the linchpins in these discussions was the colourful Theosophist, Madame Blavatsky, who enthralled both Indians and Sri Lankans. Each of the two so-called races made exaggerated claims to having founded world civilization. But unfortunately, the antagonisms that grew out of such contested but virtually make-believe origins have been the burning embers for a variety of largely political ignitions.

Other identities also came to be subsumed under the label of race. There continue to be references to Hindu, Muslim, Buddhist and Sikh races not to mention Pathan, Punjabi, Maratha, Bengali and what have you, races. This is a misuse of the term, particularly now that the very concept of race has been questioned. Nevertheless although the term is virtually meaningless, it can be thrown around to create misleading identities.

Let's look at what the texts tell us about arya. The earliest record of Indo-Aryan is the language of the *Rigveda,* thought to date to about 1400 BC. The geographical background of the composition is limited to Seistan in Afghanistan, the northwestern borderlands, and extending into Punjab and Haryana up to the Doab and northern Rajasthan. There is no knowledge of other parts of the subcontinent. This is quite unlike the preceding Harappa Culture that incorporated not only Northwestern India but Gujarat (which became the base for an active maritime trade), down to northern Maharashtra and even parts of the Gulf as in Oman where Harappan settlements have been found in the copper ore areas. A few centuries later the core area of the Indo-Aryan language had shifted from northwestern India to the western Ganga plain and then further east with references to an eastward migration. By the Christian era it was familiar to all of northern India and spreading south. The language underwent change, travelling into new areas and being used by a variety of people, not to mention the normal linguistic change that occurs in a language over many generations.

Two points are worth noticing. Existing populations in northern India were using other languages when the speakers of Indo-Aryan composed their corpus. A text of about the seventh century BC, the *Shatapatha Brahmana*, makes fun of those who could not pronounce Sanskrit correctly and replaced the 'r' sound with the 'l' sound. Because they could not speak the language correctly they are called mleccha or barbarians. Language was the demarcation between 'us' and 'them'. Secondly, Sanskrit was more often the language of Vedic ritual and was spoken by brahmanas and the learned few. The majority of the people spoke a variety of Prakrits, which were dialects of a more simple language that was akin to Sanskrit, sometimes referred to as vernaculars. The edicts of the Mauryan emperor Ashoka of the third century BC, that are found virtually all over the subcontinent, are written in variants of Prakrit and not in Sanskrit.

Interestingly, the replacement of 'r' by 'l' is also characteristic of those Ashokan inscriptions that are located in the middle Ganga plain in the heart of the Mauryan Empire. The word *raja* is rendered as *laja*. Such changes are likely because of the presence of other languages that contributed to the making of Prakrits. Even the language of a dominant group tends to soak up some linguistic elements from populations whose languages are different. And from a strictly brahmanical perspective these were all impure mleccha peoples! So who were the Aryans?

This question has troubled historians. Whoever they were they constituted part of a mixed population. There were recognizable cultural differences between the aryas, dasas, mlecchas and such like. Some fragmentary texts show similarities with the *Rigveda* but they are from outside India—from northeast Iran and from northern Syria. Contact with India from Iran and the Oxus plain dates to either the late Harappan or post-Harappan times in the second millennium BC, when these seem to have been parallel cultures. In about 1380 BC there is a fragment of a treaty from Syria with the names of deities that sound Indo-Aryan.

There are other similarities with names in the Iranian *Avesta* but with a distinct reversal of values, attributes and some linguistic sounds. For example, the devas and asuras—deities and demons—of the *Vedas* are the daivas and ahuras of the *Avesta*, but here they are the demons and deities, the meaning being reversed. The 's' sound of Indo-Aryan becomes the 'h' sound in old Iranian, hence asura is ahura. Did the three groups come from the same area and in branching off develop differences of language and culture? If so, the area that has contacts with each of these three regions is the Oxus plain. There is no evidence of a migration from India to Syria or vice versa. What complicates the argument is that languages are not static. They change with social change and especially with the assimilation of new groups. Language specialists have known for some time that there are Dravidian linguistic elements in Vedic Sanskrit, and now it is being said that there may even be Munda linguistic elements. If this is so then the linguistic analysis of these languages becomes even more important to historical investigation, since it suggests mixed cultures. The focus of the study will have to shift from examining imagined races to analyzing the nature and composition of what we call the culture of the speakers of Indo-Aryan.

The connotation of the term arya is ambiguous because it changes through history. In the *Rigveda* the composers of the hymns describe themselves as aryas and by definition, the honourable ones. Opposed to the arya is the dasa, connoting all that the arya is not. The dasa is unable to speak the Aryan language, worships alien deities, and is associated with evil and darkness. Above all the dasa is enviably wealthy and therefore is subjected to raids by the arya.

But a few centuries later the emphasis in the definition changed. Now the aryas were more frequently those who commanded respect in society irrespective of their ethnic origins or the language they spoke. Arya was used as an all-purpose honorific. Buddhist and Jaina monks were addressed as arya or ayya by their lay-followers, despite the fact that they came from various castes including those ranked low by the brahmanas. Buddhist texts also use arya as meaning the best, the highest, the most noble and therefore as an epithet for the teachings of the Buddha, (e.g. arya satya), which of course were disapproved of by the brahmanas. The word is not used in any racist sense. As a mark of respect, arya was frequently attached to terms for parents and grandparents. Sons of royalty and well-to-do families are referred to as aryaputra, the son of an arya, as a virtual title. Even the rakshasa Ravana is called thus by his wife.

This in part accounts for another turn in the meaning of the word. This time the reference is linked to the classification of Indian society into four varnas or castes in the social codes, the *Dharmashastras*. Arya is used with reference to particular varnas as a mark of status. By the early centuries AD the word arya referred specifically to those of the three upper castes (brahmana, kshatriya, vaishya) in these codes. The fourth caste of shudras in the *Dharmashastras* was generally that of non-aryas. It states that all those not included in the three upper castes were to be treated as non-aryas, irrespective of the language they speak. Language is no longer a marker of the arya. Even more interesting is the reference to children born of mixed arya and non-arya parents and the problem of defining their status. There were many permutations and combinations. The children of an arya father and a non-arya mother had arya status. Evidently, such marriages were frequent enough to demand attention from the authors of the social codes. Caste rules would have to be adjusted when new groups were incorporated requiring a new definition of arya in caste terms.

For the historian then, the identity of 'Aryan' changes radically from a supposed race to language, to status, to caste. This is not surprising because identities do change with historical change. Therefore there is also a change in the choice of identities and in the definition of an identity. But colonial scholarship treated them as static. The arya was defined for all time in terms of its meaning in the *Rigveda* and then too the meaning was mistaken and taken as race. It was argued that each caste was a separate race and that this was the most effective way of segregating races. Herbert Risley went around measuring cephalic index and nasal width in order to prove the racial equation. This was perhaps a forerunner of the attempt to prove segregation by ascertaining the genetic pattern of the four castes.

The normative codes describing the four castes were earlier taken at face value and thought to be descriptions of how society actually functioned even if such a scheme seemed much too rigid. Historical records naturally show obvious discrepancies. Each caste has its own hierarchy, allowing some flexibility and sometimes providing a mechanism for incorporating those regarded as low born into the lower levels of the top castes. This may explain why some brahmanas are either specifically excluded from or else limited to, participating in certain rituals. For example, there are stringent rules governing which brahmanas can or cannot participate in the shraddha rituals commemorating ancestors. Why this was so is not always clear. Or there is the curious reference in the *Kaushitaki Brahmana* to the dasi-putra brahmana, literally the brahman who is the son of a non-arya, dasa woman. The term is something of an oxymoron. Such persons were initially treated with contempt, but when they demonstrated their supernatural power they were welcomed as brahmanas.

The second caste, that of kshatriyas was the one that was supposed to provide the dynasties. However, political activities were relatively open and persons of other castes bid for power as well. As we have seen in the previous essay, the Mauryas appear to be included among the shudra dynasties in brahmanical literature perhaps because they patronized heterodox sects such as the Buddhist and Jaina. Some dynasties of obscure origin supported their claim to being kshatriyas by having genealogies fabricated for them linking them to ancient lineages, such as the Suryavamsha (the Solar Lineage) and the family of Rama, or the Chandravamsha (the Lunar Lineage) and the descendants of Puru. Such claims became quite fashionable after the sixth century AD when mention is made in the *Puranas* of the making of what are called 'new kshatriyas'.

It was presumed that the pattern of the four castes was uniform in the subcontinent. But in fact it differed from region to region and various occupational castes were often prominent. Thus in the Punjab the dominant caste has not been that of brahmanas but of khatris or traders. In medieval times they had problems with the peasant castes aspiring to high status. Dominant castes may formally claim a higher caste status but in fact their dominance came and comes from land and wealth. An on-going debate among historians of south India concerns the dominant caste of brahmanas in relation to the powerful vellalas, landed gentry, at various times.

Colonial scholars saw the connection between caste and religion but this did not lead to the recognition that religions in South Asia followed a pattern distinctly different from the Judeo-Christian; not that they failed to observe distinct, monolithic identities at all social levels. They are better viewed as juxtaposed sects that formed a mosaic. Harmony or discord between them, both of which feature in early texts, referred to sects and communities rather than to an overarching religious identity of Hindu, Buddhist, Muslim or Christian. There were conflicts but these were less frequent, were localized, were on a smaller scale and were easier to resolve.

As we know, another difference was that all religions—indigenous or immigrant—internalized caste. Those who converted to religions promising social equality ended up carrying the baggage of caste with them. An entire village might convert, as for example in recent years when Dalits converted to the neo-Buddhism advocated by Ambedkar, (nevertheless caste hierarchies continued to be observed). Every religion in India has its Dalits and OBCs (Other Backward Castes).

The litmus test of the centrality of caste shows up in having to conform to the caste rules of marriage circles. This means having to follow the rules of which groups can intermarry and which cannot. The rules are still generally observed. The essential requirement in this was to ensure control over women. This is made brutally clear in the decisions of the khap panchayats of Haryana to murder the young women who do not observe the caste rules of whom they may or may not marry. Or take the case of Islam where Muslim society was also fragmented. The Muslims claiming ancestry from west Asia are of a higher caste than the local converts. Despite both being Muslims there is still a distinction in caste. The ranking of castes according to occupation is also observed as it is in all religions in India. Muslims who came from elsewhere and settled in South Asia and married into local communities adapted local belief to Islam. Local custom and practice could take precedence over the Islamic law of Shar'ia, which in itself often accommodated such custom. Such communities would have had problems with a monolithic Islam. At the lowest level were the Dalit Muslims, who like their Hindu counterparts continued to be treated as polluting and were often denied burial in the graveyards of high-caste Muslims. Similarly, places of worship built and managed by Mazhabi Sikhs who are regarded as untouchables tend to be avoided by upper-caste Sikhs. Technically, once reservation is conceded to the Dalit it should be open to all Dalits of every religion.

Converting Dalits into a separate community where they could only marry among themselves meant that they were Dalits by birth and remained so all through life. Using them in the meanest occupations and declaring them thereby physically polluting to the senses, was a mechanism of ensuring a permanent supply of subordinated labour. Because they were believed to be polluting, they could live only in their section of the village. This was the most efficient ghettoization of large communities. What continues to remain unclear to the historian is why particular groups were degraded in this manner at various times in history; or why religions that claim to be inclusive of all, and supposedly treat all humans as equal, nevertheless exclude some groups as untouchable? This is surely an instance of the social structure encompassing religion. Religion rarely fights for the equality of all in material life.

For obvious reasons neither the brahmanical codes nor the construction of caste in the nineteenth century captured the reality in the functioning of castes on the ground. This is also applicable to the way religion was projected as an identity.

The construction of religious identities emerged from the textual bias of Orientalist scholarship. Since the texts were in Sanskrit and Arabic scholars were tutored by the brahmanas and the mullahs. The brahmanas highlighted the *Vedas* and the *Dharmashastras*, the others highlighted the Qur'an, the Hadith and the Shar'ia. There was little discussion of other texts or other religious groups that questioned these. Buddhism and Jainism were treated as sub-sects of Hinduism as they still are by many. Popular religion was part of the oral tradition or was recorded in languages that were not considered on par with Sanskrit such as Prakrit, or Tamil and other regional languages. That religious practices did not always follow the texts was barely noticed. It has been said of Hinduism that its essentials lie in orthopraxy—the practice of rituals, and not in orthodoxy—the theological beliefs. For the majority, observances were primary. Colonial scholarship regarded the recording of religious practices as the domain of the ethnographers and the authors of district gazetteers. There was little recognition of the fact that in complex societies there are multiple voices and they all have to be listened to.

From the colonial perspective Hinduism and Islam were two separate monolithic religions and all Hindus and Muslims observed the rules of their respective text-based religions. This may have been applicable to sections of the elite, such as court circles and heads of religious institutions. However, for the vast majority of people religion was an open-ended experience—a mixing, merging, overlapping, borrowing or rejecting of forms and ideas beyond the formal labels. Religion for the larger population lay in forms of personal devotion, in the worship of the spirits within trees and mountains, nagas, yakshis and ancillary deities of local cult shrines, in listening to the words of the bhikkhus and the Nayannars and Alvars, the Bhakti and Sufi teachers, to the stories retold from the epics and the *Puranas*, and to the conversations of those who congregated around gurus, faqirs, pirs, and other 'holy men', agreeing or disagreeing on the essentials of understanding the purpose of life and the meaning of death. There were the grand temples, mosques and churches to be visited for prayers, except that temples were not open to all. Ritual and belief because they mixed caste practices and the norms of one's sect, differed among communities that we now refer to as Hindu. These differences need detailed study in the histories of religion in India.

Religions in South Asia were generally flexible enough to allow people to worship in each other's sacred places when there was a wish to do so and if they were allowed to. My first experience of religion was when I was visiting my grandmother at the age of four. She was a devout worshipper of Vishnu, yet she took me one morning to the grave of a locally venerated Muslim holy man, a pir, and taught me how to offer flowers and seek blessings in my own way. The imprint has remained. The essence of religion concerns the worshipper, her relationship with the world around her from which her belief may come and her personal relationship with the supernatural. Today in South Asia, we unnecessarily insist on impermeable boundaries.

It is perhaps as well to remember that what came to be called 'Hindu' was the label for all that was placed together beneath an umbrella, and that which came to be called Hinduism in colonial times. The religion of Hinduism, or these many Hindu religions, as some would say, can be better described as a mosaic of sectarian belief and worship rather than a single system with a linear history. Ashoka when he speaks of what we would call religion refers to the brahmanas and the shramans (Buddhists and Jainas), as does that famed Greek visitor of the time, Megasthenes. The same is suggested by Al-Biruni as late as the eleventh century AD. Apparently it would seem that people identified themselves by their sects. As we know 'Hindu' was first used in Arabic, but initially as a geographical term and referred to the people living across the Indus river in al-Hind. It was taken from the Old Iranian and Indo-Aryan, Sindhu, and the Indos of the Greeks' name for the Indus river. It was only from about the fourteenth century or so that 'Hindu' took on a religious connotation to refer to those that were not Muslim. This brought the mosaic of sects under one awning. But the term Hinduism as suggestive of a uniform system of belief became current in colonial times.

Strictly speaking, the single identity also seems inappropriate for Muslims who by now had fragmented into many sects and communities, differentiated by the imprint of local culture and a degree of concession to it. Similarly, Buddhism too became variegated over time, ranging from Theravada to the complexities of Ge-lugs-pa in Tibet. In the case of Muslims, Buddhists, Jainas, the fact that they were religions founded by historical persons gave them a different pattern of evolution. This pattern has some parallels not with the entirety of Hinduism but with some of its sects that had their beginnings with historical founders. The history of religion in South Asia was not the same as that of the Judeo-Christian tradition.

The nineteenth-century perception of religion in India moved it from its earlier relative fluidity at the popular level into a defined pattern with indelible boundaries. This facilitated its mobilization on a large scale as and when required, as has been apparent in recent times. Having projected two monolithic religions as the major religious contribution of the Indian past, the census data was added in. There followed the theory of the majority religion of Hinduism creating a majority community and the minority religion of Islam creating a minority community—the largest and most prominent among a number of minority communities, and each was given a specific religious identity. It was then erroneously argued that the separation of the two communities Hindu and Muslim was rooted in history. Mobilizing majority and minority communities by religion led inevitably to the politics of communalism. Counting numbers and giving them religious labels was unheard of prior to the nineteenth century.

Religion became the causative factor in the interpretation of history. But religious identities have varied and changed within the same religion over time, and from one social segment to another. Periodization based on religion as the sole criterion of historical activity is a negation of history. Discarded by historians, it remains central to the creed of extreme religious nationalists, Hindu and Muslim and others, still drawing legitimation from colonial theories. Colonial scholars argued that the Hindus and Muslims belonged to two entirely separate cultures with little in common; and that the relationship was antagonistic. History became the foundation of establishing a Hindu and a Muslim identity, but the nature of religion in the subcontinent was misunderstood. It was not these identities alone that brought about the subsequent fractures in the subcontinent but they were used to legitimize the political mobilizations that led to the break-up. The pattern is almost a blueprint for colonial policy in other parts of the world as well.

Turning to yet another but different colonial reading of the South Asian past there was an insistence that poverty had been endemic to South Asia. It was attributed to the political system of Oriental Despotism said to characterize pre-modern Asia and which left little alternative. In contesting this view Indian opinion argued that poverty was recent and resulted from wealth being drained away to fuel British industry. We seem to have come full circle. The globalized market economy has been described as a form of neo-colonialism. The wealth produced in the developing world goes to enrich the national corporates feeding into multinational corporations. It cannot therefore stem the increasing impoverishment of the developing world.

Let me consider two identities associated with poverty that were not created by colonial writing but were reiterated by the colonial perspective. These were the Dalits and the forest dwelling tribes—both dating back to more than two millennia. The two were classified by colonial administration as Scheduled Castes and Scheduled Tribes. Colonial scholarship generally ignored the first but the second was reinforced through insisting on the dichotomy between the civilized and the primitive.

The British Census differentiated between tribe and caste but for Indian ethnography there was more of a continuum from tribe to caste, some tribes evolving into castes. What then has been the identity of these forest tribes? In historical records they were the mleccha, the primitive 'Other', the alternate to the civilized. A brahmanical myth of origin makes this clear. It tells of Vena, the ruler who having stopped performing brahmanical rituals was killed by the brahmanas. But a ruler was necessary. So they churned the left thigh of Vena and a short, ugly, dark man with bloodshot eyes emerged and they called him Nishad. He was banished to the forest and was associated with the Pulinda, Shabara, Bhilla and other forest dwellers, and also the rakshasas, the demons. This formulaic description of such people is repeated in most Sanskrit texts. They then churned the right arm of the dead Vena and up sprang a handsome young man whom they named Prithu. Significantly, he was the one who introduced settled agriculture and animal breeding and observed all the rituals. And the earth in gratitude took his name as Prithivi. This is a stereotypical story that occurs in many Asian cultures. The myth colours other texts. The forest dwellers are said to be hostile and to attack the armies that march through their forests. This was a classic case of the settlement encroaching on the forest and resenting the forest dwellers who resisted such encroachment. Very occasionally the encroachment resulted in a reversal of identity. The king could give a person a huge grant of forested land and the grantee would establish himself in the area, perhaps marry into the tribal chief's family and gradually build up an independent base. Such a royal family would need a carefully crafted genealogy claiming royal status, as is evident from the genealogies of the Raj Gonds and the Nagabansis of central India.

With an increase in lands granted by kings in the period after about AD 1000, the encroachments became more common. Slowly, the tribal peoples began losing their land, their forests and rivers, their animal and mineral wealth. In medieval times traders were attracted by this wealth and set up the monetary market with inevitably, money-lending. Acquisition of tribal land by the British administration requiring vast amounts of timber for the railways and other forest products associated with forested areas, such as metals and minerals, further reduced the rights. The latest predators are corporates demanding huge areas for both mining and timber. They claim to be introducing the benefits of civilization but the identity of the forest dwellers remains that of the 'Primitive Other'. The past for them is not a shared history but a remembered exploitation carried out by the representatives of civilization. These tribes are now among the most impoverished peoples in the subcontinent.

The permanence of poverty has been assumed and until recently has raised little alarm. But poverty was not what the forest tribes were identified with in earlier times. Where forest produce was available to them and where land could be used for shifting cultivation, life had a different quality. The forest was contrasted with the settlement as an alternative way of life, with its own cultural values that were sometimes even romanticized.

Today both groups have forced themselves into the consciousness of the societies where they are present. Dalits associated with Hinduism are receiving some benefits from reservations in educational institutions and state employment. Other Dalits are quite rightly demanding the same benefits. Predictably, the resentment of the upper castes is expressed in outbursts of violence against the Dalits. Private militias of the upper castes think nothing of going to a Dalit village and slaughtering Dalits knowing that they will escape punishment, as happens periodically in various parts of India. The rights of the forest tribes having been reduced to a minimum—they are now caught in a condition of continuous violence. The Naxals or Maoists claiming to speak for the tribes are battling it out with government administration in the forest habitats as well as with corporates introducing their own ways of undermining the welfare of the forest people. Caught in this crossfire, it is the tribal people whose lives are devastated.

I have been trying to question some of the identities with which we live and which some regard as historically valid. I have tried to argue that those identities that condition our lives in South Asia should be re-assessed to ascertain their validity. There is a need for recognizing that they may not be rooted in history but in other extraneous factors. And we have to remember that when history changes, identities also have to change. If the premises of the identity are no longer viable, can we continue to use the same label? Such monitoring involves a dialogue among historians and scholars but also and importantly, between them and citizens.

This would not merely be an exercise in historical research but would help us understand why an identity was initially constructed and how it was subsequently used, and why it may have become not only redundant but also perilous. Ostensibly, it may relate to race or religion, or whatever, but implicitly may be connected with other intentions such as access to power or aspirations to status. Is the identity then a mask to hide disparities, disaffections, inequities, encouraging a deviation from facing actuality? An identity is not created accidentally nor is it altogether innocent of intention.

Analyses of identities are pertinent also to the extensive and vocal South Asian diaspora. Nationals settled in distant lands often nurture identities that may well be historically untenable and outdated in the culture of the home country. But they are a source of solace to the migrant in an alien culture and underline a claim to connectedness. Such identities frequently deny the essential plurality of South Asian civilization and the intersections within it. The replacement of these identities becomes a problem of trans-nationalism.

Beyond this we might consider what the premise should be if we are to encourage the emergence of other identities given that the context of our times is not what it was a century or two ago. A nation needs identities that are broad, inclusive and that support its essential requirements of democracy, secularity, equality, rights to the institutions of welfare and to social justice. If we continue to make identities of colonial origin a part of our thinking they will continue to be the quicksand that prevents us from even aspiring to, leave alone reaching, the utopias we had once visualized.

4

IN DEFENCE OF HISTORY

From 1999 to 2004, when a BJP government was in power, there were repeated attempts to silence historians. Similar happenings could occur again. To comprehend these events requires an understanding of why it is necessary to defend history as written by historians, as also the recognition of a past that is analytical and open to critical enquiry. The historians who were verbally assaulted and physically threatened were the ones that had taken this turn in writing history in the previous decades. Their studies incorporated historical enquiry and were pointers to new ways of extending that enquiry. They widened and sharpened the intellectual foundations of the discipline of history and enriched the understanding of the Indian past. Some among those who were opposed to these historians were also mocking the discipline of history, unable to grasp the change that the discipline had undergone.

Indian history in the 1960s and 70s moved from being largely a body of information on dynasties and a recital of glorious deeds to a broad based study of social and economic forms in the past. In this there was a focus on patterns of the economy, on forms of social organization, on religious movements, and on cultural articulations. The multiple cultures of India were explored in terms of how they contributed to the making of Indian civilization, or as some historians might prefer, 'Indian civilizations'. Therefore, many aspects of this multiplicity and its varying forms—from that of forest dwellers, jhum cultivators, pastoralists, peasants, artisans, to that of merchants, aristocracies and specialists of ritual and belief—all found a place in the mosaic that was gradually being constructed. Identities were not singular but plural and the most meaningful studies were of situations where identities overlapped.

Ten years ago Indian history was moving towards what some scholars have described as almost a historical renaissance. The writing of Indian historians, ranging over many opinions and interpretations, were read and studied in the world of historical scholarship, not only in India but wherever there was an interest in comparative history. Historical interpretations at this time and in many parts of the world used methods of historical analyses that were derived from a range of theories that attempted to explain and interpret the past.

As we've seen, these included schools of interdisciplinary research such as the French Annales School, varieties of structuralism, of Marxism, Weberian concepts, and diverse other theories and there was writing on what was called 'the return of grand theory'. Lively debates on the Marxist interpretation of history, for example, led to the rejection of the Asiatic Mode of Production as proposed by Marx, and instead focused on other aspects such as whether a Marxist method of analysis could be used and if so, how it would be defined. In the period after the ending of the Cold War in the late twentieth century the interest in dialectics as a philosophical form and historical materialism as a way of understanding history began to be explored more freely. There was no single uniform reading of Marxism among Marxists, so there were many stimulating discussions on social and economic history. In the study of feudalism by Indian historians, for example, one trigger may have been the Feudal Mode of Production as developed by Marx, but the ideas of historians other than Marxists, such as Marc Bloch, Fernand Braudel and Henri Pirenne, were also central to these discussions. The intention was not to apply theories without questioning them, but to use comparative history to ask searching questions.

If those who constitute both the political leadership as well as the rank and file of political parties today, took the trouble to read, they might begin to understand that serious historical interpretation is not just a game of adopting this or that '...ism', but of attempting to use a method of analysis in interpreting the past. Gone are the days that one could talk intelligently about history to a Nehru or a Maulana Azad. They are not made like that any more. The equally serious problem is that owing to our faulty educational system in which school education has become something of a joke, there is a yawning gap between those advancing knowledge and the general public. There is no category of intellectual middle-men or women who can communicate the happenings at the cutting edge of knowledge in a sufficiently popular and reliable form so that those who are not specialists can at least follow what is happening. Consequently, there is no problem for illiterate ideas to be spread among the public, to convince them that the myths and fantasies about earlier times, were in fact realities. Stories are spun about the past and sold as history with little attempt at teaching people how to tell a fantasy from real life.

Some of the more obvious examples of historical debates relate to the question of how to investigate the reality of the past. The changing history of caste in Indian society was being studied in detail to ascertain social change and explain social disparities. It was also being viewed in a comparative sense with other systems of social organization such as those dominated by the master–slave nexus as in the Greco-Roman world, or feudal lords and serfs of the medieval European world, or the more easily recognizable class-based societies of recent centuries. Historians were asking the same questions that the Buddha had asked when told about Greek society: why do some societies have caste and others have a two-fold division of master and slave. These were questions that were concerned primarily with trying to comprehend caste as a system of organizing society before making value-judgements about it.

New themes came under the purview of historical investigation. Gender history focused on women, not merely as additional players but as primary and diverse players at varying levels of society and their role in the genesis of some social forms began to be studied. Systems of knowledge came to be examined in terms of their influence on society and their function rather than restricting their history to merely repeating the obvious—that these were great advances in knowledge. The pursuit of knowledge for itself is acceptable, but to examine its application in society and the results thereof is even more necessary. The formation and definition of a range of Indian cultures came to include the formulations of culture from communities other than elite groups and this widened the base of social history. It also influenced the extensive study of religious movements other than the well-known ones, their beliefs and rituals and their audiences. An interest in the history of the environment suggested fresh hypotheses about the rise and decline of urban centres or the impact of hydraulic changes or deforestation on settlements of various kinds.

An attempt was made through government actions to terminate this intellectual efflorescence. The blight that began in the 1990s culminated in around 2000 in an enforced effort to clamp down on the process of exploring ideas. It reached the point where a systematic attempt was made to denigrate the independent intellectual and to undermine a historical understanding of our society and its past. This attempt took a variety of forms. Sometimes it took the form of political actions, later it resorted to intervening in and closing institutions connected to academic research, and thereafter it focused on censoring books and textbooks. Each action was orchestrated to a single aim.

The political action that initiated this blight was the tearing down of the Babri Masjid in 1992. This was an attempt to insist that a single culture and a single identity—a Hindu identity, defined not by Hindus in general but by those indulging in the destruction of the Masjid—defined Indian culture. From the earlier acceptance by Hindu culture to allow variants to co-exist, the attempt now was to pick up and weave a narrow, limited, exclusive strand and define that as Hindu. Destroying the Babri Masjid was a violent, aggressive act of destruction claiming to glorify Hinduism but was a far cry from representing civilized Hindu values. What happened to 'Hindu tolerance' and the fact that Hindus in the past rarely went around destroying mosques? This activity is of recent vintage. Implicit in this act of destruction was the theory that it drew its legitimacy from history, that it was avenging the destruction of the temple at Somanatha by Mahmud of Ghazni, and thereby setting right a wrong of history, even if it was doing so after a thousand years.

This fallacious idea that the past can be changed through destroying the surviving heritage from the earlier time was of course an attack on the idea of history: for an axiom of history is that the past cannot be changed, but that if we intelligently understand the past, then the present and the future can be better directed. The destruction of the heritage of a society, as also happened in the case of the Taliban destroying the images of the Buddha at Bamiyan, was the subordination of past history to the imperatives of contemporary politics. The claim that the past could be annulled was actually a crass attempt to redefine people, their culture and their history. The effort in these instances was to create a nation moulded not by all-inclusive national aspirations as of the earlier anti-colonial kind, but instead by a narrow category labelled as 'nationalism' although it identified with a particular version of a single religion. This made it easier to impose an ideology of the sort that facilitated political mobilization and access to power of one community and excluded all others. History was being made a handmaiden to this process.

Once such a process comes into being it can be used to construct what is projected as a collective memory. Collective memories are not innate and naturally prevalent at birth. They are consciously constructed at particular historical moments for particular historical purposes. As we all know from parallel political movements that have used history in this fashion, such as in Europe in the 1930s, the notion of a collective memory encourages simplistic explanations, single agendas even for explanations of happenings in the past, and preferably a replacing of historical fact with mythology. Collective memory can be a historical or even anti-historical and is therefore a convenient tool for spreading fallacies. To call a particular mindset, or an attitude to the past, as a 'collective memory' requires a meticulous investigation of what is being presented as such to justify the description, and the reaṣon why it has been constructed and has an appeal.

The Hindutva approach to history for example, ignores all other histories and schools of interpretation contrary to it. They are all dismissed as Leftist or 'Marxist' or its equivalent. They are then replaced with a reconstruction of the past, based on dubious evidence and arguments, and which differs from the accepted mainstream history. Hindutva history draws directly from and derives its legitimacy from nineteenth-century colonial history. It draws its themes from that and the arguments are still stuck in the ideas of those times. As we've seen, the periodization of Indian history maintained by James Mill divides Indian history into the Hindu, Muslim and British periods. Mill's argument and that of many other colonial historians was that the Hindus and Muslims formed two distinct communities and that they were perpetually in conflict. This idea then contributed to the notion of the two nations—the Hindu and the Muslim—identified by religion, culminating in the creation of Pakistan.

This has been taken over by the Hindutva ideology in which the enmity of Hindu and Muslim is foundational. It is argued that Hindu civilization suffered because of Muslim rulers who oppressed the Hindus. This view is propagated despite the fact that some of the most creative forms of Hinduism such as Bhakti—the religion of devotional worship, and now the most widely practiced form of Hinduism—evolved in South India but became prevalent in North India notwithstanding Islam and sometimes with Muslim participants. That Mill's version of Indian history has been discarded on the basis of the history written in the last fifty years makes not the slightest difference to the Hindutva insistence on supporting the two-nation theory.

A major contention is that Hindus were forcibly converted to Islam. This view is based on the claims of the court chroniclers of various sultanates who keep announcing the conversion of a fantasy figure of fifty thousand Hindus. Some conversions may well have been under pressure. Others such as well-placed families, as for instance of some Rajputs, more frequently converted for reasons of social and political expediency, or else made marriage alliances without converting. Shahjehan for instance had a Rajput mother and Rajput paternal grandmother, which gives him a substantial Rajput identity. There was a time when the Rajputs were thought to have come from Central Asia, although this theory has few supporters now. In the general mélange of the Indian population it is difficult to identify those who are foreign. The characteristics of being foreign were not the same as now. But the majority of conversions were by caste—jati. These would have been voluntary and in the expectation that Islam held out a better deal of social equality than Hinduism. If large numbers of Hindus converted then the majority of Muslims were indigenous Hindus and cannot be regarded as alien. There are many contradictions in dubbing all Muslims and Christians as foreigners, apart from the fact that the definition of foreigner was not the same in those days.

There was of course no guarantee that the expectation in converting would be met and less so where a caste ranking was not terminated with conversion, as was generally the case. But what is of interest is that where a caste converted, it normally retained its rules of marriage, custom and some rituals and continued to have professional relationships with Hindu castes of its equivalence or in its social vicinity. When weavers in some north Indian towns such as Chanderi converted to Islam, they continued their earlier relationship with Hindu textile merchants. Prior to their conversion they were anyway regarded as low caste and the traders maintained a social distance, and this distance remained as before even after conversion. That every religion in India has a category of Dalits and the distancing is maintained in each, shows that conversion to an egalitarian religion was not the answer to social inequality. The social code based on jati was more powerful than religion.

The issue of conversion that was once a matter of historical debate became a political weapon that proponents of Hindutva used to threaten Muslims and Christians with. Historians have shown repeatedly that conversions did not create a monolithic, uniform community. Those who called themselves Islamic had immense variations in the practice of their religion. The Islam of the Arabs, Turks, Persians was not identical. The basic divide between the Sunni and Shi'a has continued throughout history, as also between Khojas, Bohras, Meos, Navayats and Mappilas, to name just a few. These variations enriched the culture of each community and endowed them with distinct identities of language, region and custom, identities that frequently intersected with those of other groups in the area. The hostilities that surfaced were more frequently within the sect.

In trying to understand the history of communities, whether Hindu, Muslim or any other, there are many distinctive forms that give multiple identities to such groups. These have evolved from a long process of social negotiation—some of it contentious and some of it convivial. These identities cannot be negated as in the Hindutva interpretations that sweep them all into a single religious community. Conversion resulted from a variety of reasons and these varied according to caste, occupation and region. These need to be historically investigated. Such an investigation has urgency because in India today, both in Islam as in Hinduism there is a wish to forge a new monolithic identity in pursuit of political ambitions. The process of what has been called Islamization—which some may see as a polite term for fundamentalism—is taking place in many communities. Is this a counter-point to the Hindutva now calling the shots in many Hindu communities?

Another aspect of the relations between Hindus and Muslims in the ideology of Hindutva focuses on the Muslim destruction of temples in the past. This is not denied by historians, who try and place such actions in historical perspective. The Hindutva count takes it up to 3008 but a historian's reckoning does not push it beyond 80. The exaggeration of the former speaks for itself. This was not the only activity of Muslim rulers and temple destruction has to be juxtaposed with other undertakings that were constructive and not destructive. Nor were temples destroyed out of religious animosity alone. Aurangzeb has now been converted into the icon of the Muslim destroyer of temples. Yet, there are innumerable firmans that record his substantial donations to temples and to brahmanas, as has been listed and discussed by K.K. Datta in his study, *Some Firmans, Sanads and Parwanas*. There is no record that states that any brahmana refused to receive a grant of land or money from a ruler who was destroying Hindu temples. One would expect this from self-respecting brahmanas if there was such a ground swell of resentment against him as is depicted in some modern writing. After all the brahmanas were the custodians of temples.

This is also related to the question of what we chose to recall from the past and reiterate, and what we chose to forget. The broader question is why were some temples destroyed and others conserved by the same ruler. Destroying a temple was a demonstration of power on the part of invaders, irrespective of whether they were Muslim or Hindu. We choose to forget that there were Hindu kings who destroyed temples, either willfully as did Harshadeva and other kings of Kashmir in order to acquire the wealth of the temples, or as in the case of the victorious Paramara raja who destroyed temples built by the defeated Chaulukya, as part of a campaign. In terms of numbers, Muslim rulers damaged more temples than did Hindu rulers, but the more important question is why temples became a target even where the rulers were Hindu.

My purpose in drawing attention to this is not to add up the scores, but to argue that temple destruction was not merely an act of religious hostility. Temples were places of ritual space and had a religious identity. But temples were also statements of power and were surrogate political institutions representing royalty. They were depositories of wealth and institutions financing trade and other economic enterprises. The investments of religious institutions in economic enterprise are not a recent activity but go back to the activities of those that administered the Buddhist monasteries. The temples assumed the same role when they had the wherewithal to invest. Temples also maintained social demarcations by allowing in some castes but excluding others. The cultural nucleus of at least the elite groups of a region often focused on the activities of the temple. They were, in effect, institutions with both a political and economic authority. Temple destruction and its aftermath, therefore calls for historical explanations of a wide-ranging kind. It cannot be made the justification for destroying or threatening to destroy, mosques and churches in the present day and building temples on the debris.

■

In order to assert the superiority and antiquity of the Hindu community as the indigenous and earliest inhabitants of India, the theory of Aryan identity is being revived but in a curious way. The 'Aryans' are said to be the foundation of Indian civilization therefore they have to be proved to be indigenous as well as the earliest people to give form to the civilization. Therefore they are now being equated with the authors of the Indus civilization. This contradicts the opinion of the majority of scholars who have argued that the Indus Civilization was pre-Aryan and non-Aryan. It also had very little in common with Vedic culture. It was a mercantile culture focusing on its many cities and artisanal production and trade, whereas the Vedic corpus depicts a cattle-keeping society with some agricultural activity but unfamiliar with urban culture. The Vedic corpus is rich in its depiction of an agro-pastoral culture, but this is in no way the same as the urban sophistication of the Indus cities.

The idea of the Aryan foundations of Indian civilization is an entirely non-Indian theory curiously fostered by two distinctive groups of people, European and American. As mentioned previously, one was the German scholar Max Mueller who drew on the work of European philologists seeking the roots of Indo-European languages that he combined with the fashionable (and now discarded) theories of race propounded in nineteenth-century Europe. He argued for a superior Aryan race that came into northwestern India, invaded and settled in the area from where the Aryans spread to other parts of the subcontinent. The second group was that of the Theosophists, the American, Henry Steel Olcott, associated with Madame Helena Petrovna Blavatsky, who founded the Theosophical Society in the late nineteenth century and lived partly in India to propagate Theosophy and her other ideas. They were the first to argue, as do the Hindutva ideologues now, that the Aryans of India were not only indigenous but were the fountainhead of world civilization, and that all the achievements of human society had their origins in India and travelled out from India. Vedic Sanskrit, it was claimed, was the mother language of all languages, thus reversing the argument of Sanskrit being descended from Indo-European. The Theosophical Society had very close relations with the Arya Samaj for a few years.

The thesis of Aryans being indigenous has at least two other angles to it relevant to contemporary politics. The idea may unite all the caste Hindus as being of the same ancestry and descended from the Aryans, but it excludes the Dravidian speakers and Dalits. A recent attempt to get round the first problem is the garbled attempt to argue that the Dravidian language belongs to the same linguistic group as Indo-Aryan. This is linguistically untenable. The proponents of Hindutva will surely have to think of something a little more credible. The second problem is that they run counter to the view of Jyotiba Phule and the Dalits of his time who maintained that the Aryans were alien outsiders who, as brahmanas, invaded and oppressed the lower castes of Indian society. The Hindutva argument has now shifted to saying that the authors of the *Rigveda* were the builders of the Harappan cities. They also maintain that only Hindus can legitimately call themselves indigenous since Muslims and Christians are foreigners, their religion having originated outside the territory of British India, the territory that they equate with the ancient Bharatavarsha. Perhaps one of the ways to get round this problem would be to quickly convert the Dalits and the adivasis into caste Hindus—they can then all be Aryans together.

The intention of Hindutva history is to support the vision of its founding fathers—Savarkar and Golwalkar—and to attribute the beginnings of Indian history to what they called the indigenous Aryans. This contradicts the existing archaeological and linguistic evidence of the Indo-Aryan speakers. This theory ignores all the other societies, some of which were speaking Dravidian and Munda, of which languages there are traces in Vedic Sanskrit. It refrains from defining what is an Aryan because obviously any definition would lead to many complications given the range of exceptions that would arise. It ignores the argument, now generally agreed to, that the concept of Aryan is not an exclusive, racial identity, but refers primarily to the language, Indo-Aryan and to the culture of a group recognizable by linguistic and ritual features, reflecting a merging of varied groups including migrants from the Indo-Iranian borderlands and the Oxus plain; and that the meaning and evolution of the term changed with its historical usage. The linguistic and cultural connections between those in northeastern Iran and in west Asia, are a component of the study of the Vedic language and archaeology, but we are so blinkered to anything outside north India, that we consult neither the scholarship on the *Avesta* in Iran, nor that on west Asia of this period.

Desperate attempts are being made to prove that the Vedic people and the Harappans were identical. Reading the Harappan pictograms as Indo-Aryan has failed. As mentioned earlier, the reading of archaeological evidence is forced to the extent that a damaged seal showing a Harappan unicorn was manipulated on the computer to make it look like the hind quarters of a horse, in order to link it with the horses of the Vedic sacrificial ritual of the ashvamedha. The fraud was exposed in *Frontline*. Contrary to the evidence so far excavated, which points to the origins of the Indus Civilization being located at sites in Baluchistan and the northwest, the attempt is to locate it on the banks of what some identify as the Sarasvati river. This would allow it to be called the Sarasvati Civilization, further evoking a Vedic source.

A history having been invented, the next question is how it is to be implemented? This happens at two levels. One is that of projecting this history through research institutions and the other is through the school curriculum. This was what was attempted in 2002 through a campaign that had involved the agencies of the Human Resource Development Ministry directly concerned with history such as the ICHR (Indian Council for Historical Research), and the NCERT (National Council for Education, Research and Training).

These interventions by the Ministry were politicized by statements to the effect that, earlier, these institutions were under the control of Left-wing academics so now it was the turn of the Right-wing academics to take charge. If the debate was going to be formulated in terms of leftist and rightist historians then each time the party in power changed, the curriculum and the syllabus and the topics for research, would also have to change. However, history is not a shuttlecock that can be driven back and forth in accordance with the views of governments. It also means that since procedures are not being observed, not only the curriculum but also the research programmes will change.

Excuse after excuse was made to prevent the publication of certain volumes of documents already in the press, as part of the project entitled, 'Towards Freedom'. It was first said that they had not been properly edited, then that there were no indexes, and that they would have to be cleared by yet another committee although they had already been cleared.

It was rumoured that the real reason was to prevent the publication of these documents as some showed the Hindu Mahasabha as less hostile to the British, the possibility of which has been discussed by those who have historical knowledge about the period.

Obviously, none of this should have been allowed to happen. Procedures of functioning as they were laid down and followed earlier, should have continued to be followed. The professional training in a discipline should have been respected and it should have been mandatory that professionally trained people were appointed to the agencies that determine education.

The other action relating to institutions during this period was of course even more high-handed. It took the form of arbitrarily shutting down institutions of research as and when the government wished to do so. An example of this was the sudden closing of the Kerala Council of Historical Research six months after it was founded. This was particularly unacceptable given the fact that there was a growing interest in regional history and the historians working on Kerala had been active in developing research activities. This decision was reversed through a judgment of the court. Again, the BJP in Madhya Pradesh attacked the scientific programmes of Eklavya, an educational NGO that produces school-level books on the sciences and social sciences. For all its claims to endorsing secularism, the Congress Party in practice, was sympathetic to the Sangh Parivar in this instance. If such attacks are allowed to become a pattern it will be disastrous for research and for a secular investment in Indian society. Given that there are attempts to substitute mainstream history with propaganda, it is all the more necessary to have independent bodies to counteract the hegemony of the propaganda.

To argue that Marxist historians when placed in charge of institutions bring about a hijacking of history to Left-wing ideology is a view resulting from an unfamiliarity with Indian historical research of the last fifty years. The most wide-ranging debate on pre-modern Indian history has been the debate on whether or not there had been feudalism in India. D.D. Kosambi's understanding of feudalism was a serious attempt in the 1950s to apply Marx's idea of the feudal mode to a certain period of Indian history, and yet he deviated from the model of the strictly Marxist mode. Some others used the model to varying degrees and introduced diverse forms. The major critiques of the feudal mode were initiated by Marxist historians and were later added to by non-Marxists. What resulted from this debate has been the exploration of many areas of Indian history in terms of the nature of the state, polity, economy and religion that have yielded new insights into our past. What colonial historians referred to as the post-Gupta 'dark age' is now well-lit through recent research. It has also provoked an interest in more detailed studies of regional history, which in turn have honed the focus on national history.

The confrontation among historians today is not between 'leftist and rightist' historians, nor is it about establishing a Marxist view of history, as is crudely stated by some, but over the right to debate interpretations of history. There cannot be a single, definitive, official history. If some of us feel that Hindutva history is less history and more mythology we should have the right to say so, without being personally abused, being called 'anti-national', 'academic terrorists worse than the cross-border variety' and 'perverts', and being threatened with arrest and with being physically put down. Indeed, a leading Hindutva ideologue, Arun Shourie, even sarcastically said we 'eminent historians' all had hymens that were so thick that we thought that we had retained our virginity even when we published signed articles in publications of the Left. Apart from the sheer crassness and vulgarity of this statement, if men cannot have hymens, even figuratively speaking, presumably his remark was directed at women historians. In the final analysis, history is an intellectual enterprise and does have an intellectual dimension in its understanding of the past, however much the Hindutva ideology may try and erase that and replace it with cheap jibes.

Basic to changing the Hindutva interpretation of history is the attempt to give a single definition to Indian culture, the roots of which are said to lie in Vedic foundations. This annuls the reality of Indian society being constituted of multiple cultures, in dialogue with each other. It ignores even the variant relations that have existed throughout Indian history between dominant and subordinate cultures. This sensitivity is particularly important today in forging cultural identities that are subcontinental, but at the same time incorporate the articulations of the region.

Knowledge does not consist of a body of information to be memorized and passed on. That is the concept of education in the sishu mandirs and madrassas and such like. A modern education demands questioning, skepticism and an ability to think independently and to link information. What then should we think of as the process of ensuring a transition of knowledge that is independent and draws on critical inquiry. It would seem that no dialogue is possible with government agencies. We have therefore to think of alternate strategies.

At one level one would have to work towards establishing councils of historical research in the various states so that regional histories can be treated in a seriously professional manner and not be reduced to being dependent on the patronage of politicians and bureaucrats allergic to the social sciences. The range of sources means that statements about the past have to draw from a multiplicity of records and if they contradict each other this may be the source of a new illumination about authorship and audience.

At another level it would be required of independent historians to be more involved in the teaching of history in schools, to help in drawing up a viable syllabus based on both professional expertise and pedagogy. This would not be an innovation as there are groups that have been doing just this; in some cases their textbooks have been used very effectively in state schools as well as private schools. The example of the Eklavya group comes to mind. Their work will have to be revived and continued despite the assault on them.

Ideally, the NCERT itself should be an autonomous organization, independently financed and not part of the Ministry of Human Resource Development. The same could be said of the ICHR. These organizations are now half a century old and quite capable of standing on their own and being run by members of the profession. This would allow them to play a far more effective role in advancing the discipline. And if they fall by the wayside they will have to pick themselves up and start again. They can coordinate various activities that require coordination, such as vetting textbooks and ensuring quality in every institution that calls itself a school, giving opportunities to school children to visit historical sites or become familiar with historical records, and even more importantly providing workshops for school teachers so that they can be acquainted with new research and generally make history accessible to those who teach it in schools.

In some ways the most serious challenge is the threat to close down discussion since it is an attempt to close the mind. Fortunately, it was not possible for the then government in 2002 to do so. But the attempts having been made once could be tried again. This is not a matter that concerns history alone, as it is a frontal attack on knowledge. As professionals engaged in its furtherance, it seems to me that we have no choice but to oppose it. The world has moved on since the nineteenth century and we have come to value independent thinking. There are enough historians in this country who will continue to write independently. There will be enough historical concerns growing out of the multiple cultural aspects of our society to ensure that the Indian mind is never closed.

5

WRITING HISTORY TEXTBOOKS: A MEMOIR

I wrote two textbooks on Indian history for Middle School, one on Ancient Indian History for Class VI (age group 11-13) and one on Medieval Indian History for Class VII (age group 13-14). The books were used for about forty years and were revised a couple of times. They have been replaced by other textbooks in the last few years. The story of how these books came to be written and why they were replaced touches on much that is happening to history textbooks in many parts of the world and is tied to political changes. I would like to relate the story in the context of India and in the form of a personal memoir.

▪

My first acquaintance with history textbooks for schools came about when UNESCO asked me in 1961 if I would do a review of a sample of textbooks used in the teaching of history in various schools in the Union Territory of Delhi. I had never thought of such an idea before and it interested me, so I agreed. The sample consisted of about twenty books if I remember correctly and I submitted the report fairly soon. I was appalled by the information contained in these books, with their adherence to outdated ideas and to colonial views of the Indian past, a totally banal narrative and predictable illustrations of a poor quality. I was thanked for the review and for the moment heard no further.

The review it seems coincided with a committee on history textbooks appointed by the government under the Chairmanship of Dr Tarachand. The Editorial Board consisted of the most eminent historians of that time: Professors Nilakanta Sastri, Mohammad Habib, and P.C. Gupta. The Ministry had established the National Council for Educational Research and Training (NCERT), as part of being generally alerted to the problems of school education in India. One of its functions was to commission the writing of textbooks for school. Mr M.C. Chagla, the then Minister, a thoughtful lawyer with a liberal bent of mind, was concerned that textbooks in history should not recite myths but be secular and rational explanations of the past.

It was presumably thought that if the books were to have some quality they would have to be written by, or at least supervised by, academics of recognition in the subject. Among the committee were included three senior historians from Calcutta and Delhi universities: Professor R.C. Majumdar who had written extensively on all periods of Indian history, Professor Bisheshwar Prasad who was an historian of Modern India and Dr Dasaratha Sharma whose field was ancient Indian history. Subsequently, R.C. Majumdar was made chairman of the Editorial Board and he invited me to join it, but I declined as I had just started writing the first textbook in the NCERT series.

It was decided to start with Class VI and a book on Ancient India. Quite how my name came up as a possible author is unclear to me. My initial reaction was that I wished to continue my research and not spend time on writing a textbook, and furthermore that I had no interest or expertise in writing for children. My only venture in this field was a small book of stories for children, *Indian Tales*, and this was hardly a qualification for writing a school textbook. However, I was eventually persuaded to do so by some of my colleagues at Delhi University where I was then teaching, who argued that this was a national cause and as such I should agree.

I would like to emphasize that even though India had become independent a long time ago (in 1947) the notion of a national cause was very strong in many of us. My generation had been imprinted with the nationalism of the forties and early fifties. Its essential characteristic was the enthusiasm that we were involved in the building of a new nation. We could therefore move away from conventions so as to encourage the implanting of new ideas. It was from this perspective that I agreed to write a textbook for Middle School.

The syllabus that had been worked out had two concerns: that the child should envision the ancient past as more than just the recital of conventional 'glories' and become acquainted with some of the multiple facets of life and action; and that it must be heavy with information rather than explanation. I enjoyed exploring the first but had problems with the second. But the syllabus remained the skeleton of the book.

My own research was based on a critical re-examination of the nationalist interpretation of history, emerging out of a critique of the colonial view of ancient Indian history. The colonial view had been faulted on many grounds, but the nationalist interpretation was also by now being regarded as somewhat ambivalent in relation to certain themes. There had been a hesitancy to analyze the inequities of caste, or the varied treatment of women, or the degree to which the social articulation of religions shaped societies. Whereas colonial views of the recent past were critiqued, nationalist interpretation was hesitant in critiquing the ancient Hindu past or the Islamic past which were as much in need of critical analysis as the modern. Pre-modern history had to be a narrative of greatness and glory on the whole, with little reference to that which could be prised apart and viewed without preconceptions.

The second problem was that of the amount of information a textbook should contain. There was a listing in the direction of putting in more, the argument being that at least some of the information would stick. The decision as to what could be omitted as not so relevant became a source of contention with the committee. I would try out my chapters on the age group for which they were intended and some found them heavy going and too stuffed with 'facts', which I had to then make more accessible. Arguing with a committee was not easy and there were many occasions when I wished that there had been some schoolteachers on the committee rather than only high-powered historians.

Nevertheless one kept trying and slowly the chapters began to take shape. Unfortunately, by then this committee of rather elderly historians began to lose its enthusiasm for the project, which in any case had not been a matter of great prestige or of central interest to its members. There was a quiet whiff of disdain at being involved with school textbooks, especially since they were otherwise involved in major publications of multi-volume projects, such as 'The History and Culture of the Indian People' and 'The Role of the Indian Armed Forces in World War II'. So my textbook which had been written and approved of by the Committee, rather drifted along without getting anywhere owing to the inactivity of the same Committee.

To get the project moving the ministry decided that a more active committee was required and therefore replaced the old committee with a new one. The new Editorial Board as it was called consisted of Sarvepalli Gopal as the Chief Editor, and as editors had Nurul Hasan from Aligarh University, Satish Chandra from Rajasthan University and myself, with S.K. Maitra as Secretary. The textbook project leapt into life and the first book went to press. This was *Ancient India* written for Class VI, and published in 1966. In 1968 I revised it on the basis of reactions from teachers and historians and further discussions in the Editorial Board. The textbook for Class VII on *Medieval India* was published in 1967. In the 1970s the Editorial Board commissioned further books for high-school level. These were Ram Sharan Sharma's *Ancient India*, Satish Chandra's *Medieval India*, Bipan Chandra's *Modern India* and the third book for Middle School, *India and the World* by Arjun Dev and Indrani Dev. The High School books were substantial in size and involved extended discussion. This entire set of textbooks constituted what I shall call the NCERT Textbooks (Set 1), since there were two further sets to follow.

There was a certain sense of excitement in being able to provide the kind of history that we thought contributed to the Indian child's understanding of our past. We were distancing our history from that written under imperial auspices—the writing of historians such as Vincent Smith, Thompson and Garret, and Rawlinson, or even their Indian counterparts. For Vincent Smith, Indian history led up to the inevitability of the British Empire that brought the *pax Britannica* to India. The model was the Roman Empire that Britain was said to be emulating. The heroes were kings and the sign of triumph was victory in campaigns. The historian set the pace of how events moved and separated the heroes from the villains. In ancient history a major focus had been the glorifying of the coming of the Aryans and Aryan civilization, a theme that was underlined by Indian nationalist historians as well. Medieval history meant reiterating the division between Hindu and Muslim communities and referring to them as the two nations of India.

Orientalist scholarship from the eighteenth century onwards, when it searched for histories of the ancient past in Sanskrit literature, found only one and that too of a limited kind, the *Rajatarangini,* a twelfth-century history of Kashmir. This was in part because they were looking for Enlightenment type histories. They were largely scholars in the colonial administration, such as William Jones and H.H. Wilson, who saw their role as having to discover the Indian past given that they believed there was an absence of historical writing in India. This knowledge was to enable them to understand the colony that they were governing. Incidentally, they also claimed to be bringing historical knowledge to the Indian over whom they ruled and who had lacked this knowledge from his own tradition.

They were primarily interested in codifying and translating the texts that their brahmana informants told them were the most important. These were in the main, the *Vedas*—providing information on the origins of Hinduism and the *Dharmashastras*—texts concerning the social codes and therefore focused on rules of caste and social obligations. The codification of the texts bore the imprint of European systems of classification and the translations were naturally conditioned by the intellectual and social ambience of attitudes to the Orient. These texts were regarded as containing first order knowledge about the Indian past and even Buddhist texts were not given the same importance. Access to these Sanskrit texts led to the conviction that religion was the foundational factor in Indian civilization. Where Orientalist scholars had a positive image of ancient India, it tended to be that of a golden age directed by a concern for spirituality and social harmony.

In the nineteenth century those who called themselves liberals and positivists, contested this understanding of the Indian past. James Mill and T.B. Macaulay for instance, representing what might be called the liberal-progressive view of those times, were critical of the Indian past and advocated legal measures to restructure Indian society. Some of their criticism was also meant as an aside on current British society. We have observed in earlier essays that Mill was the first author who in writing the history of British India, divided it into periods that were identified by the religions of the dynasties: the initial Hindu civilization was succeeded by a Muslim civilization and then by a British period. This periodization became axiomatic until recent times. Mill also gave currency to the idea of Oriental Despotism, that Asian societies had been ruled by despots and were static societies not undergoing any change throughout their history.

By the late nineteenth century there was a firm imperial control over India. The colonial power had succeeded in subordinating revolts of soldiers and peasants and was slowly beginning to face the emergence of nationalism from the nascent middle-class. Historical writing was necessary to contest this nationalism. It was argued that Indians had always been subordinated by alien powers and the history of India was thus a recital of invasions. Further, that the most persistent of these invaders were Muslims who settled and ruled in India giving rise to a powerful Muslim community. This inaugurated the undiminished strife between the Muslim and Hindu communities, strife that had been temporarily brought under control by the arrival of British power.

Nationalist historical writing reacted to all this, agreeing with some but disagreeing with much. A key function of nationalist history was to establish an Indian identity. This had to draw on the unity and uniformity of India throughout history. Attention to a common culture became axiomatic and this inevitably meant a historical discourse about the upper castes and the aristocracy. It was believed that these were the groups that made history. The new textbooks tried to draw attention to other groups of supposedly lesser status that also contributed to history but this was a less popular aspect of the books. Possibly the idea was not emphasized with sufficient examples.

For nationalist history the ancient past was particularly useful in constructing identities as it invariably is in all nationalist history. The sources are almost exclusively from elite groups, the period is so remote that much can be said that is imagined but cannot be questioned for lack of detailed evidence. Consequently, golden ages abound and nationalist historians took their cue from some of the Orientalist scholarship. The obsession with the Hindu golden age was such that for some the Muslim period was contrasted as one of decline, to the extent that this allowed the British to conquer India.

Anti-colonial nationalism does not always obstruct other more specific nationalisms, some of which become central to the creation of nation states. Religious and ethnic nationalisms have been frequent since the twentieth century. In the Indian situation, given the kind of history projected by colonial authors and up to a point endorsed by some nationalist historians, there was the emergence of what have been called Hindu and Muslim nationalisms—also of course entwined with the politics of the twentieth century in India. Hindu and Muslim nationalisms each argued for different pasts: the ancient past was Hindu and the medieval past was dominated by Muslim dynasties. Ancient and medieval became areas of controversy and the site of ideological struggles in defining a national history.

This difference led to the notion that these religious communities constituted two separate nations and the ensuing history was used to justify the creation of two separate nation-states. Religious nationalism takes an extreme form in communal historical writing. Pakistan is projected as a Muslim nation-state in such histories. At home, many historians are opposing political attempts to project India as a Hindu state.

The other theme prominent in the Hindu communal view of the past was the insistence on the Aryan foundation of Indian culture, a view that still prevails. Whereas in the nineteenth century it was held that the Aryan language came from across the Indo-Iranian borderlands, there is today no concession to this view among the Hindu religious nationalists. As we have seen, their claim is that the Aryans were indigenous to India, were the authors of the earliest Indian civilization—that of the cities of the Indus and the northwest—and that wherever there was a language akin to Indo-Aryan it came through Aryan out-migration from India. In 1969, members of the Parliamentary Consultative Committee wanted the textbook on *Ancient India* to state categorically that 'the Aryans' were indigenous to India—a demand that was rejected by the Editorial Board and by me as the author. At most scholars might argue that Aryan culture, if it can be recognized as that, is an evolved culture with multiple inputs from a variety of sources, some coming with migrants from the borderlands and some from those settled in the plains of the northwest of the subcontinent.

With Indian independence in 1947 came an increased interest in questions relating to the economic and social evolution of Indian society. Inevitably there was a turning to historians for information on the nature of traditional economies and social structures, and the histories of communities and castes. Historians were activated in ways different from before. There was less focus on political and dynastic history and more on social and economic history that in turn affected the discussion of historical causation. Broadening the explanations for historical change introduced many new sources and the evidence they provided enriched the scope of historical causality. And just as inevitably, pre-modern history was drawn into the circuit of the social sciences.

The study of ancient India shifted from being a subject within the fold of Indology to gradually becoming a discipline of the Social Sciences. This was a major shift away from golden ages, oriental despots and religious periodization to investigating a different set of themes that had to do with economic resources, the forms of social organization, the articulation of religion and art as aspects of social perceptions, and above all to tracking the major points of historical change in a history of three millennia. In writing about Indian achievements an attempt was made to explain the interaction of various factors and how they contributed to diverse outcomes. This shift is irksome to those who argue for a mono-causal, religion-derived cultural uniformity.

The history of 'the nation' also became a focus. Was the nation a creation of the colonial experience? Or did it emerge from factors related to modernization such as the coming of industrialization and capitalism as well as the need for a democratic and secular society? The issue was not just of building a nation which required a common history, memory and culture but also of explaining the nature of the societies and economies of the past that contributed towards the sense of a shared past. Because of a dependence on textual sources the perspective was from the elite cultures of the past. What some referred to as the 'living prehistory' of India—the cultures of the forest tribes—or that of the lower castes, received less visibility. At the same time it is necessary to recognize that the definition of the nation was largely in terms of the aspirations of what were referred to as the dominant castes and classes.

For some, the 'one-ness' of the nation lay in the syncretistic thought and action of diverse groups that fused in the idea of the nation. For others it was what was described as India's composite culture that assumed diverse social and religious units in harmonious co-existence, each giving space to the other. For yet others, the definition of one-ness was in being Hindu and this was to be protected against Muslim rule.

A history of the nation needed a central perspective. Colonial and nationalist histories had been written with the Ganga valley as the epicentre. But with the growth of interest in regional history this was becoming problematic. The image of the one-ness of the nation had also to face the demands of regional histories. The provinces of British Indian administration, whose boundaries had been arbitrarily imposed, gave way to the creation of linguistic states with more realistic boundaries based on language. This intensified regional identity since linguistic states worked their history through their own language sources as well as through manifestations of regional culture in archaeological antiquities.

On two occasions it was said that my textbooks in emphasizing the nation had not done justice to regional personalities. There was a demand for a separate chapter on Guru Nanak, whose teachings had been the foundation for Sikhism, for the books used in the Punjab; and similarly one on Shivaji the Maratha for books used in Maharashtra. On both occasions the Board felt that if the states wished to make the change it could not be stopped, even if it resulted in an imbalance in terms of the national perspective. Furthermore, since the books were intended as model textbooks they could only be a guide and could not be imposed. But it was agreed that permission from the NCERT would be required for making changes. I insisted that copyright was invested in the author and if changes were made my name as the author of the book should be deleted.

The balance between the nation and the region was a delicate one and more so when the historian was writing on a period when the nation did not exist. For such periods it was a question of dominant and subordinate states, but subordination became a sensitive matter in itself. What has now become problematic is the dominance of the identity of the region, over the smaller sub-cultures, which was earlier hidden by the national culture.

The historical change became more marked in the 1960s and 70s when Marxist historical writing encouraged a paradigm shift as did the input from other social sciences. The debates on Modes of Production among academic historians had the fallout effect of releasing more information resulting in further interpretations of social and economic history. Whether or not one participated in the debate, historical research introduced questions of state formation, the role of agriculture, the extension of trade and the degree to which changes were made by religious movements or were reflected in art and literature. Historical interest had moved towards another dimension, irrespective of whether or not it conformed to Marxist models.

The debate was largely among those who worked on the post-Gupta period from about the eighth to the thirteenth centuries, what is now called the early medieval period to distinguish it from the medieval period, the latter basically being once again the period of Muslim rule. This definition of the medieval period resembles the value-loaded categories of the earlier paradigm and is therefore not very helpful. The use of the label 'medieval' echoes the periodization of European history. As a forerunner of the medieval, the label of early medieval says little about either. The post-Gupta period had earlier been described as 'the dark age' of small kingdoms as against the previous '[the] golden ages' of large empires. In intellectual terms the darkness was dispelled because of the debate that brought to the fore the history of new kingdoms, their economies and governance and the role of local courts in defining culture. Such historians as were bogged down, by the Hindu-Muslim divide of medieval times—both early and late—rarely participated in this debate. For them the finer issues of the formation of states, or local cultures were of little importance.

For the earlier period the breakthrough came from extensive archaeological excavations. The major sites of the Indus Civilization, such as the cities of Harappa and Mohenjo-daro, were located in Pakistan. There was therefore a concerted effort to discover similar sites on the Indian side of the border and the effort met with astonishing success. The Harappa culture was far more widespread in the northern and western parts of the subcontinent than had been assumed earlier. This interest spurred on the determination to find the archaeological equivalent of the Aryan culture, a determination that continues undiminished. Such a discovery is of course not possible in the absence of a decipherable script since Aryan is essentially a language label. But all this activity gave a centrality to archaeological data and therefore to the inclusion of material culture in historical interpretation.

The colonial construction of early Indian history in concepts such as Oriental Despotism, periodization by religion, an insistence on Indian society being static and castes being races or frozen social entities, and the widespread existence of isolated, self-sufficient village communities, were the generalizations that were being systematically unwound in the new ways of investigating history. Some concepts that nationalist historiography had appropriated from colonial views, such as 'golden ages' and 'dark ages', were also axed in this new history.

These were the historical debates current in the 1960s and more so in the 1970s when the NCERT Textbooks (Set 1) were being read in schools run by the central government. Appreciation for the books lay in their more expansive vision of history, the recognition that the information they presented was reliable evidence and not wishful thinking, and that there was logic to the way in which the narrative was set out. Possibly this was part of the reason for the later criticism that they were not as user friendly for children as they could have been.

Critical reactions to their contents came from Hindu and Sikh religious organizations that felt that their respective religions and religious teachers had not been glorified. Certain religio-political organizations such as the Hindu Mahasabha and the Arya Samaj claimed that a statement made in the book 'went counter to the religious sentiments of the Hindu nationality' (whatever this may mean). In *Ancient India*, I explained that the ancient Aryans venerated the cow but like cattle-herders elsewhere, ate its flesh on ritual occasions or when honouring a guest. R.S. Sharma had made a similar statement in his textbook. The protest against this statement emanated from the Hindu political mobilization around the demand for cow protection and a ban on beef, since it was argued that not eating beef was axiomatic to Hinduism. A lengthy article in a leading newspaper argued that there was no mention of the eating of beef in ancient Sanskrit sources. I countered by quoting from texts that are unambiguous on this matter, and from excavation reports such as the *Shatapatha Brahmana* (3.1.2.21) and the excavation report of B.B. Lal on the site of Hastinapur, in *Ancient India* 1954-55, Nos. 10 and 11. The argument then turned to the question of whether it was moral to tell children that beef was once eaten by the Hindus and later forbidden. I was told off for questioning orthodox opinion and encouraging young minds to do likewise. Objections were also raised to another statement in the textbook that the shudras, the lower castes, were not always treated well. This was of course a reflection on the upper castes. But since social inequality was not a major issue in those days this comment did not lead to major objections.

Similarly, an organization of the Sikhs wanted me to reformulate what I had said about the founding and early history of the Sikh religion, to bring it into conformity with its own view :These were changes I could not agree to since they changed the historical accuracy of what was being stated in the textbook. It is worth pointing out that the objections came from religious organizations and later from political parties and not from historians.

In 1975 Indira Gandhi declared a state of Emergency that closed down free discussion. She was voted out of power in 1977 and the Janata Government—a mixed bag of parties—was elected with Morarji Desai as Prime Minister. It was expected to be a reasonably liberal government, but as it turned out was so dominated by the feuds of party factions and by issues of Hindu religious nationalism that it did not last its full term. But it did manage to fire the first governmental salvo against the NCERT Textbooks (Set 1). Morarji Desai supported and forwarded an anonymous note to the Education Minister, asking that these history textbooks be banned as they were anti-Indian and anti-national in content and prejudicial to the study of history. The note was leaked to the press and when we as the authors heard of it we decided that it should be publicly debated. We argued for the legitimacy of independent interpretations, emphasizing the proviso that they be based on reliable evidence and logically feasible explanations.

The issues that were raised by our critics were routine and predictable: why was there a mention of beef-eating; why was it not said that the Aryans were indigenous to India; where was the necessity to mention the disabilities of the lower castes; why did we not consistently depict Muslim rulers as oppressors and tyrants, and so on. For three years from 1977 to 1980 the usual Sunday papers carried articles for and against the textbooks and the issues raised. I hoped that the public debate would demonstrate that history is not just a body of facts that is packaged and handed on without change from generation to generation; but that history involves interpreting evidence, and that the evidence had grown and the methods of interpreting it had changed and become more precise and analytical as compared to earlier times.

We heard that in November 1977 a committee of reputable historians had been asked to examine the textbooks. They apparently approved of the books and their consensus was that the books should continue to be prescribed. Subsequent to this, some 'liberal' intellectuals began to criticize us heavily, focusing on one point. They maintained that writing textbooks for a state agency like the NCERT was an act of connivance with the state in the first place, therefore there was no justification in our now complaining that the books were being banned. Ironically, those who took this position were working for state-funded research institutes. At any rate nothing was done before the government fell. The joke that did the rounds of Delhi was that no action was taken to ban the books because there were many thousand copies that had already been printed and were stacked in the NCERT stores, and that the Audits and Accounts Department of the Government of India objected to them being trashed!

The issues raised by the controversy made one fully aware of the growing tension between two groups. One was that of the political parties and the organizations appropriating and claiming to represent nationalism, but obviously of the religious majority, a claim that was becoming an electoral plank. Some historians and archaeologists were sympathetic to this view. The claim was used to target the other group of professional historians who were not making concessions to the political requirements of religious nationalism. The earlier notion that anyone and everyone could claim to be writing history was being questioned by the work of the latter. This was particularly so in the writing of ancient history where it was becoming even clearer that some technical expertise in reading excavation reports, epigraphy, numismatics and textual criticism was a prerequisite to being a historian.

As the author of a textbook I felt that I had the responsibility of helping to educate a generation to think differently and in new ways about the subject. Yet I was aware that this was subjecting me to political assault. One had to debate with oneself and with one's colleagues as to the implications of this. On the issue of beef-eating, for instance, we were aware that apart from the historical importance of making the statement, it would raise political issues that had to be countered. What was made apparent was that writing a textbook was not just an academic exercise. Ancient history in particular had a primary role in the formulation of conservative identity and it vision of Indian society—even if the formulation was based on questionable 'history'. The same was true of other religious nationalisms that were seeking a political edge by reformulating history in a specific way. Those of us nurtured on the earlier anti-colonial nationalist tradition, as the members of the Editorial Board had been, had no hesitation in contesting a communalism that used only religion as a political foundation. The more sensitive question, it seemed to us, was to contest nationalism in its guise of making concessions to religious communalism. Occasional strands of communal thinking had had a presence in some aspects of the nationalist view of ancient Indian history, and this presence became more evident as it was played out in the politics of the late twentieth century.

Towards the latter part of the 1970s the structure of school education was re-organized. The books that had been written or were being written for High School in the earlier system had to now be adjusted to the new curriculum. A new Editorial Board was created with Satish Chandra as chairman; R.S. Sharma, M.G.S. Narayanan, Barun De, Sumit Sarkar and S.H. Khan as members; and Arjun Dev as Convener. This board saw the High School textbooks to completion and publication. They were viewed as a continuation of those written for Middle School and therefore part of what I have called Set 1.

The books were revised again in the late 1980s and continued in use. We had a respite of fifteen years and then the attack started up again. This time it came from a collective of Hindu right-wing nationalist organizations labelled the Sangh Parivar. It propagated its version of Indian history encapsulated in the ideology of Hindutva. (I have discussed this at some length in the previous chapter.) It came into its own successfully when the Bharatiya Janata Party (BJP) and its allies were elected to form the government of the National Democratic Alliance (NDA) in 1999. Hindutva history claims a uniform, monolithic Hindu identity for Indian civilization, often defined as Aryan, which makes it upper caste. The multiple variant and lesser cultures are either ignored or at best marginalized. From this perspective the NCERT textbooks that we had written were unacceptable and we were described as anti-Hindu, anti-Indian, traitors to the nation who were propagating perverted views that distorted the truth. Ministers of the BJP government frequently voiced these statements in Parliament—presumably so that they could abuse us and yet claim Parliamentary privilege. This assault on us—from virulent abuse to death threats—continues to embellish a number of websites on the Internet, largely controlled by wealthy Indians settled in the First World.

The attempt to proscribe the books did not succeed, so passages from them were literally and laboriously blacked out in each copy before these were sold in the market. This was followed by a more efficient idea, that of deleting such passages before printing the book. The next step was the decision to replace books and there was a frenzied writing of new textbooks in record time. The NCERT, now under the control of the NDA government, commissioned new books conforming to the Hindutva version of history, and constituting the NCERT Textbooks (Set 2), some of which were prescribed just prior to the fall of the BJP/NDA government. This was only one move among many others to terminate history as a social science and convert it into a catechism. The attitude was not one of discussing variant interpretations of history but instead terminating all other views barring those that conformed to the Hindutva version.

The BJP/NDA Government fell in 2004 and one consequence was that their NCERT Textbooks (Set 2), have since been replaced. The new government, with its core from the Congress Party and somewhat less committed to religious nationalism than the BJP, decided on a completely fresh set of textbooks, NCERT Textbooks (Set 3). However, since textbooks cannot be written in a hurry, the Set 1 textbooks were used again for the interim period. When Set 3 was ready then all earlier textbooks of Sets 1 and 2 were discontinued. Rather ironically, acrimonious criticism of the Set 1 textbooks, and arguments against their being brought back even for a short period, came from some 'liberal' historians. They did not denounce the contents of the books so much as their authors for being 'statist', in the same way as they had denounced us three decades previously. We were 'statist' because we agreed to write the books for a state agency and because we wrote them from a nationalist perspective. This echoed what had been said in 1977 almost as if there was no new way of critiquing the books. Having been previously called anti-national it was difficult to juxtapose this with now being accused of having a nationalist perspective. The historians who are authors of NCERT Textbooks (Set 3) have not yet been dubbed as 'statist'!

The NCERT Textbooks (Set 1) were seen by some as an attempt to standardize history. This is a comment that may not be easy to sustain. They were intended as model textbooks and states were free to modify them as they did in some cases. They were prescribed largely in schools run by the central government and these formed hardly ten per cent of the total number of schools. Nevertheless, the textbooks these schools use carry some influence in other broad-based teaching. Schools established by a variety of 'cultural' and religious organizations, use entirely different textbooks and some that even run riot with the subject, teaching what is hardly recognizable as history. In such schools the NCERT books are used for answering examination questions (if the school is linked to particular examination boards), but the students are told that the real history is in the fantasy textbooks.

Textbooks such as mine that had been used for forty years would inevitably have had to be replaced by newer ones more representative of another generation of historical thinking. But there is a pedagogical problem that needs urgent attention. When my textbooks were prescribed in the 1960s, schoolteachers found them different from the books they had been using. The shift away from conventional dynastic history and the introduction of comments on dominant and subordinate castes, on patterns of landownership and the use of labour, on the difference between barter and markets, on monuments not just as structures in a landscape but institutions of community life, were quite different from narratives limited to kings, courts, campaigns, territorial control and administration. We were trying to show historical interconnections in the making of a society. The concept of the society was however unitary and I, for one, felt that introducing multiplicity at an elementary stage might be confusing for the student.

Two generations of teachers taught these books, and after they were swapped, teachers had to move to teaching NCERT Textbooks Set 3. This required a far greater input into teacher training than the government or the NCERT was perhaps prepared to invest in. India has immense technical resources which state educational bodies seem reluctant to use. Yet no government should be afraid of an educated public. There could be an enlightened change in the comprehension of history by teachers and students alike if additional teaching were to be done imaginatively through radio and TV. This was worked out in some detail more than ten years ago by a group of educationists. As a member of the then Prasar Bharati Board I had submitted recommendations for the implementation of such programmes on TV and radio as part of an education channel. But not surprisingly, no interest was shown in the idea, neither by the HRD Ministry nor by Prasar Bharati.

An even more fundamental change is necessary if textbooks of quality are to survive. This narrative about the NCERT textbooks has a recurring refrain: textbooks change each time the government changes. The pattern will continue unless the legal status of the NCERT in its production of textbooks is changed. In 2005, I wrote in the newspapers arguing that we have to make bodies such as the NCERT autonomous and give them statutory status so that irrespective of a change in government they would still be able to retain textbooks of quality. But the idea fell on deaf ears. Admittedly it will be a hard fight against governments determined not to do so but at least legal support might help. If this is not done then we shall have a chameleon-like educational system that will change its colour with each change of government. The student will never know whether to state in the exam that 2+2 = 4 or whether 2+2 = 5, and may end up having to say that it could be either, depending on the political party in power.

Ancient history in particular has a special significance for contemporary times especially in developing societies. In part, this is because so much of the ancient past is still perceptible even if not immediately so. But more importantly identities, as also the heritage linked to nationalism, still hinge on the interpretation of early history. In any broader understanding of the present it helps to be informed about the past, and even more so, the remote past. That is where myths have found comfortable berths and where a well-grounded critical history has most to contribute in offering connections that are exploratory and provisional rather than mandatory.

6

GLIMPSES OF A POSSIBLE HISTORY FROM BELOW: EARLY INDIA

The nineteenth century was the age of the grand edifices of historical explanation and theoretical construction. While some of these edifices still stand firm, others are tottering. Even those that still stand often require repair and renovation, sometimes of a structural kind, in the light of new knowledge and fresh theories. The refining of concepts and theories therefore becomes a necessary part of the historical exercise and is particularly incumbent on those who, as conscientious historians, use theoretical frameworks to formulate their initial hypotheses.

Among the early sub-periods, Vedic society has been described as tribal. The term 'tribal', which we have all used in the past, has rightly come in for some questioning. Whatever precision it may once have had seems to have become blurred, so perhaps we need either to redefine it or to use more exact terms for societies that we have so far described as tribal. In its precise meaning, 'tribe' refers to a community of people claiming descent from a common ancestor. In its application, however, it has been used to cover a variety of social and economic forms, not to mention racial and biological identities: and this tends to confuse the original meaning. Even as a convention it has lost much of its precision. The more recently preferred term, lineage, narrows the focus. Although the economic range remains, lineage does emphasize succession and descent with the implication that these are decisive in determining social status and control over economic resources. It also helps differentiate between chiefships—where lineage is a significant identity, and kingship—where power is concentrated and evokes a larger number of impersonal sanctions.

The concept of vamsha (succession) carries a meaning similar to lineage and is central to Vedic society with its emphasis on succession even as a simulated lineage. Thus vamsha is used to mean a descent group among the rajanyas or kshatriyas, but is also used in the list of

Upanishadic teachers where succession refers not to birth but to the passing on of knowledge. Lineage becomes important in the structure of each varna, defined by permitted rules of marriage and kinship and by ranking in an order of status, the control over resources being implicit. The emergence of the four varnas is thus closely allied to the essentials of a society based on the central identity of lineage.

In a stratified society the reinforcing of status is necessary. But where there is no recognized private property in land, and no effective state, such reinforcing has to be done by sanctions that often take a ritual or religious form. In the absence of taxation as a system of control in the Vedic period, sacrificial ritual functioned as the occasion for renewing the status of the yajamana, the patron who orders the sacrifice.

Apart from its religious and social role, sacrificial ritual also had an economic function. It was the occasion when wealth that had been channeled to the yajamana was distributed by him in the form of gifts to the brahmana priests, and these strengthened their social rank and ensured them wealth. The ritual served to restrict the distribution of wealth to the brahmanas and the kshatriyas but at the same time prevented a substantial accumulation of wealth by either, for whatever came in the form of gifts and prestations from the lesser clans, the vish, to the ruling clans, the kshatriyas, was largely consumed in the ritual and only the remainder gifted to the brahmanas. Generosity being important to the office of the chief, wealth was not hoarded. This is a form of the economy of gift-exchange although the exchange is uneven: the priest receives the tangible gift whereas the patron can only claim the intangibility of status and spiritual merit on the completion of the ritual.

The display, consumption and distribution of wealth at the major rituals such as the rajasuya and the ashvamedha, was in turn a stimulus to production, for the ritual was also seen as a communication with and sanction from the supernatural. Embedded in the sacrificial ritual therefore were important facets of the economy. This may be a partial explanation of why a major change in the state system accompanied by a peasant economy occurred initially in the mid-first millennium BC not in the western Ganga valley but in the adjoining area of the middle Ganga valley. This change was occasioned, not only by an increase in economic production and a greater social disparity but also by the fact that the prestation economy—of making gift offerings to a patron usually associated with a lineage-based society—became more and more marginal in the latter region, and in some areas was altogether absent.

Some scholars regard the term 'peasant economy' as an imprecise concept. However, it is of some use as a measurement of change. The label of 'peasant' has been applied to a variety of categories, some of which are dissimilar. The use of a single word as a portmanteau description confuses the categories and therefore a differentiation is necessary. Eric Wolf defines peasants as transferring their surplus to a ruler which surplus is then used to support the lifestyle of the ruler and the elite.[7]

This definition seems to me inadequate, for the important point is not merely the existence of a surplus but the mechanism by which it is transferred, and it is to this that I would relate the emergence of a peasant economy. That the recognition of an incipient peasant economy in various parts of India is significant to the study of social history hardly needs stressing since concomitant with this is also the establishing of particular kinds of state systems, variant forms of jatis and new religious and cultural idioms in the area.

For the early period of Indian history the term peasant has been used to translate both the Rigvedic vish as well as the gahapati (this roughly translated as 'peasant' but more of this later) of Pali sources. But some distinction is called for. The Vedic vish was primarily a member of a clan although this did not preclude him from being a cultivator as well. The transferring of surpluses, in this case the voluntary prestations of the vish to the kshatriya, points to a stratified rather than an egalitarian society and the simile in the Veda of the kshatriya eating the vish like the deer eats the grain, would indicate greater pressures for larger gifts, prestations, offerings.

But, the transfer was not invariably through an enforced system of taxation. In the absence of private ownership of land, the relationship of the vish to the kshatriya would have been less contrapuntal, with little need of an enforced collection of the surplus. The context of the references in the *Vedas* to bali, bhaga and shulka (the offering, the share, the value), terms used in later periods for taxes, suggest that at this time they were voluntary and random, although the randomness gradually changed to required offerings particularly at sacrificial rituals.

However, the three major prerequisites governing a system of taxation—a contracted amount, collected at stipulated periods, by persons designated as tax collectors—are absent in the Vedic texts. The recognition of these prerequisites in the post-Vedic period and the collection of taxes from the cultivators by the State would seem decisive in registering the change from cultivators to peasants in which the existence of an economy based on peasant agriculture becomes clear.

The introduction of taxation presupposes the impersonal authority of the State and some degree of alienation of the cultivator from the authority to whom the surplus is given, unlike in the lineage-based society where gifts were given more informally although directly. Taxation reduced the quantity of gifts and became the more substantial part of what was taken from the peasant, but these prestations were not terminated. The sanction of the religious ritual becomes more marginal and that of the state more central, the change occurring gradually over time.

The formation of the state is therefore tied into this change. For the cultivator the change to land becoming property or a legal entity—whether his or of someone else—and the pressures on cultivation, have to do not only with subsistence but also with a provision for ensuring a surplus. This highlights the difference between appropriation in the earlier system and exploitation in the latter.

The Vedic vish was more a generalized label under which herding, cultivation and minimal crafts adequate to a household were included. Such groups were germane to the later peasant household. In effect, because the relationship with the dominant kshatriyas was based on gifts rather than on taxes, these cultivators would seem part of a lineage society in which their subservience to a dominant group arose more out of the exigencies of kinship or the ordering of clans than out of exploited labour, although the latter can be seen to increase in time.

A gradual mutation becomes evident from the frequent references in the Pali sources to the gahapati. The existence of the gahapati focuses more sharply on the presence of what might be called a peasant economy. But to translate gahapati as peasant is to provide a mere slice of its total meaning. Derived from grihapati, the head of the household, the gahapati included a range of meanings such as the wealthy mahashala brahmanas addressed as gahapatis by the Buddha, who had received as donations extensive, tax-free, arable land and is also used for those who paid taxes—the wealthy landowners who cultivated their large farms with the help of slaves and hired labourers (dasa-bhritaka).

Those at the lower end of the scale who either owned small plots of land or were professional ploughmen are more often referred to as the kassakas, from the Sanskrit word for cultivators, karshaka. The *Arthashastra* mentions tenants as upavasa and also refers to another category, the shudra cultivators settled by the state on cultivable or waste land on a different system of tenure from the aforesaid: as also the range of cultivators employed on the state farms supervised by the overseers of agriculture, the sitadhyaksha.

Gahapati, therefore, is perhaps better translated as a landowner who would generally pay taxes to the state except when the land which he owned was a religious benefice. The ownership of land and the payment of taxes demarcates this period of the mid-first millennium BC as one in which a peasant economy emerged. Traces of the lineage-based society continued in the marking of status by varna and the performance, although by now of less economic significance, of the sacrificial rituals.

That the gahapati was not even just a landowner but more a man of means is supported by the fact that it was from the ranks of the gahapatis that there emerged the setthis or the financiers. The two terms are often associated in the literature of the period and this is further attested in the votive inscriptions recording donations to the Buddhist sangha at stupa sites in central India and the western and eastern Deccan from the late first millennium BC. Gahapati fathers have setthi sons as well as the other way round. It would seem that gahapati status was acquired through the practice of any respectable profession that provided a decent income, although the most frequent references are to landownership and commerce.

This is not to suggest that trade originated with the landowning groups but rather that the commercialization of exchange was probably tied to the emergence of the gahapati. In examining the origins of trade it is necessary to define more clearly the nature of the exchange involved. Broadly, there are some recognizable forms of exchange that can either develop into commercialized exchange or supplement it. There is evidence of luxury goods exchanged by ruling groups as a part of gift-exchange. Marriage alliances between kshatriya families involved an exchange of gifts. Thus, when Bharata visits his maternal Kekeya kinsmen, he returns with a variety of gifts, including horses. This is not an exchange based on need but is a channel through which status and kinship is confirmed. It may in addition lead to other forms of exchange.

The major royal sacrifices required tributes and gifts to be brought to the yajamana which he then distributed at the end of the ritual. The description of the rajasuya of Yudhisthira in the *Mahabharata* provides an interesting inventory of valued items. Sacrificial rituals involved the gifting of cattle and possibly some gold. Boastful poets added to this horses, chariots, and on occasion, dasis (slave women), given to them by the victorious cattle-raiders whose prowess the poets had praised. These gifts became part of a distribution and exchange of wealth which in lineage-based societies formed the salient part of the wealth of those who ruled, whereas in the change to an economy based on peasant agriculture, they were merely a part of the wealth accumulated by the ruling families and the more wealthy gahapatis.

Less spectacular but more essential was another form of exchange—that of raw materials and commodities brought by itinerant groups such as smiths and pastoralists. It has been argued that the itinerant metal-smiths formed a network of connections between villages. Metal, particularly iron and iron objects were items of regular trade. The role of pastoralists in forms of exchange and in trading circuits is now gaining attention, particularly of those groups that had a regular pattern of transhumance—moving from pastures at lower elevation to those higher up in summer and returning in winter. Transactions that accompany this circuit have been described as a vertical economy. Exchange through sources of itinerant professionals was probably the starting point of the beat of pedlars that remains a continuing feature of one level of exchange in India.

Yet another category is what might be called exchange between one settlement and the next. This is a useful basis for plotting the gradual diffusion of an item as for example, the better quality varieties of pottery in archaeological evidence. The distribution of the Northern Black Polished Ware—a luxury ceramic—is an indicator of places in contact with each other. Such an exchange provides evidence not only on local trade but also on the geographical reach of intra-regional contacts. Some of these settlements may then have come to play the role of local markets, the equivalent perhaps of what the Pali texts refer to as the nigama. These in turn are likely to have been the nuclei of urban growth as in the case of towns such as Rajagriha and Sravasti in the middle Ganga plain.

Distinct from all these is the familiar picture of trade which dominates the scene in the post-Mauryan period. This is the commercial exchange between two or more centres processing and producing commodities specifically destined for trade. The organization of this more complex form involved a hierarchy of producers and traders some of whom were sedentary while others were carriers of the items traded but of a different order from pedlars and pastoralists. The picture of commercialized exchange emerges from Buddhist texts. Some monks were also involved in brade. The *Arthashastra* regards it as a legitimate source of revenue for the State. The question then arose of the degree of State interference and control that would be conducive to increasing the finances of the State.

The major artefact in this trade (other than the commodities) was coined metallic money, providing evidence of the degree of complexity and the extent of such trade and trading circuits. These early coins in some instances were issued by the nigama and in other cases may have been issued by local authorities or possibly by ruling families. In the post-Mauryan period dynastic issues gained currency, a clear pointer to the importance of commercialized exchange. However, even in this period local issues remained in circulation suggesting multiple levels of exchange.

Given these commercial activities, the control of trade routes becomes a significant factor in political policy and military annexations. Recent analyses of activities along the Silk Route linking China to the eastern Mediterranean via Central Asia have revealed a variety of levels of exchange. These ranged from gift-exchange to sophisticated emporia, in the context of political relations between tribal groups and established centres of political power, suggesting ways in which the complicated question of trade, often treated as a uniform monolith by historians of early India, may now be investigated. The Roman trade with India, as is clear from both commodities and the function of money, also spans a similar range. Diverse forms of exchange within a larger trading system suggest the coexistence of various economic levels within that system and sharpen the social contours of the groups involved.

Analyzing trade also requires locating those involved in these exchanges in the social hierarchy of the time. In the production of goods for exchange, artisans, whether individuals or in guilds, had relationships with merchants and financiers that were as diverse in form as the various categories of relationships and tenancies between cultivators and landowners. The role of the shilpin (artisan) and the shreni (guild) is quite distinct from the setthi. Their presence registers a change in the nature of the trade as does the differentiation between categories of professionals, such as the vanija (merchant), setthi (financier and merchant), and the sarthavaha, (caravaneer).

When commercialized exchange becomes active it introduces a substantial change. The investment required for elaborate trade had to be provided by a well-endowed group able to invest its surplus in risk-taking ventures. The obvious category was the gahapati who could fall back on land if the venture failed. That it turned out to be highly successful is clear from the fact that not only did the setthis emerge from the ranks of the gahapatis, but, by the post-Mauryan period, had an independent identity as financiers and gradually superceded the gahapatis.

As a result of the wealth they accumulated the setthis came to be powerful, for some of them were known to be financiers of kings and obtained in return rights to collect revenue, perhaps the prototype of what was later to become the regular form of emoluments to administrative officers. On the manifestations of trade, Buddhist and Jaina sources together with epigraphic and archaeological evidence provide a useful counterpoint to the conventional *Dharmashastra* literature of this period.

The link between agriculture and commerce is important for understanding the changes in the subsequent period. The opulence of those involved in commerce was poured into the adornment of religious monuments, monasteries and images and in the conspicuous consumption that is associated with the wealthier town-dwellers of these times. This tends to obscure the agrarian scene where one notices less of wealthy landowners and large estates and more of those with small holdings.

Small plots of land could be purchased and donated to religious beneficiaries and it seems unlikely, as has been argued, that such sales were restricted to religious donations. Small holdings together with the alienation of land could point to some degree of impoverishment among peasants. References to debt bondage (ahitaka, atmavikreta), as a regular if not frequent category of slavery, as well as the increasing references to vishti (forced labour or a labour tax), suggest a different rural scene from that of the preceding period. Oppressive taxation—referred to as pain-causing taxation—is mentioned as an evil.

This mutation was endemic to the evident change in the post-Gupta period. Where trade flourished, the resources of the urban centres and the trade routes bouyed up the system: but this period points to a declining trade in some areas. Internal commercialized trade requires the ballast of agrarian settlements and where lineage-based societies could be converted into peasant economies, the agrarian support to trade would be strengthened.

Earlier networks of exchange had permitted an easier co-existence with lineage-based societies. Their resources, generally raw materials such as elephants, timber and gemstones could, as items of exchange, be easily tapped by traders through barter and direct exchange without disturbing the social structure to any appreciable degree. On the other hand, because of the requirement of land and labour, state systems more heavily dependent on a peasant economy had to absorb these societies and convert them into peasant economies in order to extract the benefits.

Where trade declined or where new states were established, the need to develop the agrarian economy became necessary. The granting of land appears to have been the mechanism adopted for extending areas under cultivation. The reasons for this change in the post-Gupta period need more detailed investigation, particularly at a regional level. In the very useful work done so far, substantial data has surfaced. What is now required is a sifting and classifying of the data to provide more precise answers and to evoke fresh questions.

The kind of data required is that which would provide information on basic questions relating to agrarian relations. A comparative regional view would be useful. Grants could be classified in terms of type and area, the nature of the land and soil, the crops grown, local irrigation, degrees of ownership and tenancy, and who provided labour. A worm's eye view of agriculture could be better handled through inter-disciplinary research. Historians could work with soil specialists and hydrologists. The absence of field studies is unfortunate. Although it has entered into some discussions of archaeological sites it is absent among historians. An increase in data of the technical kind can assist the quality of theoretical analyses. Many of these questions could involve extrapolating from existing records but the more valuable input would come from fieldwork in the area under study. It is not for nothing that R.H.

Tawney, who wrote on the economic history of Europe, is believed to have said that the first essential of research into agrarian history is a stout pair of boots.

At another level, the analyses of the titles of grantees and changes therein might provide clues. The question of whether the peasantry was free hinges not only on the technical and legal definitions but also requires a discussion of the actual status of the peasant. Rights, obligations and dues of the grantees vis-à-vis the peasants would need to be tabulated in detail. These would provide some indications of the essentials of the prevailing system.

It is curious that there is little resort to the policy recommended by the *Arthashastra* of establishing colonies of cultivators on land owned by the state, so as to extend agriculture and thereby increase the revenue. Was the state unable to do so because it lacked the administrative infrastructure, or was it because it did not have the power to implement such a policy? Or had the economy changed to the point of discouraging the feasibility of such a policy? Instead, the state increased the grants of land to religious beneficiaries and later, but to a lesser extent, to administrative officers in lieu of a salary. This points to a need for an evaluation of the nature of the states of this period with the possibility that their formation and structure were different from the previous ones.

Was this type of state attempting to restructure the economy to a greater extent than the previous ones that may have been more concerned with revenue collecting—judging by the model advocated by Kautilya? Did the system of granting land predominate (perhaps initially) in areas where lineage-based societies were prevalent so as to facilitate their conversion to a peasant economy and where lineage could also be used for economic control? More than varna identities, jati identities would have acted as a bridge to a peasant economy and ameliorated the rupture with the lineage system. Elements of lineage have often continued even in some areas where peasant agriculture became the norm.

Religious benefices were on the pattern of earlier grants and were not strictly an innovation except that now grants were made increasingly to brahmanas and ostensibly in return for legitimizing the dynasty and for the donor acquiring religious merit. These were the stated reasons for the grant but were not sufficient reasons. Grants of this nature, as has been pointed out, were a channel of acculturation. They could also be used as foci of political loyalty.

If the grants were made initially from state-owned lands, they amounted to a renouncing of revenue. If the state was unable to administer the extension of agriculture, was the system of grants also introduced to encourage settlements in new areas where the grant was of waste land, or alternatively, of cultivated lands to stabilize the peasantry and induce increased production? Given the fact that slaves were not used in any quantitative degree in agricultural production at this time, was the system of grants an attempt at converting the peasantry into a stable productive force through various mechanisms of subordination and a chain of intermediaries?

Interestingly, the term gahapati/grihapati drops out of currency, for the system had changed and terms incorporating raja, samanta and bhogin, become frequent. Samanta had originally been the word used for a neighbour. The meaning now changed and it referred to a grantee who had received land. Bhogin was the one who enjoyed the produce of the land. The recipients of land grants had the right to receive a range of taxes and dues previously collected by the state and were soon given administrative and (some) judicial powers. This permitted them to act us a 'backup' administration where the grant was in settled areas and to introduce the system where new settlements were being established. It may in origin have been a fiscal measure but in effect became the means of controlling the peasantry.

The apparent increase in debt bondage and the fear of peasant migration would point to this being one of the functions of the large-scale grants. That the possibility of peasant migration to alleviate discontent was being slowly stifled is suggested by the fact of peasants possibly taking to revolt from the early second millennium onwards. A rise in brigandage may well have occurred in this period judging by the increase in hero-stones in some areas. These were memorials to local heroes who had died defending the village and its cattle. A qualitative change occurs when the state begins to grant villages or substantial acreages of land already under cultivation: a change that reflects both on the economy and on the nature of the state.

The need to fetter the peasantry would seem an evident departure from the earlier system and this in turn introduced a change in the relationship between the cultivator and the land now riveted in legalities and liabilities, with tax or rent no longer being the sole criterion of a peasant economy. The karshaka of this period found himself in a different situation from the kassaka of earlier times. The term 'peasant' therefore cannot have a blanket usage or meaning since the variations within it have to be distinguished.

The secular grantees were part of an hierarchical system in which they mirrored the court at the local level. This is evident from their attempts to imitate the courtly style as depicted in the art and literature of the time. Grants of land to the brahmanas as the major religious grantees rehabilitated them to a position of authority and their anguished invocation of Kalki as a millennial figure became less urgent. The codes of caste were, seemingly at least, not being overturned as vigorously as had been feared in earlier times. It is more likely that the forms were outwardly adhered to and the matter seemed to end at that point, without too much investigation into the mobility of jatis.

A new religious ideology gained popularity. It focused on the icon and the temple and asserted an assimilative quality involving the cults and rituals of Puranic Hinduism and the genesis of the Bhakti tradition. Ideological assimilation is called for when there is a need to knit together socially diverse groups. It is also crucial when there is an increase in the distancing between such groups as well as the power of some over others and the economic disparity between them.

The significance of these new cults and sects may lie in part in the focus on loyalty to a deity that has parallels to the loyalty of peasants and others to an overlord. But it would be worth examining the rudiments of each sect in its regional dimension, its groping towards a jati status and the use of an ostensibly cultural and religious idiom to express a new social identity. Were these also mechanisms for legitimizing territorial identities, drawing on sacred geography and pilgrimage routes, with the temple as the focal point?

The devotees were emphasizing what they perceived to be their equal status as devotees in the eyes of the deity. Can this be viewed as the assertion of those lower down the social scale in favour of a more egalitarian society? But its significance grows when the social background to this belief is one of increasing disparity. Movements of dissent that acquired religious legitimacy and form were often gradually accommodated and their radical content slowly diluted. The move away from community participation in a ritual to a personalized and private worship encourages the notion of individual freedom, even if it is only at the ideological level. The Vedic sacrificial ritual was a gathering of the clan, whereas forms of worship like Bhakti can be entirely based on how the individual sees his or her relationship with the deity.

In the justifiable emphasis on social and economic history there has been too frequently neglect among historians of the analysis of ideology. To study ideology without its historical context is to practice historical hydroponics, for ideas and beliefs strike roots in the humus of historical reality. To restrict the study of a society to its narrowly social and economic forms alone is to see it in a limited two-dimensional profile. The interaction of society and ideology takes a varied pattern and to insist always on the primacy of the one over the other is to deny the richness of a full-bodied historical explanation.

Ideas are sometimes analyzed as a response to social pressures and needs. This is particularly pertinent for those dealing with social history. Some of the more important literature (of the times) is suffused with a theoretical representation of society even in symbolic or ideational forms. Meanings very often do not stem from just the vocabulary but require familiarity with the cultural context of the word. Examples of this would be the levels of meaning in words such a varna and jati as they travel through time in texts such as the *Dharmashastras.* The ideological layers in the latter as codes of behaviour have to be peeled away in order to obtain a better comprehension of their ordering of society.

Central to any concern with ideology in the ancient past is the critique of religious thought, as distinct from religious practice or the organization of religious institutions. Some analyses of the *Upanishads* for instance, can provide an interesting example of this. One of the major strands in Upanishadic thought is said to be a secret doctrine known only to a few kshatriyas who teach it to select, trusted brahmanas. Even the most learned among the latter, the mahashala mahashrotriya are described as going to the kshatriyas for instruction. This does rather reverse the code but it seems not to have mattered in this context. The doctrine they discuss involves the idea of the soul, the atman and its ultimate merging with the universal soul, the brahman as well as metempsychosis and the transmigration of the soul: in fact a fundamental doctrine of this age which was to have far-reaching consequences on Indian society.

That it should have been secret and originally associated with the kshatriyas raises many questions, some of which have been discussed by scholars. It is true that the brahmanas and the kshatriyas were both members of the 'leisured classes' in Vedic society and could therefore indulge in idealistic philosophy and discourse on the niceties of life after death. But this is only a partial answer and much more remains to be explained. Was the ritual of sacrifice so deeply imprinted on the brahmana mind and so necessary to the profession at this point, that it required non-brahmanas to introduce alternatives to moksha, the liberation of the soul from rebirth, other than the sacrificial ritual? The adoption of meditation and theories of transmigration had the advantage of releasing the kshatriyas from the pressures of a prestation economy, permitting them to accumulate wealth, which in turn gave them access to power and leisure.

Alternatively, was the accumulation of these already present in the fringe areas described as the mleccha-desha (impure lands) in Vedic texts, where the sacrificial rituals for various reasons had become less important? Thus Janaka of Mithila, Ashvapati Kaikeya and Ajatashatru of Kashi could reflect on alternative ways to moksha, other than the ritual of sacrifice. This also places a different emphasis on the function of the kshatriya who had now ceased to be primarily a cattle-raiding, warrior chief.

These are not the only kinds of connections relevant to a history of the period. Upper and lower caste groups treated as monolithic, belie social reality. The tensions within these should also be noticed where the evidence suggests this. The competition for status between brahmanas and kshatriyas and the separation of their functions, although retaining their mutual dependence, is symbolized in the sacrificial ritual that becomes a key articulation of the relationship. The new beliefs discussed in the *Upanishads* reversed up to a point the sacrificial ritual, in that they required neither priests nor deities but only self-discipline and meditation. At another level, the transmigrating of the soul through the natural elements and plants to its ultimate rebirth carries an echo of shamanism which may have remained popular outside priestly ritual.

There is in the new belief the first element of a shift from the clan to the individual in as much as the sacrificial ritual involves the clan and its wealth, but meditation and self-discipline, in opposition to the clan, involves only the individual. It symbolizes the breaking away of the individual from the clan. It also introduces an element of anomie that becomes more apparent in the later development of these beliefs by various sects. These reflections were seminal to what became a major direction in Indian thought and action, the opting out of the individual from society, where renunciation is a method of self-discovery, but can also carry a message of dissent.

That the new ideas were attributed to the kshatriyas and yet included in a brahmanical text was probably because for the brahmanas to author a doctrine openly questioning the sacrificial ritual would, at this stage, have been an anomaly. However for kshatriyas wanting to be released from expending their wealth in yajanas, an alternate to the sacrificial ritual was a potentially important departure. That the doctrine stimulated philosophical discussion would in itself have required that it be recorded. Additionally, since some teachings of the heterodox reflected aspects of this doctrine, by setting it out as an important part of the Vedic corpus, it could be claimed that even the heterodox had ultimately to uphold aspects of the Vedic tradition. Such an argument is made many centuries later, in modern times. This assumes that the Upanishadic doctrine preceded the heterodox teachings, but it may have been the reverse.

This was to become yet another technique by which orthodox theory in subsequent centuries sought to disguise ideas contradicting its own position. The Buddha not only democratized the doctrine but also nurtured the idea of karma and samsara, actions in this life determining the quality of rebirth in the next, a generally held belief that explained social inequities. For him the link was through consciousness as he denied the existence of the soul. But his negation of the soul (atman) introduces a contradiction of the doctrine as visualized in the *Upanishads.* Such contradictions were current at that time. The positing of a thesis and an anti-thesis prior to arriving at a possible synthesis, became a characteristic feature of philosophical debate and was reflected both in empirical disciplines such as grammar as well as in more abstract analysis.

The relating of ideology to historical reality, as historians are now doing, can result not only in new ways of examining an historical situation and be used to extend or modify the analysis from other sources, but can also help in confirming the reality as derived from other sources.

Such a study, incorporating elements of the deconstruction of both material culture and ideas, would sharpen the awareness of concepts and theoretical frameworks. Historical explanation then becomes an enterprise in which the nuances and refinements of concepts and theories are a constant necessity, not only because of the availability of fresh evidence from new sources but also because of greater precision in our understanding of the categories which we use to analyze these sources.

II

CONCERNING RELIGION AND HISTORY

CONCERNING RELIGION AND HISTORY: AN INTRODUCTION

If we limit history to the recitation of facts it remains somewhat distanced and unconnected to our lives in the present. One of the areas where this link between the past and the present needs investigation is that of religion in the past and now. Earlier, modern historians had limited the history of religion to studying what the sacred texts of each religion say, and to information on how the religion was organized. But the significant aspect from a historical perspective is also to ascertain what this organization grew out of and how it impinged on society. This has been a recent subject of study. When one begins to think about the relationship of religion and society in these terms then one also begins to see how crucial the analysis of this link to the assessment of society as a whole is. The significance is even more noticeable in the way religion is used in present times in various forms of nationalism. The changes in the discipline of history were making it intellectually far more stimulating and nuanced than before. Other demands came to be made on the knowledge of historians. But apart from this, history—more than the other human sciences—was essential to political ideologies that appeal to the past for legitimacy. This it does because the identity of a society in modern times draws on its perceptions of history, and this is particularly marked in the experience of nationalism.

The questioning of colonial and nationalist interpretations has also to do with the historical change brought about in the process of modernization, in which we have been and are currently, participating. The crucial fact of the change is that the survival of a nation is dependant on its preferably being a secular democracy, a mutation that is ultimately inevitable, irrespective of how many decades it may take. Among the dramatic changes is the emergence of capitalism (which it was once thought could be bypassed), accompanied by industrialization. The nature of these changes could differ through the experience of the market economy, neo-liberalism and globalization, but change there has to be. This unsettles existing social norms and structures in variant ways in different societies, an aspect that should be treated as the logical counterpart to modernization brought by capitalism. What is open to us is to avoid the brutalities of the change. For this we have to focus on enhancing the potential of the more humane aspects of this mutation, a focus that is often deliberately set aside. We allow the brutalities to overtake us and thereby annul what could be the more creative aspirations. I am assuming that it may be possible to have a substantial change in the political economy without brutalities.

The relevance of the questions posed is bound to affect the social sciences. The coming of nationalism in India, as an activity opposed to colonial rule and moving towards the expulsion of the colonial power, led inevitably to inducting history as foundational to the ideology. At first this was to be just the intellectual ammunition needed to give an inclusive identity to nationalism, but parallel to it were the identities of religious communities with a political agenda that often corroded nationalist ideology and surfaced as communalisms.

Identity

Nationalism implies the coalescing of smaller groups into a larger inclusive identity that incorporates the lesser ones. The coalescing includes that of the territories of the smaller groups. It refers itself back to a shared history of all those that constitute the nation. The Indian national movement was based on these ideas. It broke when religion was given priority, splitting the groups that had earlier come together, resulting in the division of the territory and ultimately the denial of a shared history, all of which reversed the constituents of nationalism.

Nations are not easily forged since many identities have to be coalesced. History is thought to provide past identities and in the process history comes to be contested. Often enough we are imposing present identities onto the past. Those that select a single identity from the past—be it religion, caste, language or whatever—and then project it as their take on national identity are in fact negating nationalism. Identity politics, where one identity is chosen, is often associated with extremism of a kind that harbours fundamentalism and destroys the more positive changes expected of secular democratic nationalism.

Historical change brings various communities into prominence and democratically by ensuring that all citizens have equal rights, and none is considered as a primary citizen with special rights. The manipulation of history to legitimize community identity becomes essential to communalism demanding special rights, the more so when it dominates politics. The contestation is between historians trying to defend history from communal manipulation and those insisting on ideologies that support fundamentalist versions of the past. The history that has raised the maximum controversy in this context is that of pre-modern India and particularly that of the early period.

Nationalism

Eric Hobsbawm encapsulates the link between history and nationalism when he states that historians are to nationalism what poppy-growers are to heroin addicts! All nationalisms require and search for utopias from the past and the more remote periods of history are chosen, partly because there is less detailed evidence on such periods and therefore it is possible to fantasize more freely about them. Except that these days we historians, with our new methodologies, tend to disallow the fantasy and run into problems with the fantasy-makers. Political ideologies focusing in particular on what they call 'cultural nationalism'—and this is common to many societies apart from the Indian—blatantly exploit history.

In India there have been and continue to be a variety of ideologies that claim to be forms of nationalism. These include the avowedly secular inclusive Indian national movement against colonialism, whose secular credentials by and large held, although occasionally they were somewhat opaque. But this more secular Indian nationalism seems to be slowly receding, being overtaken by various religious nationalisms such as the Hindu, Muslim, and Sikh—incorporating varieties of fundamentalism.

The objection to applying the label of nationalism to what may be viewed as these 'lesser breeds without the law' is well taken. Nationalism is secular and the term should refer only to the one Indian nationalism. But the lesser ones have grown, nourished on the theory sponsored by colonial thinking that the religion of a community was and has always been, its identity, and that this qualified it to be called a nation. Politicians such as V.D. Savarkar and M.A. Jinnah, toeing in their later years the line of British colonial policy, regularly referred to the two nations of the Hindus and the Muslims. Religious communal organizations have appropriated the label of nationalisms—thus the references to Hindu, Muslim and

Sikh nationalisms. Strictly these are not nationalisms but fundamentalist religious identities. They are now referred to as nationalisms since that is the term they claim, even though it does not apply. Both Hindu and Muslim communalists had their organizational bases in the 1920s such as the Muslim League and the Hindu Mahasabha. Despite it being in essence anti-nationalist, the two-nation theory is now effectively not questioned, if anything it is once again being endorsed by some political parties.

Communalisms

The nationalism of a religious community is not Indian nationalism, irrespective of which community it may refer to. This argument was made in the 1940s and quite correctly against 'Muslim nationalists', but seventy years later a man proclaiming himself to be a 'Hindu nationalist' is taken as synonymous with an Indian nationalist.

When nationalism is reduced to identity politics and priority is given to a religious community, then it follows that the history sought will be a history that focuses on the particular religious community that is being projected as that of the primary citizen. So Hindu nationalism/communalism refers itself back to the pre-Islamic period and claims an unbroken continuity from Harappan times, tracing its origins to the golden age of the early past when Hinduism is said to have been dominant. Questioning this theory is not welcomed and those that do so are dismissed as 'Marxists', intended as a form of abuse (!), or else targeted with the most crass denunciation. The golden age, it is maintained, was terminated by 'the Muslim invasions' followed by a period of tyrannical Muslim rulers whose actions are portrayed in brutal terms.

Muslim nationalism/communalism, familiar in Pakistan, traces the origin of its history (subsequent to the Indus Civilization)to Mohammad bin Qasim's campaigns in Sind in the eighth century AD, and the history prior to this is seen as largely irrelevant. Some historians in Pakistan disagree with this position, but the focus remains mostly on the history of the subcontinent under Islamic rulers. Muslim rule is praised as having benefitted India. And so the story goes on and on. Some Sikh nationalists wanted the history of the Punjab to start with Guru Nanak. The attempt at an exclusive focus on Shivaji in Maharashtra derives from a similar kind of sentiment.

Religious organizations the world over have never been averse to playing politics, accessing and controlling power and setting themselves up as parallel governing structures. The Catholic-Protestant conflicts in Europe are an obvious example. This has also been known to the history of religions in India, although until recently historians have tended not to examine this aspect of organized religion, possibly because the conflicts were not on the same scale as those of the European. Now the scale has become more apparent what with political parties organizing communal riots, destroying mosques and banning books that do not conform to the views of religious conservatism. Any threat to the control of religion is proclaimed as a threat to the religion itself. No distinction is made between the religion of an individual and the political use of religious organizations.

Yet this distinction is crucial to any society. An individual has the right to her belief and her way of worshipping a deity of her choice, provided this does not harm anyone else in that society. This of course is the ideal although it may not always work in such a harmonious manner. Some forms of worship can cause conflicts. Religion encourages community worship that bonds the worshippers and perhaps serves psychological needs. Some aspects of religion can be humane and conducive to the well-being of everyone but these tend to receive lip service from the majority. Sometimes it is fear of the unknown that creates a God, or alternately the awe of the universe that is overwhelming. Mystery is perceived by the individual and can be articulated in religious poetry and music.

Organized religion, however, is different from the religion of the individual. Religious organizations may begin with the finest values but many succumb to other pressures and turn into tyrannical bodies. When this happens religion moves away from its root purposes and turns into an organization encouraging hatred and violence and opposing the initial values with which it had itself started. The defence of such a religion then requires an 'enemy', generally chosen from within society although it can be external to it—the Sunni fundamentalists attack the Shi'as, supporters of Hindutva organized by the Sangh Parivar attack Christians and Muslims. Human rights, social welfare or social justice are not the concerns of such religious organizations. Welfare relates only to their followers, if at all. Justice is subjected to observing the code of the religion. Belief and ritual get subsumed into religiosity. All this becomes an area of contention against secularism, that neither denies nor rejects religion, but insists on the priority of social ethics based on equal and universal human rights, and social justice based on uniform civil laws. Religion is not required for these values to prevail.

Religiosity

Religiosity, often described as excessive religiousness, is of course different from religion. The end purpose of religiosity is seldom worship per se, but is more often the means of demonstrating wealth and power. Religiosity binds the gullible with superstitions and ensnares them with the false promises of fake gurus thriving on media attention and magnanimous donations. Those who have faith and seek genuine teachers are frequently left by the wayside. One has only to see what Hindutva and the Sangh Parivar have done to Hinduism, what the Taliban and the mullahs have done to Islam, what the supporters of Khalistan have done to Sikhism, and what the Goa Inquisition did to local catholic Christians, to realize the change. The secular critique is not of religion as such, but of those who exploit religious faith for political and other gain.

The history of a religion therefore, is not limited to what the texts may say. Many religious texts incorporate the same values of moral behavior, tolerance and discouraging violence. Historically, new religions emerge when there are ideological differences that result in social conflict and the new religion attempts to douse the embers. The problem comes when the religion is associated with those in power, for then, religion also becomes a party to political competition or to moral corruption where it prevails. The historian therefore has to constantly place both the texts and the activities of a religion, in the context of what is happening in the society to which they refer. The relationship between a religion and its social activities may not always be complimentary to the religion. And when this is exposed, the religious organization tries to stifle the views of those that do so, as we have witnessed in recent decades.

Some religious 'nationalisms' resort to the euphemism of calling themselves cultural nationalists, arguing that their organization is neither religious nor political but cultural. The implication is that 'culture' is neutral and apolitical. This makes no sense, as culture relates itself to social groups and their self-expression. The statement is in any case denied by such nationalisms generally being the pivot of those political parties that are based on religious identities. This identity is defined by the social strata whose cultures are being appropriated by the particular organization Culture also has an identity defined by whose culture is being appropriated by the particular organization. An obvious example is the RSS, the ideological propagator of Hindutva. One of its leaders, B.S. Moonje, stated that its organization was modelled on the Italian Fascisti, which together with Mussolini, had greatly impressed him. Its continuous stepping into political waters could hardly hide its political intentions. These are now amply clear in its role as the pivot of the BJP. Such 'cultural nationalisms' oriented to religious identities have had a long innings.

Another manifestation of cultural nationalism comes from the Indian diaspora that uses various Internet websites run by certain NRI organizations to mobilize opinion and spread 'the message'. There is an element of pathos in their clinging to what they believe is the idea of India, even if it is passé. This is strongly coloured by the religious nationalisms of the home country, be they Hindu, Muslim or Sikh and these religious nationalisms are in turn reinforced by the belief and the substantial financial contributions that come from abroad. It is projected as their claim to a culture superior to that of the host countries where they have settled. Alienated as they are from the host culture the image of a utopian past of the homeland is evoked, even if it is an out-of-date one. The enemy however is not the host country—which it dare not be since the concerned NRIs are living there—but those in the home country who oppose the politics of religious fundamentalism. The material success of such NRIs makes them the role model for those of the Indian middle class aspiring to success in the home country, and their ideology is also imbibed by their Indian counterparts. The intention is to redefine the particular religion to make it less flexible and to define civilization in religious terms.

The concept of Indian civilization was equated by some European Orientalists with things Hindu and its definition lay in the Hindu religion and the Sanskrit language, and the territorial boundaries of British India, all inherited from colonial scholarship. The concept was not questioned nor was it argued that Indian culture consisted of many strands not just the one. The strikingly unique feature of the plurality of cultures in India, that distinguished Indian civilization, went unheeded in the desperate attempt to identify a single culture and give it priority. Today historians recognize that the hallmark of a civilization is not its rigid boundaries but its porosity, and that civilizations can only thrive when there is an inter-connectedness between them that enhances the communication of ideas and practices. That is perhaps one reason why for historians the concept of civilization is something quite else than what was meant by the term in the nineteenth century.

The fundamentalist versions of religions mock the idea of religion. For instance, Hindutva replaces the freedom of individual belief by conformity to a uniform belief and practice. Its organization and ideology has suggested the influence of the Semitic religions. It also encourages the community's competition in religiosity by constant reference to what it constructs as the Hindu tradition. The sensitivity and fluidity of worship in some aspects of Hinduism as prevalent especially among the lesser castes, are brushed aside. Pre-modern Hinduism had its warts—big and small—as do all religions, but its subtleties were richer than what is now being thrust on its believers. Hindutva is in many ways the antithesis of Hinduism, and aims to create a society that is narrow, bigoted and inward looking, in which the co-existence with those that differ, such as the minority communities of various kinds, is becoming increasingly impossible, as demonstrated by the frequency of communal riots. These inevitably lead to the ghettoization of the targeted community, as has happened subsequent to such riots, and the exclusion of such communities from living in an integrated society, as happened in Gujarat after the communal riots of 2002. Ghettoization, as one knows from the European experience, has the potential of facilitating barbaric solutions, and does solve the problems of differences in patterns of living.

7

COMMUNALISM: A HISTORICAL PERSPECTIVE

A critique of communalism in the context of India is often mistaken for a critique of religion. It therefore needs to be emphasized that communalism is a phenomenon of recent times, when communities are identified by religion and this identification is brought into play as a substantial political articulation. This is distinctly different from the past when community identities ranged over many perspectives apart from religion, such as caste, region, language and occupation. Religious communities were also labelled differently with labels such as brahmana and shramana (referring to the heterodox sects of Buddhist, Jainas, etc;). The indication here was that the teaching and the propagation through monks differentiated the two. The terms continued to be used for many centuries. Al-Biruni visiting India in the early eleventh century speaks of the brahmanas prevailing in India, and the shamaniyya who had propounded a religion hostile to that of the brahmanas in previous centuries and in Iran and Central Asia. This was obviously Buddhism.

The secular critique of communalism is not an opposition to religion but to the abuse of religion. As the emotional and psychological need of an individual to worship and belief, religion is not objected to. But when religious expression demands the setting aside of other values that a society requires, then it has to be criticized. Religion has its place in society but should not be given pre-eminence since it is, in social terms, only one among the other requirements that go to make a worthwhile society. Social justice, for instance, among the other requirements has priority. Where religion overrides social justice, there it has to be put back in its place.

Religion can be used as a mechanism of controlling society through the institutions that it establishes, particularly educational institutions. These can be propagating a philosophy that deliberately opposes the secular and the rational, and therefore can be questioned. When groups associated with religious organizations or with political parties that draw on religious identities, start demanding that certain books, films, plays, lectures, social behavior are either hurtful to the sentiments of a particular religion or are violating what are referred to as 'Indian values and tradition' and therefore should be censored and banned, there religion has gone beyond its boundaries and turned communal. Those who make these claims are generally associated with political organizations, observing an extremist agenda using religion, or are self-appointed 'spokesmen' of religion-based organizations. What makes such groups unacceptable is that they are violent to the extent of assassinating those that do not accede to their demands. Both the threats and the violence have been increasing over the years. Communal ideology defines groups as religious communities and it maintains that this identity wipes out all others. Communalism is the political exploitation of a religious ideology. Therefore a critique of communalism is not an attack on religion *per se,* but on the political use of religion or the abuse of religion. Communal politicians however always use the easy ploy and accuse those who critique communalism of being anti-religious.

Religion can be the legitimate belief of an individual in a deity and in what the individual hopes that the worship of that deity may bring. This aspect of religion is often not the concern of the historian although it could be in some instances. What historians are interested in is seeing the way in which religious organizations establish institutions in order to control the functioning of society, as a parallel system attempting to influence governance. These range from some institutions pertaining to civic and social welfare, but generally many more that cater to political ambitions and interface with political groups and ideologies. In the past these were institutions financed by royal grants. They could act as a catchment area of support for the ruler or could alternatively develop into a focus of opposition. The negotiations between religious institutions and political authority, going back to past times, make for a fascinating history.

In a modern society, governance and social control are not the functions of religion but of civil administration acting in accordance with secular laws for the benefit of society. Some may argue that it does not matter if a religious organization sets up schools, colleges, universities, hospitals, workshops as charitable institutions, since these are needed. But there is always a need for caution since no religion is altruistic and is interested in ideological control, ultimately extending over a large part of society.

The communal ideology insists that the separation of communities identified by religion, also has its roots in the past. This further implies the denial that social systems cut across religious identities. History is brought in as an attempt to provide a justification from the past as was first done by colonial scholars. Mill's periodization made a deep imprint on modern Indian thinking, in diverting it from the more significant issues of the connections between the past and the present.

For the Muslim communalist there is a reversal of history. Pre-Islamic Indian history is unimportant and irrelevant. History becomes relevant with the establishment of Islam. This of course creates immense problems for historians who wish to toe the official line in an Islamic state such as Pakistan. They record pre-Islamic history, but have to dodge the question of regarding it as ancestral. Whereas the Hindu communalist refers to Indian history linked to Islam as the history of foreigners, for Muslim communalists the identity of being foreign is a mark of status. Among Muslim castes, priority was given to the very few that claimed to be of Arab, Persian or Turkish descent, as against the many who were local converts. Even with the coming of Islam, where the 'Muslim period' is seen as the golden age, the attempt is to trace historical roots back to the early history of Islam. The alternate preference is to seek longevity as a nation where this can be taken to an extreme as in *Five Thousand Years of Pakistan* by Mortimer Wheeler, which was an attempt at giving historical legitimacy to the new nation but it posed an uncomfortable proximity to a non-Islamic past.

Doubtless the question will become even more difficult for Sikh communalists and others of similar ilk, who would like to claim roots in more recent times, and the subordination of earlier history will pose a bigger problem. If the history of the Punjab becomes significant only with the birth of Guru Nanak, as some like to argue, there is considerable evident history that would have to be wished away. Books that analyze the organizations propagating Sikhism, if they are critical in their assessments, get proscribed. Where such books cannot be banned, as in North America, their authors are targeted.

The ideology of Hindu communalism argues that since the Hindus form the 'majority community' they are therefore the inheritors of the past and claimants to dominance in the present. It is also claimed that religious tolerance and non-violence in relation to religion are characteristic of this community, however intolerant and violent such groups may be today. A particular 'tradition' is regarded as the Hindu tradition and this underlies the comprehension of culture and social values. The Hindu communal ideology also seeks to redefine Hinduism as Hindutva, literally Hinduness, in a form appropriate to political mobilization. These kinds of attitudes are not limited to Hindu communalism, but occur in other forms of communalism as well. The increasing popularity of Islamization has visible symbols of identification. The symbols of the Sikhs are recognized. The term 'majority community' for the Hindus has come to be accepted even by those who do not subscribe to the communal ideology. It goes back to the British Indian Censuses when the numbers for every religious community were counted. But a little historical exploration might help us understand these terms. As we have seen, the term 'Hindu' is an invention of the Arabs going back to the Iranian and Greek names for the inhabitants living in the land beyond the Indus, al-Hind. It is in origin a geographical term and it was later given a religious connotation. The label 'Hindu' came from non-Hindu usage and was later taken up by the Hindus themselves.

The reason for this appears to be the fact that those who identified with the various sects that went to make up the 'Hindu' had no common term by which they identified themselves. The sense of a single religious community cutting across caste, region and language with a common creed, rituals and a single sacred book, was absent. The nearest perhaps was the notion of the common caste and cultural identity of those who observed the 'varnashramadharma', the social code of the four castes and the four stages of life; but this emphasized the segregation and segmentation of caste society, rather than the all-inclusive sense of a religious community.

The rigid exclusion of what were called the unclean shudras and untouchables, was very different from the present day political wooing of these groups by the upper castes. The appropriation of the Islamic label, 'Hindu', by the Hindus in order to identify themselves, seems to have begun from about the fourteenth century, but nevertheless used only in limited regions and among certain castes.

The Hindu view of the Muslims was also expressed not in religious terms but in ethnic, geographical and cultural identities. They were referred to as 'Turushkas,' usually Turks from Central Asia, or 'Shakas,' 'Yavanas,' Greeks and others from West Asia, and 'mlecchas', outside the social pale of caste. Initially Mussalman/Muslim was not used, and only later came the colonial usage of calling them Mohammadans. The Hindus do not appear to have seen themselves as a unified community, but rather preferred the identity of castes, sects and regions. This hypothesis can be confirmed or otherwise by an analysis of the self-perception of such groups in the literature of the second millennium AD in various regional languages.

Some communities did manage to cut across this segmentation. The brahmanas of the sub-continent, for instance, identified themselves through language and ritual apart from caste, even though the use of these in various ways led to multiple gradations within their ranks. The renouncer and the wandering ascetic were often familiar figures on the edge of many landscapes, although language frequently determined their effective boundaries. The recognition of the social system of *jati* as caste, created a larger identity and one that included a variety of castes and sects pertaining to various religious affiliations. But even in this the hierarchical pattern of the caste structure varied from region to region. The dominant caste was not invariably the same all over and the jatis did not follow identical rankings in every part of the subcontinent.

The notion of a Hindu and a Muslim community as defined today was tied to the Census. Its political necessity emerged from the colonial view of Indian society and became crystallized through the competition for political power and access to economic resources between various groups in a colonial situation. There was need to change from a segmented identity to a community which cut across caste, sect and region. This social need also required a reformulation of what had come to be called the Hindu religion and this was part of the attempt of various socio-religious reform movements of the nineteenth century. The Hindu religion that took shape came to be called Hinduism.

To establish the implicit antiquity of the community as well as its demarcating characteristics that made it different from other communities, it was argued that among its essential features was a spirit of tolerance and non-violence. These values were picked up from the normative tradition but were posited as being descriptive of the reality of social relations.

However, historical facts suggest otherwise. It we read the edicts of the Emperor Ashoka, a constant refrain is that of the plea for tolerance and particularly tolerance among the various religious sects, often summarized in the phrase *bamhana-samananam,* 'brahmanas and shramanas', where the enmity between the two is compared by Patanjali to that between the snake and the mongoose. If tolerance and co-existence prevailed, then there would not have been this repeated plea.

Somewhat later in time, in the *Rajatarangini* of Kalhana, there are references to the persecution of Buddhists, particularly by Shaiva sects. Still later, in the late first millennium and early second millennium AD, there is evidence of the persecution of Jainas in the south and, again, particularly by Shaiva sects. Jaina monastic centres were appropriated, Jaina temples were desecrated and images removed, and Jaina monks not only ridiculed but impaled and beheaded.

This intolerance has been ignored for a variety of reasons. It is generally dismissed as more of a sectarian rivalry rather than religious intolerance. It is argued that the Hindu community as a whole was not responsible for such acts but only one sect among its many. But, for the situations where this intolerance and persecution prevailed, it was of a substantial kind. Places of pilgrimage were sometimes locations of violence. This may be explained as due to the large takings in money and gifts at such places, made as offerings to the custodians of temples, or as conflicting claims to a following by various groups of ascetics. Given the propensity of ascetic 'godmen' today for property and material wealth, this may also have been an aspect that goes back into history.

If the Shaivas were intolerant, the Vaishnavas seem to have been less so, being an assimilating sect. In either case less powerful religious sects tended to get absorbed in a process of acculturation, probably in a harmonious manner but sometimes in confrontation. This came to be viewed as the Hindu way of coping with other sects. What is interesting is that in our times it is Vaishnavism that has become the better organized and the more fierce, judging by the mobilization and activities of 'Rama-bhaktas' over issues like the Ramjanmabhoomi. What were noticeably absent in the earlier acts of intolerance were jihads and inquisitions. But today we have the organized communal riots. However, the absence of extreme behaviour does not cleanse the record, for the latter shows the presence of a potential if not actual extremism. Looked at historically, tolerance and non-violence were not what set Indian civilization apart from others.

Hinduism is closely tied to caste. Conversion to non-Hindu religions or the contours of sects within Hinduism are often determined by caste considerations. The arranging of marriages and inheritance of property according to caste rules is a normal procedure but the rules may vary according to the religion. However when it comes to caste hierarchy and the exclusion of Dalit groups, this is characteristic of every formal, organized religion. Hindus, Muslims, Sikhs and Christians all demarcate untouchable castes, irrespective of whether or not religion teaches the equality of all believers. This becomes the practice in India even of those religions originating outside India and where this characteristic does not preval in other places where the religion prevails. Not only does this throw a deep shadow on religious tolerance in India but it also points to intolerance within religions in India being an established belief and practice. The intolerance is not of belief but of the social origins of the believers.

Communal ideologies claim to base themselves on an appeal to tradition. But tradition, as is well known, is not a given package of ideas and practices. Traditions are invented or are put together through a selection of items from the past and the selection is deliberate and frequently relates to the social underpinnings of the group involved in present times. Each of the communal ideologies is careful to pick items from the religious beliefs and practices applicable to its community. And the traditions therefore are socially segregated as well.

In the case of Hindu communalism, upper caste beliefs and practices are seen as more attractive and obviously appeal to those who in the past have been excluded socially. Thus, the rituals of brahmanism are at a premium and are looked upon as the core of tradition. The ban on beef eating and the insistence on cow protection become important issues in later centuries. At a certain point in history these were manifestations of the upper caste and of the orthodoxy. What remains an unanswered historical question is why and when this practice was discontinued, and later became a slogan for communal mobilization when organizing confrontations with the beef-eating communities.

In such situations, communalism attempts to imitate upper caste mores and gives the illusion of upward mobility to the socially inferior group now being reunited with the community. It acts as a kind of all-purpose 'sanskritization'—the theory that one form of upward mobility was for the lower castes to imitate, when they were able to, the life-style of the upper castes. Nevertheless, the actual differences of economic and social status remain. These are not done away with because this is not the purpose of communalism. The pose may be egalitarian, but the reality remains conservative and socially differentiated.

It is sometimes argued that within the context of a religious community, if people are declared equal then communalism has a democratic component. But in the insistence on the return to the practice of what are seen as religious laws, there is a return to conservatism and an anti-democratic system. It is as well to remember that sacred laws, whether they be the precepts of the *Dharmashastras* or of the Shar'ia or Hadith, were promulgated to support and further a hierarchical society and are therefore by their very nature opposed to democratic rights.

Communal ideologies, because they use religion for political purposes in the context of a changing and modernizing society, also attempt to refashion the religion. This is evident in recent trends in Hindu communalism. By way of an example, there is a serious attempt to historicize its mythologies and beliefs, an attempt that did not exist in earlier times. The Rama and Krishna janmabhoomi movements trying to locate the birthplace of each are clear indications of this. In medieval times the locations varied and were left vague. Today there is a determination to give precise locations and calculate precise dates. What we tend to forget is that historicity was not central to the narratives in the epics and *Puranas*. Epic characters were converted into avataras of Vishnu many centuries ago in a successful effort to use popular epics to propagate the worship of Vishnu, a technique common to much religious literature.

This was attempted again by the socio-religious reform movements of the nineteenth century, when, in imitation of the Semitic model, there was an attempt to endorse monotheism, to postulate a historical founder or teacher for the religion to provide it with a historical base, to emphasize a single sacred book (often the *Gita*), to suggest or invent some kind of congregational worship, and to introduce the notion of conversion to Hinduism. The problem with conversion is that it requires a caste identity, for otherwise the person converted can only be classified as a lowly mleccha—outside caste; and caste identities come with birth into a caste—jati. Hence the Arya Samaj adoption of conversion to Hinduism involves the ritual of shuddhi, purification. The search for historicity makes it necessary to locate the central figure in space and time and indicate a precise location for a janmabhoomi, birthplace.

Yet, the great strength of Vaishnavism in the past was precisely its ahistoricity, where the historical fact of the existence of Rama or Krishna was irrelevant to the beliefs and practices of the devotee. This is what made a number of the Hindu sects unique in the religious experience of civilization and gave to them a distinctively different character—a character that is now being eroded.

In this refashioning of the Hindu religion, there is an attempt to dictate to all Hindus what their religion should be. As such it cuts away from the major strength of the Hindu sects of the past that spanned an entire range of belief and practice, from atheism to animism. The narrowing of this identity can only detract from the quality of the religious experience.

The claim to places being historically associated with the biography of the avataras has also to be seen as an attempt to claim valuable property and to control vast resources provided by the offerings of pilgrims and the estates of temples. That this was a recognized source of income for important religious places of worship is also referred to in the past. The claims to such locations are now made because some Hindu organizations see themselves as powerful. But if others claim the same rights to their sacred sites that were taken over by Hindu sects, it is seen as a law and order problem—witness the struggle to keep in tact places of worship jointly visited by both Hindus and Muslims. And then there was the struggle of the Dongria Kondhs to defend their sacred hill of Niyamgiri from being mined for bauxite by both the government and the corporate multi-national, Vedanta. If religion is so primary and conducive to tolerance, then should it not have stopped the defacing of what is a sacred site to the Kondhs. It is the equivalent to destroying a temple. Both should be decried and double standards should not be applied.

Comparable to this has been the recent move to revivify disused mosques in Delhi and elsewhere. The ones chosen are either those with a property potential or else those which have a demonstration effect politically. This move is again intended to test an assertion of power. Religious buildings, whether temples or mosques, when desanctified for many decades if not centuries, and brought under the protection of the Archaeological Survey of India, become part of an historical heritage and are not therefore negotiable for being used again as places of worship. Such buildings should not be surreptitiously brought into religious use as is being done in many places. The temptation is great as monuments when they become places of pilgrimage, apart from attracting devoted worshippers, are also conducive to gathering wealth through offerings and through commerce.

In the historical process of modernization that we are undergoing with the building of a nation-state and other similar experiences, there is a premium on the annulling of segmented, segregated groups and the restructuring of society with larger identities. It is not secularism which brings about the communalization of our society, but the deliberate choice of a religious identity which can be used in the game of numbers related to democratic representation and by which groups aspiring to power can manipulate the system. The minorities adopt the same pattern by converting each into a single conservative body, then threaten society, and then negotiate a political status.

The choice before us is not limited to the defining of the larger community only by a religious identity. We can choose to organize our society along different lines where concepts such as a majority community and minority communities, each with their attendant rights, is seen as divisive and merely allowing a change of persons in power but doing nothing to ensure the well-being of society. Communalism does not bring about an improvement in social and economic levels since this is not part of its programme; it is fundamentally a hunt for power.

If a demonstration of this is required, we do not have to look far. Our northern neighbour, Pakistan, was created in the matrix of Muslim communalism and it was believed that a religious identity was sufficient to build a nation. Not only did the breaking away of Bangladesh upset this calculation, but the strife within Pakistan and the incipient sub-nationalisms of Baluchistan and Sind or the repeated killing of Shia's, have demonstrated the ineffectiveness of a religious identity backed by a religious community providing the basis for a secure nation.

That communalist ideologies attract a following, again has to do with a particular historical situation. Nationalism of the anti-colonial variety that provided the ideological magnet in the earlier half of this century is now seen as irrelevant in India. There is therefore a search for a new ideology.

This is a particular requirement among those sections of society, such as the urban middle classes, who have experienced some degree of affluence but who have in the process had to change their life style or move away from what they were taught to accept as traditional values, and who are facing increasing competition to retain their place in the sun. In such a condition of insecurity and loss of ideology there is a turning towards a replacement. The notion of a religious community defined by this group provides it with the necessary ambition to reach for power and covers this striving with a garb of pious sentiment and religiosity.

Communalism also disallows the possibility of uniform civil laws that would go a long way towards easing social interaction. In earlier times, when societies were hierarchically organized and privilege was the hallmark of the few, customary law prevailed in the segmented groups, particularly at the lower levels, and the state safeguarded customary law. But communities are in any case not sacrosanct and heritable. They are created and they change over time. Today, with the demand for the equality of all before the law and the equal access of everyone to rights, customary law can no longer prevail. This particularly affects the rights of women in marriage and inheritance, and their rights to property. We have recently seen the confrontation between believed customary practice and the Civil Code in the action of the khap panchayats against breaking marriage rules relating to caste. This is a testing of the power of patriarchy. Conventional religious laws insist on a subordinate status for women and that is now unacceptable.

We already have claims to different personal laws and doubtless more can be created if various communalisms so require it. But in the perpetration of such laws we violate basic human rights. Equal rights do imply a uniformity of laws and this in turn implies at least a different concept of society. Given the nature of the society we aspire to, it would be tragic if we were to be strangled by the entrails of communalist ideologies playing with the politics of power, and were to become vulnerable to the actions of religious fundamentalisms.

8

RELIGION AND THE SECULARIZING OF INDIAN SOCIETY

Religion in the Indian subcontinent was, and is, a different experience from that of Europe and elsewhere. But it was redefined by colonial scholarship so as to make it comprehensible to those who saw it from a Judeo-Christian perspective. This definition was not averse to Indian scholars and to those who gave form to the socio-religious reform movements of the nineteenth century. This definition now prevails among its influential practitioners and observers. If anything it has been taken even further in making it resemble the Semitic religions. However, it does not explain the earlier practice of religion nor the presence of the variety of religions in India.

Secularism, that constitutes the second theme, has been variously defined. Since most Indian religions lack a Church the question of Church and State relations would not apply. However, this does not mean that secularism has no role in India. As we have noted earlier in this book, the definition prevalent in India, is that secularism means the co-existence of all religions irrespective of their status. As an extension of this idea it is said that secularism, since it excludes divine sanction, is alien to Indian civilization, the assumption being that everything in Indian civilization requires divine sanction.

I would like initially to suggest that a distinction be made between secularism and the secularizing of a society. I see secularism as an ideology whose concern is with secularizing society, and although it accepts the presence of religion this presence does not receive priority. It is distinct from religion, but not opposed to it, since its concern is with the rights and obligations of the individual in the context of multiple social relationships, in other words of the individual as citizen. The secularizing of a society moves towards giving a new direction to the identity of a citizen.

As ideology, secularism neither has an organizational base, nor can it be politically imposed. It has to evolve from rights to citizens and changes in society and its laws appropriate to these. This requires a readjustment of the social control exercised by various traditional authorities, which includes religious authorities. Nevertheless, secularism does challenge religious fundamentalism, in as much as the latter attempts to re-assert membership of a formal religion as the sole identity of the citizen. Religious fundamentalism is primarily a political condition that wears the authoritarian cover of a religion, and can only be terminated by ending the political inducement it offers and by undermining its claim to being the unquestioning authority over all codes.

The secularizing of society suggests a process of graduated change that endorses the kinds of values that may lead to a secular society, but the process may or may not be deliberately directed towards this. Secularizing society requires the state and civil society to ensure that social ethics assume both the equality of all its citizens and their welfare. This requires that codes be sanctioned not by religious authority, but by a civil authority. This authority would have primacy over the registration of birth, marriage and death, although religious rites could certainly be performed if so wished; and the laws governing inheritance would be part of the universal civil code. Social justice in particular would not come under any religious jurisdiction. This would extend to schemes of social welfare—such as education, employment and health—initiated by the state. In short, it should be possible for any Indian to exercise his/her rights as a citizen without seeking the sanction of any religious identity. Both the Hindu Code Bill and the Muslim Personal law and such like, would have to be replaced by a uniform, universally applicable civil law having jurisdiction over marriage and inheritance, and ensuring gender justice.

If the interface with religion is important to secularism then the more pertinent question is whether the religion's concerned can accommodate themselves to the secularizing of Indian society. Although it is anachronistic to look for ideas similar to secularism in pre-modern societies, it could be helpful to locate elements in traditional religions and thought that would be conducive to a secularizing process. What emerges from such an investigation is that religious sanction was not invariably required to establish social laws since there were exceptions and there were differences in customary practice. Furthermore, the priority given to civil law in contemporary times is one of the major characteristics of a modern society. To that extent it does involve a new way of looking at the relationship between law and society.

Definitions of Indian religions in the last couple of centuries have generally assumed that the prototype of the Semitic religions would apply. This is particularly problematic for religions indigenous to India. In addition, it is problematic in terms of how religion is practiced in the sub-continent. The primary religious identity in pre-modern times was that of the religious sect rather than that of formal singular religion. There is a complex history of varieties of accommodation or of contestation among the various sects that also shape the forms they take. They are not therefore, self-contained entities and have not been so in popular practice.

The public articulation of religion is related to social institutions. Consequently, one aspect of religion in India is the degree to which the institution of caste as the basic organization of Indian society, structures religion. Every religion reflects an acceptance of caste in differing degree. Some Hindu sects are obsessive about caste others are more flexible. Islam and Sikhism have denied it in theory but conform to much of it in practice, particularly in rules of marriage and of inheritance of property. Caste implies diverse customary codes of identification, and these often differentiate the practice of religion even within the same formal religious identity. Some religious sects formulated and furthered caste organization and some opposed it in various ways. Many rituals were practiced only by particular castes in particular locations. A section of people, now referred to as Other Backward Caste Hindus (OBC) and of course the Dalits, were not permitted to worship in the sanctum of Hindu temples. Even now, some temples deny them entry. Their beliefs and practices have inevitably differed from those of upper-caste Hindus, although attempts are being made in recent times to iron out differences and present uniformity. Recruiting tribal groups into Hindu society in Gujarat at the time of the Godhra genocide in 2002, by various agencies of Hindutva, was not just religious conversion as they could be used politically.

Hinduism is perhaps better seen as a mosaic of religious sects rather than a single uniform religion along the lines of a monotheistic Judeo-Christian type of religion. Sectarian differentiation can arise as a break-away from an established practice of a religion. Equally often there has been the assertion of a higher status by a caste accompanied by a change in religious practices imitating those of the higher castes. As has often been said, it is not the belief system that has to be uniform within each caste but rather the practice of the ritual, therefore, orthopraxy is more important than orthodoxy.

Religious sects in India have distinct identities. Some that have been included within the umbrella label of Hinduism are nevertheless at varying distances in belief and practice from each other. There are other practices and identities in the other religions of India such as in Islam, Sikhism, Christianity, Jainism and neo-Buddhism, each with a different take on religion and on secularism. Most of these have their forms of fundamentalism as well—be it Hindu, Islamic or Sikh. Their institutions establish their agendas vis-à-vis both state and society, and they use a religious identity for political mobilization as and when they need to.

The process of secularizing society can draw on traditional ways in which social relationships were articulated. Central to the values that governed most societies was the concept of social ethics. The definition varied, as for example, between Brahmanism and Buddhism. The *Bhagvad Gita*, for example, would not, on any account, have been the message of the Buddha. Whatever the message of the *Gita,* the fact that it had to be endorsed by a vision of the divine, would disqualify it as appropriate to secularism. One wonders where social ethics went when bodily pollution became a reason for casting out certain social groups and reducing them to servitude. As a contrast to this, and essential to the meaning of secular, would be social ethics focusing on social equality and human well-being, but without claiming divine sanction.

The insistence on viewing secularism as the reverse image of religion has detracted from its origins linked to modernity and to nationalism, to its articulation in the nation-state, and more directly to democratic values. Secularism and democracy are intrinsically interwoven. In theory, nationalism redefines social codes to make them inclusive and universal. To that extent it opposes exclusive religious identities, except where nationalism itself endorses a religious identity. However, this is not a characteristic only of modern times. There were occasions in the earlier past when social ethics presuming the equality of all, had primacy in debates on social codes and some of these did not seek a divine mandate.

If such an ethic endorsed social values broadly of a kind underlying the secularizing of society, then this would suggest, not a secular society in early times, but a potentially proto-secular presence in a culture. It may not always have been present in practice but could be referred to as a principal. This might be useful when drawing upon a tradition.

This proto-secular presence in India, as it might be called, did not come from the text-bound, established formal religions of Vedic Brahmanism, Puranic Hinduism, Islam and Sikhism, but from ideologies that were distanced from these formal religions or were even opposed to them. This presence asserted an alternative structure of social ethics where caste distinctions were initially at least irrelevant to religious ritual and were not a primary value. Such ideologies had a substantial following and included Buddhists, Jainas, and a range of diverse free-thinking sects. These have been swept into the general category of Hinduism but need to be distinguished very clearly. They represent a gradation ranging from opposition to distancing and for a variety of reasons. These have constituted a substratum that was distinct from the formal religions and have been present since the earliest times to now. This substratum has been articulate and popular with large numbers of people, but is not given its due recognition because in our times they do not constitute formal religion. Instead they are often arbitrarily and as a fragment, fitted into one or other of the formal religions.

For example, early Buddhism had a substantial following and there was much in Indian culture that has been imprinted with it. Patronage came in part from royalty but more from householders—small-scale land owners and merchants. For almost a thousand years its presence was almost hegemonic. By the late first millennium AD, Buddhist centres in India had dwindled to a few pockets, or else had been so transmuted that the initial teaching had moved into the shadows. Brahmanism as the hegemonic religion replaced Buddhism. The *Puranas*, refer to the shramanas as mahamoha, those who delude people with their erroneous teaching. This was despite the fact that some Puranic sects grew out of an interface between the two.

The centrality of its interpretation of social ethics was pre-eminent in early Buddhism. The emphasis was on the relationship between the individual and society, and on ethical equality, not endorsing the Brahmanical rules of caste as a divinely ordained inequality. However, the Shramanic sects did not attempt to eliminate caste from society. The Brahmanical varna-ashrama-dharma, the caste ordering of society, insisted on a hierarchy of status and identity in a system of castes and this determined social behaviour and obligations. The hierarchy of social status was controlled through rules of marriage and social obligations and the specificity of rituals. Divine sanction was the source of legitimation. The observance of caste regulations is so insistent in brahmanical texts that obviously there must have been violations else the insistence would not have been necessary. The Buddhist ethic to the contrary, envisaged social behaviour as being determined by ethical norms conducive to universal well-being, irrespective of caste and divine sanction.

Even though subsequent to his death the Buddha was deified and deities were incorporated in Buddhism, nevertheless the understanding of the social ethic remained a constant factor. My concern here is not with the discussion on the liberation of the individual from rebirth, but with the ethic governing the relationship between the individual and society. The two are not disconnected. Living according to the precepts of the middle way may not be enough to preclude rebirth but would ensure a better rebirth than otherwise.

The existence of deity was not central to the discussion of social behaviour. The kernel of the Buddha's teaching drew on causality to explain the human condition and proposed the practice of the middle way as a partial solution. There was no immortal soul therefore impermanence was pervasive. The Buddhist dhamma was the universal ethic of family and community privileging non-violence, tolerance and respect for the individual. These values applied equally to all since they assumed the equality of all and the inter-connection of all sentient beings. The ethic was encapsulated in conduct towards various social categories such as parents, friends, teachers and those for whom the individual worked and those who worked for the individual.

The explanation in Buddhist sources of how political authority and the state came about reflects the same concerns. The utopian beginnings of human society gradually gave way to a dystopia. This was caused by the emergence of families as discrete social units and by their claims to private property. It eventually became necessary for people to elect one among them to ensure protection from mutual greed and to enforce the laws that were applicable to all. The mutual interdependence of temporal and spiritual power is rejected by the early Buddhist tradition. In later centuries the Buddhist Order, the Sangha, negotiated with those that wielded political power to establish its own authority. This was not the equivalent of a Church since it was technically the community of Buddhist monks, with no intervention of deity.

The upholding of dhamma was said to be the most important duty of the ruler and even of the universal monarch—the chakravartin. An attempt was made at propagating some of these ideas by the Mauryan emperor Ashoka but at the level of imperial polity it did not survive his reign in any direct way. Nevertheless, it has been viewed as a threat to the Brahmanical vision of society. The appeal of the Buddhist ethic was maximally to the householder, perhaps the most effective patron of Buddhism. Equality was assumed since wealth was acquired through labour, effort and righteous means. The ruler had to provide sustenance for the poor apart from ensuring good administration and general prosperity.

It is also significant that Buddhism and Jainism acknowledged the right of women to become nuns. This was not absolute freedom but at least it permitted a way of life alternate to the conventional one. The frequency of donations at Buddhist places of worship, by nuns and by women donors, often on behalf of their families, would suggest that they had more freedom than just the choice of joining the Order.

Buddhism, even when patronized by rulers did not establish a new social order. But it provided an alternate ideology to the Brahmanical order and thus indirectly legitimized many non-brahmanical and often lower caste movements that preached an ethic similar to the Buddhist. Some among these movements gained sanction for this ethic through the intervention of deity, but there were others that made no reference to deity. The questioning of deity particularly in the context of social ethics was not limited to the Buddha. Such views persisted as parallel schools of thought among sects well into later times.

Many ancient texts referring to and describing the religions of India mention two categories: the Brahmanic and the Shramanic. The latter, mainly Buddhism and Jainism, subsumed other non-Brahmanical groups. The Brahmanical religion underwent much change. Vedic Brahmanism constituted the orthodoxy. Its focus was the elaborate sacrificial ritual lasting sometimes up to a couple of years and conducted by a hierarchy of brahmana priests. By the first millennium AD, although it was still venerated, it began to be superseded by the popular religion described by modern scholars as Puranic Hinduism. The major gods and rituals changed—with Indra and Agni giving way to Shiva and Vishnu—and the innovation of worshipping icons in shrines and temples. It was a competitor of the Shramanic religion and its flexibility allowed it to absorb a variety of myths and practices of various groups of people. The resulting multiplicity of sects encouraged the osmosis of ideas and practices but discourged the notion of an over-arching religion recognizable as a uniform belief system. New sects emerged. Migrant sects from elsewhere such as the Sufis who trickled in from Persia in the early centuries of the second millennium AD, gave rise to further sects in India. The dialogue between Sufi and Bhakti teaching was reflected in many of the religious trends in this period. Some sects had been and were renunciatory, others evolved into new castes often asserting a higher status than previously.

The period after the thirteenth century saw a scatter of religious teachers—the gurus and the pirs—who had the largest followings of mixed Hindu, Muslim and other groups, up until the last century. These teachers cut across caste and formal religions. There emerged a distinctive Guru-Pir tradition in Indian religion, unfortunately not given the attention it deserves because much of its teaching was oral and it attracted the non-elite person in the main. The impact of this tradition is evident on all the formal religions even when they opposed these teachings. The message they endorsed was that of social equality rather than caste hierarchies, and a concern for the human condition—the message that appealed to those who saw themselves as the subordinated but not the defeated.

The renouncer in Indian society as a figure of moral authority reaching beyond a single religious identity also has a bearing on social ethics. Mysticism apart, many more renouncers were concerned with the mainsprings of society and how these could be directed towards the welfare of its constituents at all levels. This moral authority lay not only in challenging deity—as in the many myths of ascetics threatening to overthrow a god or gods fearing the power of the ascetic—but also in legitimating political and social protest. Gandhi's adoption of the symbols of asceticism was not just an individual quirk. He was using, consciously or subconsciously, the continuation of a long tradition of linking moral authority, as distinct from religious authority, with protest.

I have tried to argue that religion in pre-colonial India had, and in some ways continues to have, a different structure and trajectory from religion elsewhere, both in form and in relation to society. Therefore, as a prelude to the interface between religion and secularism, we have to re-examine our definitions of religions in India.

The current debate on secularism is not a radical departure from some ideologies of pre-modern Indian society, but the emphases and mechanisms are naturally different. The definition of religion in India has been partial, based as it has been largely only on the study of the belief systems and ritual practices as described in the texts used by the dominant castes and elite groups. This was further strengthened in the colonial projection of Indian religions as monolithic, static, uniform entities, virtually unconnected to any social context.

The colonial state recognized only the formal religions of what it called Hinduism and of Islam and contoured them in keeping with its own perspectives on Indian religion. Colonial ethnography collected data on the supporters of the Guru-Pir religious articulation in the Gazetteers and Censuses. There was also data available in the regional languages. Yet, ironically, the distinctive identity of such groups was not recognized. They were marginalized and excluded from the construction of Indian religion. Their articulation was both oral and textual but not always written in the language of the cultural mainstream.

The notion of monolithic religions of the majority and the minority communities tended to shuffle everyone into monolithic identity slots. With the coming of nationalism there was a turning to these identities especially when drawing upon tradition and cultural heritage. Secular nationalism in the anti-colonial struggle was followed closely by Hindu and Muslim nationalisms. These were less concerned with confronting colonial power and more with confronting the other religious nationalism. They were seminal to the current communalism which apart from its political agenda, has no place for religious articulation that cannot be firmly located in one of the two monoliths. Battles over places of worship frequently occur often accompanied by violence. These are places where earlier adherents of all kinds of religious sects would worship together, and where religious identities had been ambiguous and blurred.

Muslim 'nationalism' succeeded in establishing a state—Pakistan.

Hindu nationalism is anxious to make India into a Hindu state, which so far has been evaded. Religious nationalism is not so distant from religious fundamentalism and is therefore hostile to secularism. Interestingly, Hindu nationalism has reformulated Hinduism and calls it Hindutva. I have referred to this elsewhere as Syndicated Hinduism. This has been called an attempt to 'semitize Hinduism' by giving it a format and organization that approximates the Judeo-Christian. Doubtless the rationale is the belief that a religion organized in this way is more effective for modern political mobilization. The search for a historical founder has not met with success, there never having been one. The authority of a single sacred text is being sought but meets the same problem. Congregational worship has been introduced to create a sense of community. There have been attempts to establish an ecclesiastical organization as a surrogate Church, to dictate the beliefs and laws of the religion. Multiple deities weaken the claim that a monotheistic God is embedded in the worship of one out of many deities. A monotheistic God implies a different understanding of the role of deity than one among a number of deities. Further, to boost nationalism, the enemy of the nation has to be targeted and the choice for this can be the Muslim or the Christian. This was made only too apparent in the genocide of Muslims in Gujarat in 2002 and the assault on Christians in Odisha and other areas. Islamic fundamentalism provides a gnawing parallel often used to justify retaliation by other religious fundamentalisms.

The noticeable increase in religiosity is in part due to the changed condition of society where we now are part of the market economy required of current globalization. There is a visible expansion of the middle class with a greater competition among people to join it. Those that succeed improve their material life and need to exhibit their success through lavish spending on religiosity among other things; those that do not succeed, feel the insecurity of having competed and lost and turn to religion for solace. Globalization increases insecurity and reverses the economic system with which people were earlier familiar. Providing rational solutions get dismissed when the mood is to propagate irrationality and superstition. It is noticeable as to how many otherwise urbane middle-class men go around with red mouli threads and black threads tied to their wrists, and wear cheap rings set with monga or other 'auspicious' gemstones, to ensure their success and well-being.

Secularism in India faces the fundamentalism of various religions—Hinduism, Sikhism, Islam. These are movements that wish to retain control over the institutions of society and force an observance of religious laws rather than civil law. The control extends to denying lower castes access to social justice on more than one occasion. This opposes secular values. Secularism in India has to contend with religious institutions and caste dominated ones, which up to a point are a manifestation of religions attempting to control society. It also has to contend with a rather weak attempt by the state to ensure human rights and social justice for lower castes, Dalits and women, such rights if strongly backed would reinforce secularism, since secularism has the same aspirations. But the effort should not stop with just a demonstration of upward mobility by a few through the internalization of upper caste religion and culture ways. On a larger scale it has preferred conversion to what is now being called neo-Buddhism. It can be viewed as part of a continuous tradition although it has to be kept from becoming a historical anachronism.

In conclusion I would like to reiterate three points : if religion is to be treated as a counterpoint to secularism then the form of the religious articulation that is being contested has to be defined for each society. In formulating the meaning of secularism for the present, ideologies from the past that might assist in this formulation could be drawn upon. And since secularism as an ideology is associated with the nation-state it becomes part of the emergent institutions of this historical change. Inevitably secularizing society requires defining citizenship through creating a new identity, an identity based on essential human rights being equally and justly available to all citizens.

9

SYNDICATED HINDUISM

The term Hinduism as we understand it today to describe a *particular religion* is modern, as also is the concept that it presupposes, both resulting from a series of choices made from a range of belief, ritual and practice that were collated into creating a label for this religion. Unlike the Semitic religions (with which the comparison is often made, although the comparison could also be with Buddhism and Jainism closer home), which began with a structure at a point in time and evolved both in relation to and within that structure, and as reactions to historical situations, Hinduism (and I use the word here in its contemporary meaning) because of its fluidity, has taken shape more closely in relation to the latter. This took the form of variations articulated in a range of sects that gave identity to religious belief and practice. This is partly why some prefer to use the phrase 'the Hindu religions' (in the plural) rather than Hinduism. All religions react to historical situations but Hinduism perhaps more so, since its initial structure did not follow a rigid path. Comparisons with Semitic religions, especially Christianity and Islam, are not fortuitous since these have been catalysts among some contemporary Hindu thinkers searching for a structure. Interaction with historical circumstances bringing about change are more easily seen in individual Hindu sects rather than in Hinduism as a whole. Yet there has been a general reluctance on the part of scholars of Hinduism to relate the manifestations of Hinduism to their historical context and to changes in society.

The religion is however among the most ancient but with a remarkable continuity in some of its features, unlike others. The study of what is regarded as Hindu philosophy and its religious texts and beliefs has been so emphasized as to almost ignore those who are the practitioners of these tenets, beliefs, rituals and ideas. As the subject of nineteenth century ethnography these aspects were merely juxtaposed with the texts. Furthermore, the view has generally been from above, since the texts were earlier composed in Sanskrit and their interpreters were brahmanas. But, precisely because Hinduism is not a linear religion, it becomes necessary to look at the situation further down the ranks of society where the majority of its practitioners are located. The religious practices of the latter may differ from those at the upper levels of society to a degree considerably greater than that of a uniform, centralized, monolithic religion, which is how it has been projected since colonial times.

Discussions on Hinduism have tended to be confined to Hindu philosophy and theory. But the manifestation of a contemporary, resurgent, active movement, largely galvanized for political ends, provides a rather different focus to such discussions. As we have seen, the new Hinduism that is being currently propagated by the Sanghs, Parishads and Samajs, and carries the name of Hindutva, as given to it by V.D. Savarkar, is an attempt to restructure the indigenous religions into a monolithic, uniform religion, rather paralleling some of the features of Semitic religions. This seems to be a fundamental departure from the essentials of what may be called the indigenous Hindu religions. Its form is not only in many ways alien to the earlier culture of India but equally disturbing is the uniformity which it seeks to impose on the still existing variety of Hindu religious articulation.

My attempt here is to look at some of the significant directions taken by various Hindu sects through history and try and relate these to historical and social change. The study of what is regarded as Hindu philosophy and thought has its own importance but is not of central concern to this article. The manifestation of religion in the daily routine of life draws more heavily on social sources than on the philosophical. I am also arguing that the reformulations of Hinduism in colonial times have encouraged the direction that the religion is now taking.

Religions such as Islam or Christianity do diversify into sects but this diversification retains a particular reference point—the historical founder and the teachings embodied generally in a single sacred text or a group of texts regarded as a Canon. The area of discourse among the sects in these religions is tied to the dogma, tenets and theology as enunciated in the beginning. Buddhism and Jainism are up to a point similar except that their non-theism has led to some debate on whether they qualify as 'religion'. However, all these see themselves as part of the historical process of the unfolding of the single religion even though they may have branched off from the mainstream.

Hindu sects generally had an origin related either to their particular founder or founders or to a cult, focusing on the centrality of a deity, and the working out of their own system of beliefs and rituals, that could, but need not be, related to other existing systems. Only at a later stage, and if required, were attempts made to try and assimilate some of these lesser sects into the dominant sects through the amalgamation of new deities as manifestations of the older ones and by incorporating some of their mythology, ritual and custom. Subordinate sects sought to improve their status by a similar incorporation from the dominant sects if they were in a position to do so.

What has survived over the centuries is not a single, monolithic religion but a diversity of religious sects that we today have put together under a uniform name. The collation of these religious groups is defined as 'Hinduism' even though the religious reference points of such groups might be quite distinct. There was a time when Hinduism was a convenient general label among some scholars for studying the different indigenous religious expressions. This was when it was claimed that anything from atheism to animism could legitimately be regarded as part of Hinduism. Today the Hindutvavadis look upon atheists and animists with suspicion and contempt and regard them as unacceptable. The label 'Hinduism' is now being used in a different sense.

Hinduism as defined in contemporary parlance is a collation of beliefs, rites and practices consciously selected from those of the past, interpreted in a contemporary idiom in the last couple of centuries and the selection conditioned by historical circumstances. This is not to suggest that religions with a linear growth are superior to what may apparently be a religion with an ahistorical trajectory, but rather to emphasize the difference between the two.

In a strict sense, a reference to Hinduism would require a more precise definition of the particular variety referred to—Vedic Brahmanism, Puranic Hinduism, Bhakti, Tantrism, Brahmo Samaj, Arya Samaj, Shaiva Siddhanta, or whatever. These are not comparable to the sects of Christianity or Islam as they do not relate back to a single sacred text or its narrative and its interpretation, but allow of alternative texts and rituals. Nor do they focus on a single monotheistic deity common to all. Many are rooted in ritual practices and beliefs rather than in texts alone. It has been argued that a characteristic difference is that Hindu sects relate more to orthopraxy than to orthodoxy. Hinduism, therefore, is not just a religion with a trajectory moving from a beginning to an evolution from Harappan through Vedic, Puranic and Bhakti forms. In this it differs from Buddhism, Jainism, Islam and Christianity.

Its origin has no distinct point in time. The *Vedas* were regarded as the foundation until the discovery of the Indus Valley Civilization in the 1920s when its origin was then pushed back, but so far with some ambiguity, since the decipherment of the pictograms is awaited. There is no historically attested founder, no text encapsulating the teachings of the founder, and initially no organizational base, all of which reduces its historicity. This of course makes it easier to reinterpret if not to recreate such a religion afresh as and when required.

Many of these features, absent in the religion as a whole, do however exist among the various sects which are sought to be included under the umbrella-label of Hinduism which makes them historical entities. But, then, not all these sects would accept certain rites, beliefs and practices as essential. Animal sacrifice and libations of alcohol would be essential to some but anathema to others among the sects that the census labels as 'Hindu'. The yardstick of the Semitic religions that has been the conscious and subconscious challenge in the modern recreation of Hinduism would be inappropriate to an understanding of what existed before.

Historically, we know little for certain about the Harappan religion that flourished in the Harappan cities except for a suggested fertility cult involving in some places the worship of abstract icons and female forms and symbols, and the possibility of a priesthood performing rituals to legitimize authority. The decipherment of the pictograms will hopefully tell us more. It was earlier thought that with the ascendance of Vedic religion the Harappan became a substratum religion, some facets of which surfaced in later periods. Another tentative suggestion, however, has been that some elements of the Harappan religion may have been picked up by the Vedic. As has been pointed out there is the interesting category of dasi-putra brahmanas (the sons of the dasis) who are clearly not regular Vedic brahmanas in origin. They are initially dismissed, but when found to be favoured by the gods, are readily welcomed to the brahmana fold. The Vedic texts perhaps incorporate elements of this religion but nevertheless emphasize the central role of their own religious ideas such as those of the sacrificial ritual or yajna, and the gamut of deities, involving the fire-altar and the soma cult. A substantial element of shamanism can also be noticed in the Vedic corpus.

The Vedic religion requires belief in specific deities, in the *Vedas* having divine sanction, in the immortality of the soul, as also the centrality of the performance of the yajna, the sacrificial ritual. The brahmana is the intermediary between men and gods, and worship focuses on rituals without images and performed in locations that change with each performance. There are therefore no icons and no temples. Because of the pivotal role of the brahmana it is sometimes referred to as Brahmanical Hinduism or Vedic Brahmanism to distinguish it from other forms that followed, such as Puranic Hinduism. The Vedic texts and the *Dharmashastras* are said to constitute the norms for Brahmanism and the religious practices for the upper castes. A characteristic belief concerns the afterlife. The soul was said to transmigrate to another body after death and one's destiny in the next life was determined by the quality of one's actions in this life—the theory of karma and samsara. This was the theory that was said to make people conform to the norms out of fear of what was to come in the next birth. But not everyone accepted this. There are repeated references to an eternity in either heaven or hell, as among the heroes celebrated on hero-stones or among the characters of the *Mahabharata*.

The latter part of the first millennium BC sees the rise of various sects, some of which become substantial religions, that distance themselves from Brahmanism and disagree with its basic tenets. Brahmanism is therefore differentiated from these many of which had an organization of shramanas, monks. The term Shramanism was used for these religions and particularly for the Buddhists and Jainas. The Buddhist and Jaina texts, the inscriptions of Ashoka, the description of India by the Greek traveller Megasthenes in the fourth century BC, the accounts of the Chinese pilgrims in the first millennium AD and coming up to the writing of Al-Biruni in the eleventh century AD, all refer to two main religious categories: the brahmanas and the shramanas. The identity of the former is clear. The latter were the Buddhists, Jainas, Ajivikas and a number of other sects associated with both renunciatory orders and a lay following, who explored areas of belief and practice different from the *Vedas* and *Dharmashastras.* They often preached a system of universal ethics that spanned castes and communities, denied deity as well as the divine sanction of the *Vedas* and some rejected the existence of a soul. The Shramana sects tended to be splinter groups breaking away from the main organization, known as the Sangha. This differed from the tendency to segment religious practice by caste or by ritual that was often required of Brahmanism. The segmenting of sects is of course common even among historically evolved religions but the breaking away still retains the historical imprint of the founder, the text and the institution. Shramanic religions tried to prevent segmentation in their attempt to universalize their religious teaching.

The hostility between Brahmanism and Shramanism was acute. The grammarian Patanjali, when speaking of natural enemies and innate hostility, refers to this characteristic of Brahmans and Shramanas as being in the same category as the hostility of the snake and the mongoose and the cat and the mouse. This indigenous view of the dichotomous religions of India is referred to even at the beginning of the second millennium AD when Al-Biruni speaks of the brahman and the shamaniyya.

Brahmanism maintained its identity and survived the centuries with few fundamental changes, even after the decline of Buddhism. Maintaining the continuity was difficult in view of changes within its followers. This was possible because it was well-endowed with grants of land and items of wealth through extensive royal patronage, which in turn reinforced its claim to social superiority and enabled it further to emphasize its distance from other castes and their practices. The extensive use of Sanskrit as the language of rituals and learning gave Brahmanism access to high political office and proximity to the royal courts. This again supported its exclusive status. The use of Sanskrit gave it a pan-Indian character, the wide geographical spread of which provided both mobility as well as a strengthening of its social identity. Being the language of the elite and of the upper bureaucracy, the new kingdoms that mushroomed throughout the subcontinent in the first millennium AD provided ample employment opportunities for brahmanas both as ritual specialists and in the administration.

But Vedic Brahmanism became increasingly an upper caste religion. The more popular religion was what has come to be called the Bhakti tradition. The message of the Bhakti tradition, articulated in the first millennium AD and continuing into the second, is sometimes traced at the philosophical level to the *Bhagvad Gita*, which text although historically post-Buddhist, was interpolated into the *Mahabharata,* thus giving the *Gita* both antiquity and currency. The *Gita* moved away from the centrality of the sacrificial ritual and instead emphasized worship through devotion to the deity, and to selfless action projected as the need to act in accordance with one's svadharma, the dharma of one's caste, even if such action entailed violence. The arbiters of svadharma remained the brahmanas. This ensured the centrality of the caste code. Dharma now became the key concept. Dharma was also a key concept in Buddhism but with a different meaning that referred to a universal social ethic of equal respect for all persons and beliefs.

Historically, the early evidence of a popular articulation by men and women of a Bhakti-type religion comes from south India, from about the seventh century AD. The sentiments expressed are somewhat similar to those that come from worshippers in north India but later in the second millennium AD. This shift of emphasis from Vedic Brahmanism provided the root for the emergence of a number of Bhakti cults—Shaiva, Vaishnava, Shakta, and others—which flourished from the first millennium AD, and provided the contours to much that is viewed as traditional Hinduism, or Puranic Hinduism as it is now beginning to be called. The Shiva Bhakti of the Pashupatas, the Shaiva and Vaishnava Alvars and Nayannars of the Tamil speaking region, the Shaiva-Siddhanta and Lingayats, the teaching of Jnaneshvara and Tukaram in Maharashtra, of Kabir, Suradasa, Mira and Tulasidasa in what were to be the Hindi speaking areas, of Chaitanya and Shankaradeva in eastern India, of Lalla in Kashmir, all these are often bunched together as part of the Bhakti stream. In fact, there are significant variations among them. Some accepted the earlier style of worship and practice, others were hostile to the Vedic tradition; some objected to caste distinctions and untouchability, whereas for others such distinctions posed no problem. Some discouraged worship in temples, going on pilgrimages and observing the upper caste dharma. A few felt that neither asceticism nor renunciation was a path to liberation from rebirth whereas others were committed to these. Kabir and Nanak infused Sufi ideas into their teaching. These major differences are rarely discussed and commented upon in modern popular writing that is searching for similarities in the tradition. Yet these dissimilarities were to be expected and were in a sense their strength.

The Vedic deities of Mitra, Varuna, Indra and Agni slowly gave space to the main Puranic deities—Shiva, Vishnu, Durga together with a host of lesser ones all located in a complex pantheon from which the worshipper could choose. The deities now had iconic forms and many were housed in temples that had begun as small shrines and evolved with patronage into vast structures. The rituals of worship also changed. Generally only caste Hindus could worship in the temples, and some lower castes were disallowed entry.

The Bhakti sects were in some ways the inheritors of the Shramanic tradition, their rise in part inspired by this tradition and to some degree gradually replaced it in places where it was declining. They arose at varying times over a span of a thousand years in different parts of the subcontinent. They were open to all castes and were organized along sectarian lines. They were however limited by the language that they used which was the regional language. They did not evolve out of some original teaching or spread through conversion; rather, they arose as and when historical conditions were conducive to their growth, often intermeshed with the need for particular castes to articulate their aspirations. There was variation in belief and practice and a lack of a conscious identity of a religion across a subcontinental plane. Similarities were present in some cases but even these did not lead to recognition of participation in a single religious movement crossing regional boundaries. With the growth of the Bhakti cults, the worship of the iconic image of the deity gained popularity, possibly influenced by the emphasis on the icon in Buddhism and Jainism. Whereas the Greek account of India by Megasthenes in the fourth century BC, does not refer to any images, the later Chinese and Arab accounts of the first millennium AD make icons a feature of the indigenous religions.

This was also the period that saw the currency of the Shakta sects and Tantric rituals. Regarded by some as the resurgence of an indigenous belief associated with subordinate social groups (gradually becoming powerful), it was clearly popular at every level of society including the royal courts. The attempt earlier in the last century to sweep it under the carpet or to give a respectable 'gloss' to its rituals, or its manifestation in the art of the period, is largely because of the embarrassment these might cause to middle-class Indians heavily influenced by puritanism and somewhat titillated into imagining erroneously that Tantric rituals were pornographic. The hesitation to investigate and understand such cults also stemmed from the attempt to define Hinduism as the Brahmanism of the upper castes, where such cults were thought to be somewhat alien.

Another manifestation of indigenous religion is what is sometimes euphemistically called 'folk Hinduism'—the religion of the Dalits, tribals and other groups at the lower end of the social scale. This is characterized by a predominance of the worship of goddesses and spirits (bhuta-preta), represented symbolically and often aniconically, and with some rituals performed by non-brahmana priests for a variety of reasons, not least among them being that since the offerings and libations consist of meat and alcohol they would be regarded as polluting by brahmanas. Needless to say, some of such groups would not be able to afford the costly donations required of a brahmanical yajna. For the upper-caste Hindus these groups were (and often still are) regarded as mlecchas or impure, and certainly not a part of their own religious identity, however insistently the Registrar-General of the census or politicians may try to include them as such. Hindu missionaries proselytizing among such groups lay a strong emphasis on the prohibition on meat-eating and consuming alcohol.

The word dharma became central to an understanding of the religion. It referred to the duties regarded as sacred which had to be performed in accordance with one's varna/jati and sect and which were not identical for all. The constituents of dharma were conformity to ritual duties, to social obligations and to the social norms of family and caste as stipulated in the *Dharmashastras.* Neither theology nor ecclesiastical authority is prominent, and this points to another difference between Hinduism and the Semitic religions. The performance of sacred duty heavily enmeshed in social obligations and rituals was so important that absolute individual freedom only lay in renunciation.

But, the significance of this dharma was that it demarcated between the upper castes—the dvija or twice born—for whom it was the core of the religion and the rest of society whose conformity to dharma was rather left in abeyance, as long as it did not transgress the dharma of the upper castes. The non-dvija were thought of largely as neither requiring nor practising any dharma: they were adharma, lacking in dharma. The attempt today in trying to redefine Hinduism is the implicit attempt to hold up the dharma of the *Dharmashastras* as essential to this religion, even for those traditionally regarded as adharma.

Hindu missionary organizations, such as those attached to the Ramkrishna Mission, the Arya Samaj, the RSS and the Hindu Vishva Parishad, taking their cue from Christian missionaries are active among the adivasis (Scheduled Tribes), the Dalits and other backward communities. They are being converted to Hinduism as defined by the upper caste movements of the last two centuries. Some time ago there was a difference of opinion among those of the upper castes as to whether such converts can be regarded as Hindus even on conversion. The first problem would be that of assigning them a caste. The proponents of Hindutva had contrary views about this. What is important to such missionaries is that these communities be ready to be labelled as 'Hindu' in any head count, whether of the Census or of a political party. That this 'conversion' does little or nothing to change their status as adivasis, Dalits and so on, and that they continue to be looked down upon by upper-caste Hindus is of course of little consequence.

This perhaps accounts in part for the statements made by some upper-caste Hindus today that Hinduism in the last one thousand years has been through the most severe persecution that any religion in the world has ever undergone. The need to exaggerate the persecution at the hands of the Muslim is required to justify the inculcation of anti-Muslim sentiments among the Hindus of today and to claim victimhood. There is a forgetting of the various expressions of religious persecution in India prior to the coming of the Muslims, particularly between the Shaiva and the Shramana sects. The persistence of untouchability is another and more continuous manifestation of religious and social persecution, which is conveniently ignored. This was a persecution in which every religion in India indulged, even those claiming social egalitarianism. In fact, far from persecution, the last one thousand years in the history of Hinduism has witnessed the establishment of powerful Hindu institutions and religious sects : the Shankaracharya mathas, and most of the wealthy and powerful ashramas and similar institutions attempting to provide an ecclesiastical structure to strengthen conservatism; the powerful Dashnami and Bairagi religious orders of Shaiva and Vaishnava origin, vying for royal patronage and frequently in confrontation; the popular cults of the Nathpanthis; the extremely significant sects of the major Bhakti teachers and others such as Nanak in dialogue with Sufis; and, more recently, the very influential Brahmo and Arya Samaj, and other socio-religious reform movements that have been channels of giving power and authority to Hinduism in our times. The facts of Hinduism that are regarded as essential today, have been nurtured more in the last thousand years than in the previous millennia.

The establishment of some of the sects that accompanied these developments often received wealthy patronage from Hindu and Muslim rulers, which accounts for the prosperity of the temples and institutions associated with these sects. Where then is the severe persecution? The last thousand years have seen the most assertive thrust of the major 'Hindu' sects. The more innovative sects were in part the result of extensive dialogues between gurus, sadhus, pirs and Sufis, dialogues that were sometimes confrontational and sometimes most creative. If by persecution is meant the conversion of Hindus to Islam or Christianity, then it should be kept in mind that the majority of the conversions were by caste and from the lower castes and this is more a reflection on 'Hindu' society than on persecution. Upper caste conversions were often motivated by political alliances and hardly due to persecution. The Mughals at one point were more Rajput than Mughal, given the marriages between them. Tragically for those that converted on the assumption that there would be social equality as claimed in the new religions, this turned out to be a false dream. The lower castes remained low in social ranking and had to carry their caste identities into the new religion where they continued to be subservient.

Mention is made of some Muslim rulers destroying temples and breaking idols, and where this is so it should be mentioned, but two other facts should also be mentioned. One is that iconoclasm and idol-breaking was also practiced by Hindu rulers in pre-Islamic times, although it was not resorted to so commonly. And secondly there were also some Muslim rulers—not excluding Aurangzeb—who gave substantial donations to Hindu sects and to individual brahmanas. There was obviously more than just religious bigotry or religious tolerance involved in these actions. The reasons for the one or the other have to be investigated. Hindu kings of Kashmir looted temples and broke images when they were financially strapped, a Paramara raja destroyed Chaulukya temples, and a

Rashtrakuta king tore down a Pratihara temple as a statement of victory. The looting of images from the royal temple was resorted to for the same reason when concluding a campaign in some Deccan wars. Complex political reasons conditioned Mughal-Bundela relations: a Bundela raja murdered Abu'l Fazl at the request of Jahangir, and later when relations turned sour between the Bundelas and Mughals in the reigns of Shah Jahan and Aurangzeb, the temple at Mathura was damaged. The temple became the political pawn in the conflict.

Nor should it be forgotten that some Hindu rulers also exploited the temple as a source of wealth. Those who refer to Mahmud of Ghazni's destruction of Hindu temples and the carrying away of their wealth generally prefer to ignore the statement of Kalhana in the *Rajatarangini* that Harshadeva, an eleventh century king of Kashmir and therefore a close contemporary of Mahmud, defiled and looted temples when he required funds for the State treasury. The devotpatananayaka, officer in charge of uprooting the gods, was appointed to seize the images and the wealth of temples. Given the opulence of most temples, such evidence may be forthcoming from other areas as well. The wealth stored in temples required some to be walled in and defended almost like fortresses.

The religious intolerance of royalty flavoured with politics often taking violent forms is not unknown in many societies. Possibly what muted religious intolerance among the larger number of people in India was the link between religion and caste which confined it to being a local event. Communication of news was in any case relatively limited. For example, knowledge about the raids of Mahmud of Ghazni, was generally confined to the areas he visited.

The European adoption of the term 'Hindu' gave it further currency as also the attempts of Catholic and Protestant Christian missionaries to convert the Hindu/Gentoo to Christianity. The pressure to convert, initially disassociated with European commercial activity, changed with the coming of British colonial power when, by the early nineteenth century, missionary activities were either surreptitiously or overtly, according to context, encouraged by the colonial authority. The impact both of missionary activity and Christian colonial power resulted in considerable soul searching on the part of those Indians who were close to this new historical experience.

One result was the emergence or establishment of a number of groups such as the Brahmo Samaj, the Ramakrishna Mission, the Prarthana Samaj, the Arya Samaj, the Theosophical Society, the Divine Life Society, the Swaminarayan movement, et al., which gave greater currency to the term 'Hinduism'. Some were influenced by Christian missions and some reacted against them; but even the latter were not immune from their imprint. There was a dialogue between upper-caste Hindus and Christian missionaries. There were fewer Hindus converting to Christianity than had converted to Islam. The Protestant colonizer seems to have been more interested in extracting wealth from the colonized whereas the Catholic colonizer was counting converted souls.

The more subtle imprint was through educational institutions run by missionaries that were necessary for the emerging middle-class. Many who were attracted to these new Hindu 'samajs' had at some point of their lives experienced Christian education. In the organization of the educational institutions of the Arya Samaj, for example, the Christian missionary model was evident. The Shaiva Siddhanta Samaj in south India was inspired by the nineteenth century interpreter of Shaivism, Arumuga Navalar, who was roused to this vocation after translating the Bible into Tamil. The movement attracted middle-class Tamils seeking a cultural self-assertion and was to that degree a parallel to many of the other movements in the country. The impact of Orientalism in creating the image of Indian, and particularly Hindu culture, as projected in the nineteenth century, was considerable and religion was a major part of that image. Orientalists who were sympathetic drew heavily on the culture of Sanskrit texts and extended this to include the larger part of Society, which should more correctly have been excluded from these descriptions.

Some among the groups in dialogue with Christian theologians attempted to defend, redefine and reformulate Hinduism on the model of the Christian religion. They sought for the equivalent of a monotheistic God, a Book, a Prophet or a Founder and congregational worship with an institutional organization supporting it. The implicit intention was to annul the definition of the Hindu as being 'the Other'. The monotheistic God was sought in the abstract notion of brahman—the universal soul with which according to the *Upanishads* the atman, the individual soul seeks union and moksha: or else with the interpretation of the term deva or deity which in early English translations was rendered as God, suggesting a monotheistic God. The worship of a single deity among many others is not strictly speaking monotheism, although attempts have been made by modern commentators to argue this. Unlike many of the earlier sects that were associated with a particular deity, some of these groups claimed to transcend deity and reach out to the Absolute, the Infinite, the Abstract. This was an attempt to transcend segmented interests in an effort to attain a universalistic identity, but in social customs and ritual, caste distinctions between high and low continued to be maintained.

The teaching of such sects drew on what they regarded as the core of the tradition: the Atman-Brahman relationship allowing freedom from rebirth, which theory of action and rebirth (karma and samsara), was projected as common to all Hindus although this was not strictly so. The search for a single sacred book led some to adopt the *Bhagvad Gita,* others preferred the Vedic texts, especially the *Upanishads,* and yet others the *Mahabharata* or the *Ramayana.* The single founder or teacher being an alien idea, the closest possibility was the teacher-figure of Krishna in the *Gita.* But Krishna was neither a Prophet, nor a Son of God, nor a historically established figure as was the Buddha. Congregational worship was systematized and became the channel for propagating these versions of Hinduism. Rituals practiced in common and the singing of hymns jointly became essential to the ritual. The discarding of the icon by both the Brahmo and Arya Samaj was almost a knee-jerk reaction. It was seen as a pollution of the original religion but possibly the jibe of idol worship may have enhanced this reaction. This last was not a new feature since some Bhakti teachers had also referred to the irrelevance of worshipping icons. A prior reaction to the icon but resulting in the virtual substitution of a Book for the image was, and is, the centrality of the Guru Granth Sahib in Sikh ritual. Much of the sacred literature had been orally preserved and served a variety of social and religious ends. Some texts, most likely secular in origin, such as the *Mahabharata* and the *Ramayana,* had been converted into religious texts by making Krishna and Rama avataras of Vishnu. The narration became the actions of a deity. Interpolations could be added as and when required, as for example, the *Gita.* This, however, remains different from the centrality of the Book in the Judeo-Christian and Islamic religions. These new groups of the last two centuries were also in part the inheritors of the older tradition combining social aspirations with religious expression and establishing new sects. But at the same time they were trying to create a different kind of religion and gave further currency to the term Hinduism.

Traditional flexibility in juxtaposing sects as an idiom of social change as well as the basic concepts of religious expression now became problematic. In the absence of a single 'jealous' God, demanding complete and undiluted loyalty from the worshipper, there were instead many deities in various degrees of importance to the worshipper, some of which survived over time, and others that faded out. Thus, the major Vedic deities, declined with the rise of the Shaiva and Vaishnava sects in the first millennium AD. Shiva and Vishnu have remained major deities supported by various sects although not always in agreement with what the deities represent for them. This has not prevented the creation of fresh deities as has been witnessed in recent decades with the very popular worship in northern India of the goddess, Santoshi Ma.

The attitude to deity would in part explain the argument that it is not theology that is necessarily the most important aspect of Hinduism, but the mode of worship. The Vedic yajna was a carefully orchestrated performance of ritual with the meticulous ordering of every detail, down to the correct pronunciation of the words constituting the mantra. Worship as Bhakti and the rituals required in Puranic Hinduism, emerging in the first millennium AD, focused on the icon and its location, the temple, or else just on the worshipper seeking deity. The emphasis on oblation and sacrifice from the yajna was now transformed into sharing in the grace of the deity and devotion to the deity.

The deity was conceptualized in a variety of ways—abstract, aniconic, an image, or an image elaborately sculpted and housed in an equally elaborate temple; and devotion could also be expressed in various ways. There was a limited requirement of uniformity in methods of routine worship or who participated in the ritual. There was little ecclesiastical order involved and no centralized church. The caste of the worshipper conditioned his/her entry to the temple and to some extent the ritual and worship. The caste of the priest, the contents of the offering, and the language and form of the prayer were also considered. The diversity of shrines and temples in a village are in part a reflection of this.

The question of conversion was unimportant to Hinduism since caste was a significant factor and recruitment to caste was by birth. The Arya Samaj introduced 'shuddhi' or purification rites for Dalits wanting to convert to becoming caste Hindus, but this was problematic and therefore short-lived. In the absence of conversion, sects grew through segmenting off or through assimilating other cults or amalgamating similar sects. The religious sect was also an avenue to caste mobility. Origin myths of middle and lower castes often maintain that the caste was originally of higher status but a lapse in the ritual or an unwitting act of pollution led to a loss of status. Imitation of higher caste norms or the dropping of caste obligations would normally not be permitted unless justified by the creation of a new religious sect. The conservative might initially have regarded the latter with some hostility but if the sect became socially and economically powerful, it would be accommodated.

The absence of conversion accounted for the absence of the distinction between the true follower and the infidel or pagan. Yet, distinctions of another kind were more relevant and were sharply maintained, particularly in sects with a substantially upper caste following. Those who were outside the social pale or the mlecchas, such as untouchables, tribals, Indian Muslims and Christians, foreigners, those observing the social mores of the foreigners and even upper castes who did not conform to dharma regulations, were automatically excluded. They were polluting because they performed neither the ritual duties nor the social duties required by the codes. That they were prohibited from doing so, such as entering the temple, did not prevent their being excluded.

It is often stated that one is born a Hindu, i.e. into a particular caste whose regulations are to be observed, and one cannot therefore be converted to Hinduism. Caste identity cannot be changed although one can join a sect of one's choice, provided it has no caste restrictions. The idea of conversion was debated in the nineteenth century when this was seen as a way of expanding the numbers of Hindus. This became serious when numbers were counted of the majority and minority communities. Previously it had been maintained that each sect had its own regulations, obligations and duties that often drew both on religious antecedents and social requirements. Gradually, if a sect acquired a large following cutting across castes, it tended to become a caste in itself. An example of this is the history of the Lingayat sect that today is also a politically powerful caste.

There was one category of persons that had its roots in religious articulation and which could legitimately transgress the caste code, and these were various renunciatory orders, who were recruited from any caste, although a few of these did have caste restrictions. Although theoretically they were open to all, needless to say members of the upper varnas were preferred by some in the initial formation of the sect for reasons of status and patronage. Open recruitment was possible because renouncers were expected to discard all social obligations and were regarded as being outside the rules of social codes. Renunciatory sects were generally not expected to maintain a caste identity. Joining such an order was also in some cases the only legitimate form of dissent from social obligations. The multiplicity of renouncers in India has therefore to be viewed not merely as inspired by otherworldly aspirations but also with the nature of the links between social forms and dissent. The Shramanic religions were similar to these sects in that they did recruit members from a range of castes although, as was the case also with Indian Islam, Indian Christianity and Sikhism, the original caste identity was known, especially in the crucial social area of marriage connections.

Sects battened on patronage, whether royal or from others. Even the renunciatory orders were not averse to accepting wealth that ensured them material comforts as is evident from the many grants given to such orders scattered across the Indian landscape over the last two thousand years. The wealth ranged from small donations of money and labour for the construction of buildings, to extensive areas of cultivated and fallow land. Such orders were dependent on stable societies for alms and for establishing their institutions. Joining a renunciatory order was not necessarily switching to asceticism. It was often a change in the pattern of life for it still required a reciprocal relationship with society. Where they built institutions such as the sangha, the matha, and the khanqah, these gave the orders access to political power, resulting in the intertwining of politics and religion. There were a few, however, who stayed with the original intention of concentrating on thought, meditation or scholarship. Where these institutions were centres of literacy they became a powerful agency of social control. In addition to economic wealth, these institutions had access to political power and the intertwining of politics and religion was obvious. A significant texture of Indian social and religious history in the second millennium AD has been given less attention than it deserves because of the focus on Hindu-Muslim relations in this period and especially at elite levels, to the exclusion of the more pertinent investigation of the interaction of society and religion in the activities of all these sects, not to mention politics.

Caste identities, economic wealth and access to power also contributed to providing the edge to sectarian rivalries and conflicts. Xuanzang and Kalhana speak of confrontations between Shaiva sects and the Shramanas—earlier the Buddhists and later the Jainas. Such actions go back to Mihirakula and Shashanka who in the northern India of the mid-first millennium AD are remembered for their destruction of Buddhist monasteries and the killing of monks. Early in the second millennium AD, Karnataka witnessed the destruction of Jaina temples by Shaivas and the sixteenth century records a similar series of events in Kakatiya territory. It seems that once the Buddhists and Jainas were virtually out of the way, hostility among the Hindu sects was not unknown, even between ascetic groups, as is evident from the pitched battles between the Dasnamis and the Bairagis over the question of precedence at the Kumbha Mela. Such antagonism was not that of the Hindu against another religion, but that of a particular sect expressing its hostility towards others. Tolerance and non-violence therefore have to be assessed also in terms of sectarian aggression. It is true that there were no Inquisitions, except for the Catholics in Goa organized by the Portuguese authorities. This was partly because dissent could be channelled into a separate sect that, if it became a renunciatory order, could lose some of its social sting. In addition, there was no centralized church whose supremacy was endangered. However, social oppression of an extreme kind, justifying itself by theories of pollution, replaced the inequities of an authoritarian church or polity. The quality of intolerance meted out to those regarded as polluting and therefore untouchable was possibly the most extreme ever known. The ancient world tended to have little compassion for the under privileged who were kept subordinated in every civilization.

Religious violence is not alien to Hinduism despite the modern myth that the Hindus are by instinct and religion a non-violent people. One suspects that the genesis of this myth was in the romantic image of the past in some Orientalist scholarship, and in the requirements of nationalism stressing the spiritual superiority of Indian culture of which non-violence was treated as a component. Non-violence as a central tenet of behaviour and morality was perhaps most widely discussed in the Shramanic tradition, that of Buddhism and Jainism. Not that this tradition was able to prevent violence but at least it was brought to the fore. These were the religions that not only were allowed to decline but were persecuted in some places. One is often struck by how different the message of the *Gita* would have been and how very much closer to non-violence if Gautama Buddha had been the charioteer of Arjuna instead of Krishna. Gandhiji's concern with ahimsa is more correctly traced to the Jaina imprint on the culture of Kathiawar. Sporadic killing apart, even the violence involved in the regular burning of Hindu brides for dowry in the city of Delhi, as of late, does not elicit any powerful and consistent condemnation against the perpetrators of such violence from the spokesmen of Hinduism.

Sectarian institutions acted as networks across geographical areas, but their reach was limited except in the case of the major institutions such as those of the Dasnamis, the Bairagis or the Nathpanthis. Bhakti as a religious manifestation was predominant throughout the subcontinent by the seventeenth century; yet, curiously, there was little attempt to link these movements to forge a single religion. This was partly because the sects tended to use the local language which imposed geographical limits on them and also because there was no ecclesiastical organization to integrate this development.

Attempts at building institutions were made by the founders of certain sects, the most prominent being Shankaracharya when mathas, monastic type orders, were established and institutions founded in various parts of the sub-continent, the pithas. In part, these were in imitation of the Buddhist sangha and the recognition of the need for an institutional base, even though some have seen them as a means of holding back the spread of Buddhism. However, this was not exactly a grassroots popular movement. The matha was in some ways the more organized version of the ashrama, with an emphasis on formal learning, whereas the ashrama generally had a wider range of activities. The current versions of some of these institutions have run into heavy weather given the goings on that are being revealed, some of them being of anything but a religious nature.

The emergence of Bhakti has been linked by some scholars to what have been described as the feudalizing tendencies of the time. Parallels have been drawn between the loyalty of the peasant to the feudal lord being comparable to the devotion of worshippers to the deity. The Bhakti emphasis on liberation from rebirth through devotion to a deity and through the idea of karma and samsara was a convenient ideology for keeping subordinate groups, subordinated. It was argued that they might suffer in this life, but by observing the dharma—the social code and the required ritual—they would benefit in their next birth. The onus of responsibility for one's condition was therefore on oneself and not on society. The emphasis on the individual's liberation from rebirth gave the individual an importance that was absent in real life and therefore served to maintain quiescence.

Interestingly, this explanation of karma is not acceptable to some lower caste groups who, while supporting the notion of rebirth do not accept that they were born low because of misdemeanors in a previous birth. Common as is the belief in karma and samsara among many sects, it did not however preclude the growth at a popular level of the concepts of heaven and hell as is evident in the widespread references to svarga and naraka, going back to early times. In the same *Mahabharata* where the protagonists go variously to heaven or hell, Krishna preaches the centrality of rebirth and the system of justice associated with it. The hundreds of hero-stone memorials in the peninsula and western India from the early centuries AD onwards, irrespective of the sectarian affiliation of the hero, generally depict him being taken up to heaven, to spend eternity with the apsaras. Whether it be apsaras or houris the aspiration of spending an eternity with them sprang eternal in the male breast!

The segregation of social communities and the relatively distinct religious identity of these led to the possibility of each group leading a comparatively self-centred existence. The clash could come in the competition, for patronage. This might partially explain the notion of tolerance with which the nineteenth century invested indigenous Indian religions. However, sectarian rivalries did exist, sometimes taking a violent form, thereby projecting a different picture of the past.

Nor is this lack of tolerance strikingly enhanced with the coming of

Islam. Within the broad spectrum of Puranic religion and the Bhakti sects there was dialogue between some of these and Islamic sects. Curiously, although some Islamic popular belief was internalized, particularly among sects identified with the socially less privileged, there was little serious theological interest of a mutual kind. But then Brahmanism by and large was remarkably uninterested in the ideas that came to India via different religions and philosophical schools. The intellectual curiosity seems to have been mainly in knowledge pertaining to astronomy, mathematics and medicine. There are few major studies of Islam in Sanskrit or in the regional languages until much later. References to the Muslims were either to Turushkas/Turks in the early sources, which was the correct ethnic identity of the earlier rulers, or more generally to mlecchas and yavanas. Similarly, the more learned among Muslim authors such as Al-Biruni and Abu'l Fazl tend to summarize Brahmanism when they discuss the Hindu religions since this was socially the most prestigious. There is little detail of the other sects except in a very generalized way. Abu'l Fazl refers to the strife among the various indigenous religions that he attributes to diversity in language as well as the hesitation of Hindus in discussing their religion!

The confrontation of Islam and Hinduism, as we've seen, is often posed as two monolithic religions, face-to-face. In fact, for both, the experience was probably bewildering to begin with, since the recognizable institutions were rather different. There was no single ecclesiastical authority among the Hindus as a whole to which Islam could address itself. It faced a large variety of belief systems of which the most noticeable common feature to Islam was idol-worship—but even this was by no means uniform. Hence the frequency with which references are made preferentially to castes and ethnic communities—Rajputs, Jats, Zamindars, etc.—in the context of the indigenous religions rather than to Hindus, which term was gradually coming into use.

It is said that the Hindus must have been upset at seeing Turkish and Mongol soldiers in their heavy boots trampling the floors of the temples. The question is, which Hindus? For, the same temple if it was now entered by mleccha soldiers was open only to upper-caste Hindus and its sanctum was in any case barred to the majority of the population who were regarded as the indigenous mleccha. The trauma was therefore more in the notion of the temple being polluted rather than the confrontation of one religion with another.

I have tried to argue that if one is attempting to understand Hinduism in a historical way then one has to see it as far as possible in its pre-colonial forms. The distinction between the two traditions of Brahmanism and Shramanism are significant. These separate identities were carefully maintained. In the eyes of the former the latter were obviously inferior and for this one has only to look at texts of brahmana authorship of the second millennium AD referring to monks and mendicants. It would be worth investigating whether the term Shramanism and its derivatives applied only to the Jainas after the decline of Buddhism, or whether it included other sects of what I have called the Guru-Pir tradition that may have had some similarities with Shramanism. Brahmanism also maintained a distinction between itself and other 'Hindu' religious sects such as those associated with the Bhakti and the Shakta movements that, although not Shramanic in the strictest sense, were nevertheless the inheritors of some of that tradition. The separateness of the two was narrowed, from time to time when historical situations demanded it although it was not amalgamated. The coming of Islam imposed a formal closeness on them. For the first time, all indigenous cults referred to as Hindu carried the connotation of 'the Other'. Despite this the independence of the sects was not affected.

The bigger crisis came with the arrival of European Christianity riding on the powerful wave of colonialism. In the projected superiority of the Semitic religions, it was once again the 'Hindus' who were regarded as 'the Other' and this again included both the Brahmanic and the Shramanic traditions. This time the dialogue was with Brahmanism, since Buddhist monks no longer existed in India and the Jaina munis were initially ignored. Of the social groups most closely associated with power, the upper castes were the genitors of the new middle class, and among them, the brahmanas were seen as representing the Hindus.

Inevitably, the Brahmanical base of what was seen as the new Hinduism was unavoidable. But merged into it were various bits and pieces from upper caste belief and ritual with one eye on the Christian and Islamic models. Close links with certain nationalist opinion gave to many of these neo-Hindu movements a political edge that remains recognizable even today. It is this development that was the parent to the present-day Syndicated Hinduism as I choose to call it, that is being pushed forward as the sole claimant to the inheritance of indigenous Indian religion.

It goes without saying that if Indian society is changing, then its religious expressions must also undergo change. But, the direction of this change is somewhat alarming. The emergence of a powerful middle-class with urban moorings and a political reach to the rural rich would find it useful to bring into politics a uniform, monolithic, Hinduism created to serve its new politics and requirements. Under the guise of a new, reformed Hinduism, an effort is being made to draw a large clientele and to speak with the voice of numbers.

The appeal to the middle-class would be obvious. To those lower down in society there would be the attraction of upward mobility through a new religious movement, a pattern that has a familiar ring. But the latter, having forsaken some of their ideologies of non-caste religious sects, would have to accept the dharma of the powerful but remain subordinate. A change in this direction would introduce new problems as it has already begun to do. In wishing away the weaknesses of the old, one does not want to bring in the predictable disasters of the new.

It would seem that the major asset of what we call Hinduism of the pre-modern period was that it was not a uniform monolithic religion, but a juxtaposition of flexible religious sects. It was characterized by plurality, a characteristic that is now being annulled. Flexibility was its strength and its distinguishing feature, allowing the existence even of non-caste, anti-Vedic groups who disavowed the injunctions of the *Dharmashastras,* which nevertheless had to be included within the definition of what has now been called Hinduism. The weakening or disappearance of such dissenting groups within the framework of at least religious expression would be a considerable loss. If Syndicated Hinduism could simultaneously do away with social hierarchies, this might mitigate its lack of flexibility. But the scramble to use it politically merely results in the realignment of castes, now connected with equations of class.

Syndicated Hinduism draws largely on Brahmanical texts, the *Vedas*, the epics, the *Gita* and accepts some aspects of the *Dharmashastras,* and attempts to present a religion appropriate for modern living, although claiming at the same time that it encapsulates ancient tradition. This contradiction ends up inevitably as a garbled form of what is said to be Brahmanism with motley 'values' drawn from other sources, such as bringing in elements of individual moksha, liberation, from the Bhakti tradition, and of course Puranic mythology and rituals. Its contradictions are many. The call to unite under Hinduism as a political identity can be anachronistic.

Social and economic inequality was accepted as normal by Vedic Brahmanism and whether one approves or disapproves of it, it was an established point of view. To propagate the texts associated with this assumption and yet insist that they are appropriate to modern values of democracy and secularism is hardly acceptable. Some religions like Islam and Christianity claim to support social egalitarianism. Others like Buddhism restrict equality to the moral and ethical spheres of life. The major religions arose and evolved in societies and in periods when inequality was a fact of life. The social function of these religions was less to change this inequality and more to try and ameliorate the reality for those who found it harsh and abrasive. The acceptability of these texts will continue for those that live by them as texts of their faith, but what modern life is underlining is the difference between faith in the entirety of what they teach or the need to select from them what is relevant to a changed time. This in itself calls for a wider discussion.

Further, as a proselytizing religion, Syndicated Hinduism cannot accept a multiplicity of religious manifestations as being equally important: clearly, some selected beliefs, rituals and practices will have to be regarded as essential and therefore more significant and others jettisoned. This is a major departure from the traditional position. Who does the selecting, and from what sources, and to what purpose, also becomes a matter of considerable significance.

All religions give rise to heresies with which they contend and thereby clarify and hone their own ideas and intentions. In India there has been the heterodoxy of Nastika thinking, that is, those who deny deity, and are opposed to the conservative views of the Astikas who believe in gods and the sanctity of the *Vedas*. This has been an essential part of religious and philosophical thought for two and half millennia. The Shramanic tradition played a role in this for many centuries. It led to contestations, but the heresies remained, crucial to new thinking. Now Hindutva disallows its views being contested or the presentation of alternative views, and does so quite brutally in terms of verbal abuse and of physical assaults on those that disagree with it.

Hindutva claims to represent indigenous Indian thought opposed to western interpretations of Indian religion, traditions and culture. The claim is that colonial scholarship used its understanding of Indian culture for political purposes to justify colonialism. Yet Hindutva is doing precisely the same by reformulating Hinduism along the lines suggested by colonial interpretations in order to facilitate its use in political mobilization. It uses colonial constructions of the Indian past such as the theories of James Mill and Max Mueller to further its programme of political control. The exploitation of history becomes a significant dimension of its attempt to appropriate the understanding of the past.

Another factor of increasing importance to this Syndicated Hinduism is the 'Hindu' diaspora. As we know, 'Hindu' communities settled outside India experience a sense of cultural insecurity since they are minority communities, frequently in a largely Islamic or Christian society as in the Gulf or in Europe, North America or the Caribbean. Their search is often for sects which will support their new enterprise or, better still, a form of Hinduism parallel to Christianity and with an idiom comprehensible to Christians which they can teach their children (preferably, we are told, through Hindu Sunday Schools and video films). Such communities with their particular requirements and their not inconsequential financial support will also provide the basis for the institutions and the ecclesia of Syndicated Hinduism.

The importance of this 'diaspora' is clearly reflected not only in the social links between those in India and those abroad jointly supporting the new Hinduism, but also in the growing frequency with which the Sanghs, Parishads and Samajs hold their meetings abroad and seek the support and 'conversion' of the affluent. Conversion is new and aggressive, both among 'native-born' Indians and whites. This is not to be confused with the guru-cult in affluent societies where the attempt is less to convert people to Hinduism, but more to suggest to them methods of 'self-realization' irrespective of their religious affiliations—at least in theory.

The creation of this Syndicated Hinduism for purposes more political than religious, and mainly supportive of the ambitions of a new social class, has been a long process in the last hundred years or so and has now come more clearly into focus. Social groups in the past have expressed their aspirations in part by creating new religious sects. The emergence of Syndicated Hinduism is different both in scale and scope and is not restricted to the creation of a new sect but a new religious form seeking to collate all the earlier sects. The sheer scale and the motivation call for considerable caution. Syndicated Hinduism claims to be re-establishing the Hinduism of pre-modern times: in fact it is only establishing itself in a different format and in the process altering the historical and cultural dimensions of the indigenous religions and divesting them of the nuances and variety which was a major source of their richness.

Attempts to insist on its legitimacy increase the distance between it and the indigenous religious articulations of Indian civilization and invest it with the ingredients of a dangerous fundamentalism. With each aggressive stance, based on the false alarm of Hinduism in danger (as when five hundred 'Hindu' untouchables were converted to Islam at Meenakshipuram in 1984 out of a population of five hundred million 'Hindus'), this Syndicated Hinduism forces a particular identity on all those who are now technically called Hindus. But not all would wish to participate in this identity. What I have tried to argue is that there is a difference between religion and religiosity and that we are now being subjected to the latter in a major way. There is also a difference between Hinduism and Hindutva. The Hindu it seems, is being overtaken by the Hindutvavadin, who is changing the essential nature of the religion. There is something to be said for attempting to comprehend with knowledge and sensitivity and not just the verbosity of glorification, the real religious expression of pre-modern Indian culture, before it is snuffed out.

III

DEBATES

Invented Theories

One of the principal statements of the colonial understanding of Indian society was that of describing it as a static society that underwent no change whatsoever, throughout its history. A static society meant that the description of society would remain the same for long periods. Therefore the Hindu period could well last for two if not three thousand years without change. It also meant that early Indian society had no consciousness of history since an awareness of history requires recognition of historical change. Historians influenced by anti-colonial nationalism, contested some colonial interpretations, but these views were not among them.

Two theories from among those propounded by colonial scholarship were continued unchallenged by the successor historians of the early twentieth century. Both have been run threadbare and have been rejected by later historians, but remain resilient in the identity politics of today. One was the equating of the identity politics of religious communities with nationalisms as has been discussed above. The other was the projection of the Aryan race and its culture as the author of Indian civilization and therefore foundational to its creation. As we've seen, this theory was influential through the writings of Friedrich Max Mueller, the Sanskrit scholar, and at the popular level through its propagation by Colonel Henry Steel Olcott, the Theosophist. Max Mueller maintained that the Aryans came from Central Asia but Olcott insisted that they were indigenous, and were the cradle of Indian civilization which they took to other parts of the world. This view does not reflect indigenous scholarship, as is claimed by those that support it today. Based on this theory it is argued that the superior cultures of the past have an Aryan authorship; hence the need to insist that the Harappans were Aryans, irrespective of whether or not the evidence supports the argument. If Aryanism was the foundation of Indian civilization it had to be indigenous, that is, it had to originate within the boundaries of British India or else it would count as alien—as indeed it was so declared by Jyotiba Phule, an early social reformer of nineteenth century Maharashtra. Needless to say Phule is not a hot favourite in Hindutva circles. And furthermore, there is now a need for the latter to insist on Aryan being indigenous in order to associate Hinduism with the earliest beginnings, despite the definition of 'Aryan' having mutated from Vedic times to the later centuries, as indeed also in historical thinking over the last two centuries. 'Aryan' and 'Dravidian' used as terms for peoples confuses language and race since these are language labels, and should correctly be used as, 'Aryan-speaking people' and 'Dravidian-speaking people'.

Secularism

The Partition of India in 1947 enhanced the support for nationalism based on the religious identities of communities. The rhetoric of secular anti-colonial nationalism was to the fore, but as we examine it now, there were weaknesses in the formulation of secularism that were not recognized at the time. This was in part because the generally accepted Indian definition of secularism, as we have seen, skirted the requirements of a secular society and was in essence not focused on democracy and social justice. In India, secularism was defined as the co-existence of all religions. That religions have an unequal status and that some are more equal than others—are in effect socially dominant and therefore endorse inequality—was ignored in this definition. Furthermore, the concept of majority and minority communities defined as religious their numbers with arrived at from Censuses held since 1872, contradicts the idea of a secular society. The argument requiring models from the past invariably refer to Ashoka the Mauryan emperor and Akbar the Mughal emperor, without considering whether what they propagated was actually a secular society, or whether their insistence on religions having to co-exist arose from the requirements of imperial systems governing a society of multiple religions and plural cultures. Whereas the co-existence of religions was an admirable aspiration for those times, it remains insufficient in today's world that demands equal rights for all citizens. A secular society would be one in which the identity would be that of the Indian citizen and the function of religious communities would be confined to matters of religion and segregated from state functions. A secular India would not entertain Hindu/Muslim/Sikh nationalists as being equivalent to Indian nationalists since the very definition is not the same.

The need for the political mobilization of the Hindus required the re-organization of Hinduism as a religion fit for such mobilization. This introduced the centrality of converting Hinduism into Hindutva. Needless to say not all Hindus need to conform to the beliefs of Hindutva, nor do they, but it is an effective way of organizing a religious front to oppose other religious groups or even secular ones, as has been done again and again in the last half century. This is a period that has seen violent contestations between Hindus and Muslims, Hindus and Sikhs, Hindus and Christians. This does not add up to the co-existence of all religions in a secular society.

Such contestations are sometimes sparked by claims to what could well be property disputes but are presented to the public as claims relating to the particular religion, valid for both historical and present times. The questioning of these claims is seen as an affront to the religion making them. In the case of Hinduism, the more dramatic occasions have been in relation to Rama as a deity and the *Ramayana* as a sacred text. In the case of Muslims it is often linked to the symbols of being Muslim and of opposition to what is said in the Qur'an. When secular historians attempt an analysis of a religious text with a dispassionate inquiry as is required of historians, they are abused, and accused of hurting the sentiments of those that believe the text to be sacred. It should be understood that the world of the historian working on religious texts and that of the believer for whom the texts are sacred, are two distinctly different worlds and should not be confused. The latter cannot deny space to the former. All texts have to undergo such inquiries in the course of their being used as historical evidence. On the one hand the historicity of the religion is reiterated and on the other the historical analyses of the foundational texts are objected to. This has brought into focus the entire plethora of hurt sentiments by a variety of political groups claiming to be defenders of the various religions.

Interpretation of Texts

Some of the articles in this book discuss the manner in which religious 'nationalisms' interpret or object to certain historical texts. Items are picked out from the *Mahabharata* and the *Ramayana*—to be used for political mobilization; or there is a particular projection of an event such as the raid of Mahmud of Ghazni on the temple of Somanatha/Somnath. The dates of the epics have been contested since a long time and the more conservative attempt has been to take them back to remote antiquity. Historians try to date the core of each epic by relating it to the kind of society it represents as known from other sources, and the segments added on are investigated in terms of the society they depict or the artifacts they mention. It is thought that since evidence for them is lacking in earlier periods, signet rings were probably unknown to India prior to the coming of the Indo-Greeks at the turn of the Christian era. Would the reference to the signet ring in the *Ramayana* date to this period, as was suggested by the archaeologist H.D. Sankalia?

Epics are initially rooted in oral traditions and at a later date converted to written form. This may possibly have coincided with the oral being closely related to societies where the system of clans prevailed and caste was less prominent, to the written becoming part of the royal courts in kingdoms that emerged when the clan society was in decline. The two processes could have covered a sizeable period of time. Indian epics however, had a third dimension. Starting as popular narratives of clans and heroes they acquired a sacred character when Rama and Krishna became avataras of Vishnu. Their initial powerful impact as epic literature gave way to a different kind of impact as sacred texts. The insertions into the texts have been much commented upon. The chief editor of the Critical Edition of the *Mahabharata,* V.S. Sukthankar, has demarcated the earlier 'narrative' component in the story from the 'didactic' infusions. However, for those who regard these as the texts of their faith, for them naturally, the entire epic is seamless.

Re-editing by various poets is a familiar activity common to virtually all epics. The Greek epics of Homer were not immune to this. Segments are either allowed to fade out or alternatively new ones are added in. Something as simple as a qualifying adjective can result in a different emphasis on a nuanced statement. The metre of the verse has to be correct and this can act as something of a control, unless the addition is in itself an entire segment. Therefore, it becomes difficult to ascertain a specific time for the entire enterprise. Generally a range of dates is suggested such as 400 BC to AD 400. But not all scholars accept this, some arguing for a shorter period around the turn of the Christian era. In the last century both the epics have been subjected to critical editions, where a comparison of all the different recensions—of which there are a large number—helps define the core epic.

The *Ramayana,* perhaps because it was shorter with a more compact story, lent itself early to a political role. It is a simple story in which the demarcation of good and evil is projected in an open way. The hero/deity Rama is, in comparison with Krishna, a gentle, casual person, barring his harsh treatment of Sita. The story was reflected with variations in many versions that differed from the one of Valmiki—especially the Buddhist and the Jaina versions, not to mention other later ones in the regional languages. The *Jatakas* for instance are a valuable narrative collection from the Buddhist Pali oral tradition whose value is enhanced by their seeming to be used as a source of stories by poets and others in the writing of narrative texts in Sanskrit.

Ancient Texts and Politics

Repeated attempts are now being made to establish the authenticity of only the Valmiki version, denying the others. The TV presentation of three decades ago went a long way to establish the Valmiki version with little said about other versions. We seem not to recognize that one of the admirable achievements of Indian civilization has been the acceptance of the juxtaposition of variants. Life is not governed therefore by an either/or choice in everything. There is always something else—the variant. Perhaps this is due to the absence of Satan, which apart from excluding the notion of original sin, disallows a perpetual duality. Can good and evil be seen as contingent?

The familiarizing of people with other versions and explaining why they were composed, are in present times dismissed by claiming that alternate versions of the story other than that of Valmiki, hurt Hindu sentiment. What also gets dismissed thereby is that this was a narrative that travelled not only all over the Indian sub-continent, but also all over Asia. It was adapted to local cultural patterns wherever it went, adding both to the richness of the original narrative and to the narratives of the host culture. The dismissal of this aspect of the text denies to the Indian of today any awareness of the potentiality that this text held in the past.

The most blatant use of the *Ramayana* for politics and vote-garnering was the movement launched to destroy the Babri Masjid at Ayodhya in 1992, claiming that it was located at the exact place where Rama was born. There is of course no historical evidence to support this claim, or for that matter even the historicity of Rama, although the benefit of doubt is often given in the latter case. This uncertainty stands in sharp contrast to the pillar locating the birth place of the Buddha erected subsequently by Ashoka Maurya, or the references to Jesus Christ in the works of Roman and Jewish historians of the first century AD, or even the near contemporary historical records of Muhammad. Religions rooted in the lives of historical figures involve histories in a different way, as compared to the worship of imagined religious figures, which although equally efficacious in religious terms, may not require historicity.

Another attempt was made more recently to use the *Ramayana* to create a political controversy. This was over the Ramasetu/Ramasethu, or the so-called bridge or causeway linking Dhanushkodi to Sri Lanka between the Gulf of Mannar and the Palk Straits, and supposedly built by his monkey allies under orders from Rama. The controversy brought out the irrelevance of actual location and chronology to the believer, and its central importance to the historian. That the name Lanka for the present-day Sri Lanka was not in use until the early centuries AD, is telling evidence on the date of the *Ramayana,* if Lanka is to be identified with modern Sri Lanka. The description in the text of how the causeway was constructed is hardly conducive to accepting its feasibility. The politicians of Hindu 'nationalism' insisted that they would not allow a channel to be excavated through the rocks under the sea to allow an easy passage to shipping which otherwise has to circumvent southern Sri Lanka to reach the east coast of India. The supposed 'setu' was said to be a national heritage associated with a deity. That may explain why it has no visibility!

Looking Afresh at Somanatha

An example of a different kind is illustrated in the treatment of the raid of Mahmud of Ghazni on the temple of Somanatha. This does not involve a contradiction between faith and history and none of the texts that provide the evidence are sacred texts. Here the issue is one of using a historical event for promoting a contemporary political ideology. The exploitation of history is only too obvious but is of a somewhat different kind from that which used the *Ramayana* story. From the historian's perspective this piece of historical investigation that involved a variety of texts emanating from various kinds of persons, also showed how perceptions of and interests in, an event can differ, and that this difference has also to be examined by the historian.

Colonial historians initially wrote an account of Mahmud's raid on the Somanatha temple. Subsequently Indian historians continued with the same narrative without further questioning the sources. The argument was that the raid had created a trauma in the Hindu community in relation to the Muslim and planted the seed of a permanent, increasing hostility and intense aggression between Hindus and Muslims that never died down. This reading was based on the chroniclers of the Delhi and Deccan Sultanates who in giving their version of the event had to exaggerate not only the triumphal aspect of the raid itself but also the ensuing aftermath of the victory of Islam. That the descriptions of the raid in these chronicles contradicted each other apart from being exaggerated, seems not to have bothered the chroniclers nor the historians of modern times.

That other sources on the history of Somanatha—such as lengthy inscriptions in Sanskrit, Jaina chronicles of the history of the Chaulukyas of Gujarat, popular compositions of northern India that referred to Mahmud—were not consulted by historians was because they were conditioned to end the Hindu period at AD 1000 and switch to the Muslim period after that, which meant that sources in Sanskrit were only associated with the Hindu period and the Muslim period meant reading only the sources in Persian, Arabic and Turkish because, as we've seen, James Mill's periodization has remained ingrained in the study of Indian history. Had historians read as sources the post-Mahmud Sanskrit inscriptions or the Jaina chronicles also in Sanskrit, they would have realized that the religious authorities of Somanatha, far from suffering a trauma were involved in profitable commerce with Arab and Persian Muslim traders. These sources also suggest that at that time religious hostility was not between Hindu and Muslim, but lay in the competition for royal patronage between the Shaiva brahmana chief priest of the temple and the Jaina minister of the Caulukya king. The Islamic intervention in the temple in the form of building a small dome in one place dates to a later time when the temple itself was in a dilapidated condition.

On the question of the collective memory of the Hindu trauma, this is mentioned for the first time not in any Indian text but in a debate in the House of Commons in 1843, when the British Parliament was debating Lord Ellenborough's Proclamation of the Gates. References were made in the debate as to how traumatic the raid must have been for the Hindus. This idea, it would seem, was picked up by K.M. Munshi of the Indian National Congress who encouraged its becoming a political slogan in the mid-twentieth century, encapsulating the collective memory of the Hindu trauma. The story of course continues into our times with the tearing down of the Babri Masjid being justified as avenging the raid on Somanatha, albeit, a thousand years later.

This illustrates a contemporary political use of an event from the past. For the historian there is also the other dimension in this construction, namely, the viability of the concept of a collective memory. If it is viable then how are such memories constructed over time? Memories are individually remembered and, as we all know, a memory can be imprecise and ambiguous. Collective memories have to be deliberately constructed by a group of people consciously referring back to a particular event and remembering it in a particular way. Such constructions have a specific time and place and initiators. Obviously in any raid there are clashes and violence as there must have been in this raid, but this experience did not qualify for it to be called a long-lasting, unabating Hindu trauma.

Reformulating Religions

With all this emphasis on religious extremisms and the political exploitation of religion, one has to ask another historical question. In what ways did the formulation of religions undergo change in order to accommodate the religion to modern-day politics, very different from the politics of earlier times? It would introduce a change in the end purpose of religion. The attempts to inject issues of faith and belief as legitimate components of history would naturally distort history. What is noticeable is the presence now of extremism in the larger space of all Indian religions.

Historical changes affect the structure and functioning of religion and religious organizations. Disjuncture breaks continuities as with colonialism and that brought changes in the various religions. Thus Islam, now declared a minority religion, had to adjust to a changed status. This was less applicable among those Muslims of the middle and lower castes whose belief and ritual were already mixed, reflecting their location and those among whom they lived. Examples of these come from many parts of the subcontinent. Ancestry in a trading community as was the case with many, gave them a different take on their religious and social identity. Others claimed links with various Sufi sects that also traversed a range of relations of closeness to or distance from, orthodox Islam. Upper caste Muslims felt the change. Anxious to demonstrate power they chose the path of using religion as an agency of political negotiation, not disapproved of by the colonial power. The pattern echoes something of the past where the lower castes tended to merge but some of the elite differentiated themselves from both the lower castes and from other religions.

If there is a greater acceptance of Hindutva as representing Hinduism among Hindus, there is also more Islamization among Muslims with a conscious statement of Muslim identity, and the same has happened among the Sikhs. Religious extremism comes to the fore in moments of conflict, but its residue remains, even if somewhat opaque at times. We have witnessed the demonstration of all the extremist forms of these religions in the politics of recent times. Is the rise of fundamentalism in more than one religion in India a reaction to the initial one as it is frequently explained, or is it a move towards the political ambition of all communities identifying themselves by religion? The political use of religion requires its reformulation so as to make it viable for political mobilization. Such reformulations, whether Hindutva or Islamization, make belief and practice more inflexible, and as such are a curb on the freedom and justice of the many. The fundamentalist form is best accommodated to dictatorships and what may euphemistically be called 'controlled democracies'.

The change is perhaps easier to recognize with references to the Hindu community. In earlier times the statement of identity was linked more to caste and sect—although the two were not always distinct—than to an over-arching religion. Hinduism, as it came to be called in the colonial period, had been used in the past for political mobilization but only in segments taking the form of sects, and then too for a limited and often localized social outreach. The single label that incorporated caste and sect gave it a wide-ranging universality that facilitated its use for mass mobilization.

Where a historical founder is lacking, as in Hinduism, it becomes advantageous to argue for the historicity of the human incarnations of deity and to bring together the different sects as being the manifestation of one universal deity. There were many sects and many sacred texts, so a single one was sought—often the *Bhagvad Gita*—with its message of doing one's caste duty as the fundamental ethic. The absence of a Church and ecclesiastical authority has been partially met by Councils of Dharmacharyas and heads of religious organizations. The structure of Christianity suggested a model. And indeed many centuries earlier there had been attempts to adopt the organizations of monastic orders similar to those of the Buddhists and Jainas to better propagate the religion.

The two public agencies that could help inculcate meaningful social values that might result in a more caring society and politics are of course education and the media. The content of what it taught in schools and colleges, with rare exceptions, is generally abysmal. Yet it does not take much for there to be an intelligent interest in the school curriculum by educationists preferably in conversation with parents. This would be particularly important in issues pertaining to human rights and social justice.

Many of these issues are relevant to the foundations and the self-perceptions of a nation and, as such, permeate all of life. The response to these ideas is related to how we educate the next generation. The present-day focus on community identities centred on religion has diverted attention from the fundamental notion of inequality that has governed our history, namely, that those societies regarded as beyond the pale, had a permanently low status and were treated as inferior beings, what we today refer to as Scheduled Castes and Scheduled Tribes. They were excluded from caste thereby allowing them their own social codes. But the justification of the exclusion was by declaring them to be physically polluting or beyond the bounds of civilized society. This converted them into permanent servitors of caste society, living on its edges or in isolation. They have had to force their presence onto the Indian middle-class consciousness, either as the Dalits have done through demanding concessions in the educational system and government jobs, or as with the tribal people unable to withstand Naxalite pressures on their home ground. Caste society has only itself to blame for the current civil strife. A dilute democracy heavily flavoured with corruption, can do little and the bravado of claiming to shoot the revolutionaries backfires before even the first shot is fired.

We often forget that the raising of questions or of evaluating the potential of unconventional views, is in itself, conducive to fresh thinking and to that extent, educative. We are supposed to be teaching ways of reasoning and not catechism. The objection to and putting down of alternative views usually comes from groups with fundamentalist religious commitments and political affiliations and aspirations, who use the occasion to demonstrate their muscle power. This has been on the increase in the last twenty years with the frequency in banning books, some of which are on university reading-lists. A recent example of this was the removal of A.K. Ramanujan's essay on the many versions of the *Ramayana* story, from the History syllabus in Delhi University. The decision was taken by the Academic Council presided over by the Vice-Chancellor. This has precedents in the earlier attack on history via the NCERT textbooks by a BJP government and the more recent 'editing' of Social Studies/Politics textbooks by the UPA II government over the issue of political cartoons. It becomes all the more necessary to have an autonomous NCERT beyond the clutches of government that has the power to vet all textbooks used in various schools. At least the less qualified books can be commented upon even if they are not removed, so that parents know when their children are being taught from sub-standard textbooks and thereby being short-changed.

The removal of Ramanujan's essay is a reflection, however, on the academic professional and his/her bending or not, to the demands of those that administer and govern. Instances of encroachments on academic freedom are not new but in the years soon after independence they were less frequent. The politics of religion and caste raise the spectre of hurt sentiments which it is claimed can be allayed by banning books, defacing paintings and statues, censoring films, vandalizing libraries, abusing and harming in various ways those individuals that expose these claims or disagree with fundamentalist positions, and destroying whatever else one chooses to. The frequency, the violence and the abuse that goes with it has increased, and the root of the problem receives little attention.

The space for liberal values has shrunk enormously and those who take even mildly independent positions tend to be harassed especially at the hands of state governments of every political party. Some of the latter try and maintain a façade of not being dictatorial, others openly bare their teeth.

The media could play a more effective role as the platform for debate, a role it is reluctant to perform. Newspapers which once commented extensively on various activities are now more given to entertainment and commercial advertising. Admittedly this is what brings in the finances, but why should it require the dumbing down of intelligent commentary on the Indian world? The visual media, initially described by some as 'the idiot box', has perhaps risen above the description but is now obsessed with the one-byte pattern. Discussions more often than not are shouting matches where the more loud-voiced panelists and anchors reduce the rest to almost being spectators; the loud ones usually have little to say of substance. For those that have something to say, there is not enough time to develop an idea. Evening after evening the circus goes on and one waits for a weekly programme that may be more informative and might raise thought-provoking questions. The focus is on political personalities. Others who also exist are tucked away into non-prime time moments or the equivalent of half-a-byte.

To assume that the audience has a low IQ and cannot concentrate on a subject for more than a few minutes which is basic to many programmes, is insulting but objections to this assumption are not voiced. When the 'Maoist menace' was at its height, various experts from the capital gave their views. It would have been more to the point to have had people from the tribal groups speaking about their problem of being caught between the state and its opponents. Or when there was an objection to allowing mining in the Niyamgiri area should there not have been a discussion between those actually objecting and those wishing to encroach? It would be salutary for the Indian middle class to know that there are many Indians who do not share their culture, and to understand why they do not; and that they are not just the left-overs from history but that they have their own viable cultures that they value, and that other Indians have to respect these cultures as they do their own. And that they cannot just be swept into the mainstream, they have to be persuaded to join in as equal members.

Or there was the more recent absurdity of the Archaeological Survey of India, a professional body of archaeologists, digging for gold at the command of its authority, at a location determined by the dream of a godman. This was surely the occasion for some relevant discussion on the difference between legitimate archaeology and hunting for hidden treasure. TV channels could have dispensed with the incoherent shouting of disciples of the godman. Instead they could have picked up the interest in archaeology to explain how excavations are done and its relation to history and society, instead of the endless interviews with the disciple of the godman. Single bytes can add up to an indigestible meal, but perhaps not for the corporates who own the media.

But the matter goes beyond education and media to the larger concerns of society. The construction of a social ethic is foundational and the discussion on such an ethic goes back many centuries. There was basic contention between the Brahmanical and the Buddhist definitions of a social ethic. Whereas the former projected it as a concern of the individual in the context of conforming to a structured caste society, the latter saw it as pertinent to the relationship between individuals and in their lives with each other, irrespective of sect or caste. The social ethic is an important aspect of governance as we know from the edicts of Ashoka Maurya to other statements of later times. In some instances religion and caste are accepted but are marginal because the ethic applies to all of humanity irrespective of these identities. In other cases there is specific concern for certain castes and sects that receive lavish grants of land, but little is said about the rest of society. Today we can try and choose the ethic that ensures the welfare of society.

10

WHICH OF US ARE ARYANS?

The theory of Aryan race arose out of European preoccupations and preconceptions and was applied to the early Indian past as part of the colonial interpretation of Indian history. As a theory it is not put forward in Indian texts to explain the foundations of Indian culture. The culture it refers to is upper caste culture. It is associated with those that are the ritual specialists and those that control resources. It broadens out in its meaning and in post-Vedic times refers to those that are to be honoured and respected. In its historical interpretation it is now treated, at the popular level, as the bedrock of Indian civilization. Whereas scholars working on the European past have questioned this theory, we in India hold fast to it and those who attempt alternate interpretations are welcome only in academic circles.

The European search for its own identity gained momentum in the eighteenth century. This was in part the result of a groping towards the concept of the nation-state that made it imperative that there be individual identities for the various states, although stemming from a common origin. In looking at the past, the roots of European civilization were taken back to what was regarded as the miracle of Greek culture, which since then is seeking origins in even earlier cultures. Nationalist thinking tends to search for origins in antiquity and the age of the civilization with which it claims links, is constantly pushed back.

The discovery of the Orient had been commented upon at the popular level through the writings of European travelers, merchants and missionaries. Gradually, classical scholarship, the views garnered through the writings of earlier Greek and Latin authors, was added to this and it conjured up the Orient as the epitome of luxury and of mythical beings and activities. In the colonial age the interest shifted to those who were using the origins of languages and their comparative study –philology—as a method of arriving at the common ancestry or the roots of European culture, a mood which was best captured in the

Romantic movement in German literature. Thus when, at the end of the eighteenth century, William Jones declared that there was a similarity in the structure and vocabulary of Sanskrit and Greek (an idea which had been floated even earlier), it fell on fertile ground and became the basis for a large number of theories regarding the origins of European and Indian culture.

In the nineteenth century therefore, the Indologist (a term used originally for non-Indians studying India) came into his own. Using comparative philology as the method for obtaining the data, a common original language, Indo-European, was proposed as the source for a group of related languages that included Sanskrit, Old Iranian, Greek, Latin, Celtic and various other European languages. Comparative philology became important to the reconstruction of the Indian past. Having arrived at a common language, it did not take long for the language to be seen as the expression of a common race, the Aryan race. Given the newly discovered 'race science' in nineteenth century Europe, language was regarded as major evidence of race.

The equation of language with race is not particular to the Indo-European and Aryan situation. It has been extended to other regions as well, such as the equation initially made between Bantu speakers and the supposed Bantu race in Africa. There is of course no basis for such an equation and there is no support for the argument that those who speak an Indo-European language must belong to the same Aryan race. It is equally difficult to define, with even a remote degree of precision, what the Aryan race might be. In the latter part of the nineteenth century, the fallacy of equating language with race was recognized, and despite statements to the effect that the two cannot be equated, the idea had caught the imagination of people and could not be dislodged. Even some scholars such as Max Mueller who were well aware of the difference occasionally confused the two.

In the mid-nineteenth century, Arthur de Gobineau expanded on the idea of the Aryan race which he identified with the European aristocracy. His influential book on the inequality of human races had natural appeal, particularly to the aristocracy that was in decline in Europe, and also to groups gradually replacing this aristocracy but wanting nevertheless to be regarded as having a special status. Gobineau argued that the fairer races were pre-eminent because they were instrumental in creating and spreading culture largely through the conquest of others. But conquest, because it required settling in new areas, led to the mixing of races and hence to decline. This theory was to have disastrous consequences in Germany in the twentieth century.

Many of those working on the early Sanskrit texts, such as the *Vedas,* read the word arya as having a racial connotation. For example, Max Mueller's discussions encouraged the idea of a superior Aryan race subduing the inferior indigenes and settling in India. Although at a later stage he argued that race and language were separate, it was by then too late to make the distinction, for the theory of Aryan race was becoming the established explanation for much of the reconstruction of early Indian history.

Language groups were now equated with race and there were references to not only the Aryan but also the Dravidian and the Austro-Asiatic races, based on the various languages spoken in different regions. Even the origin of caste society was explained as an attempt at racial segregation where, ideally, each caste constituted a different race and racial purity was maintained by forbidding inter-marriage. Thus the argument could be stretched to maintain that the upper castes, and especially the brahmanas, were lineal descendants of the Aryans.

It was, however, in the reconstruction of early Indian history that the theory of Aryan race had its biggest impact. It was argued that the foundation of Indian civilization was laid by the coming of the Aryans. This took the form of an invasion of the north-western part of the Indian subcontinent to begin with and the subjugation of the existing populations often described as Dravidian, because of the presence of Dravidian languages in the southern region. The Aryans were seen as conquering northern India and pushing the Dravidians into the peninsula and the south, leaving pockets of the Austro-Asiatic and some Dravidian speakers in central India. Cultural history involved the spread and establishment of the Aryan race over the sub-continent.

The term arya is more frequently used in the Vedic and Buddhist texts to refer to one who is respected and regarded as an honoured person. It referred to those who spoke Sanskrit and observed the varna regulations. But in the nineteenth century reading of the *Rigveda,* the counterposing of the arya with the dasa was interpreted as a racial demarcation. The dasa, it was argued, is differentiated, among other characteristics, by physical differences as well. So the term arya was used to refer to those of the Aryan race and the dasa to those of the indigenous races. The pre-eminence of the aryas was explained by reference to their being the conquerors. The term varna, which literally means colour, but which was probably used in a symbolic sense, as is suggested by the colours of the castes listed in other texts, as white, yellow, red and black, was nevertheless taken literally to refer to differences in skin colour and this, in turn, was sought to support the argument that caste was a form of racial segregation.

Some scholars described early Indian society as living in idyllic village communities characterized by harmony and a lack of aggression. There was a representation of some levels of Indian society being primitive in the romantic sense. Such descriptions were extended to contemporary nineteenth century India, as for instance in some passages in the writings of Max Mueller, which he could happily do as he (like James Mill) never visited India. Part of the reason for this depiction of ideal communities was that such village communities were seen as similar to the village communities from which the peoples of Europe had originated. The Indian present was seen as reflecting the features of Europe in its infancy. India, like Asia generally, was viewed as 'the Other' of Europe, perhaps also because it was necessary for there to be an 'Other' so that Europe could create its own identity. Such 'othering' could either conjure up a positive romantic image of Indian society as viewed by the German Romantic poets, or a negative and dismal one as projected by the Utilitarian philosophers and by Hegel in his later writings.

The history of early India therefore became a channel for propagating European views on the origins of peoples and cultures more generally. Thus even the culture of non-European societies was conditioned by the prevailing debates in Europe. This was in part an aspect of Orientalism where the use of knowledge as a form of power was implicit. The recreation of a colony's culture and image of itself in terms of the Orientalist paradigms was a mechanism of control by the colonial power, as has been suggested by Edward Said in his study of Orientalism. Thus for Lord Curzon the furtherance of such scholarship and knowledge was what he called the necessary furniture of empire.

The interpretation did not have to be reductionist in terms of the colonial framework but it tended to conform to its essentials and there is little attempt at any critique of this framework among earlier Orientalist scholars. Much of the detailed scholarship on early India, which was a legitimate means of discovering many aspects of the past, came from those who were employed as officers by the East India Company either in India or in England, such as William Jones, James Mill, H.T. Colebroke, H.H. Wilson and James Prinsep, and later, by Her Majesty's Imperial Government such as Alexander Cunningham and Vincent Smith. As such, therefore, they were unlikely to question the interpretations supporting colonial policy.

Even when nationalist historians in India began to question some of the colonial paradigms, the theory of Aryan race was not among these. It could be argued that as many Indian historians who had been influenced by the ideology of nationalism, came from the upper castes (brahmanas, kshatriyas, and kayasthas) and from the middle class, the theory of Aryan race appealed to them as it supported their claims to social superiority. It also suggested that Sanskritic Indian culture sprang from the same roots as that of the colonizing power. According to Keshab Chandra Sen, the coming of the British to India was symbolic of the meeting of parted cousins.

Even those who were opposed to what they regarded as upper caste interpretations of the past, also accepted the theory, but turned it to their own use. Thus, thinkers such as Jyotiba Phule in Maharashtra, and others who were members of the non-Brahmin movements in south India, maintained that the lower castes were the original inhabitants of India and that the upper castes, descended from the incoming Aryans, were foreigners. Once again it was assumed that the speakers of a particular language constituted a different race from the speakers of another language. Phule's interpretation introduced the relevance of caste as well. Despite the denial of the equation of language with race by scholars, this equation was firmly embedded in both European and Indian views of the Indian past.

The Theosophist view of the Aryans being indigenous is prior to the Hindutva view and this is not originally an Indian theory, but the creation of European commentators on the roots of Indian culture. Indian scholars of pre-colonial times, commenting on the *Rigveda*, such as Sayana, made no such reconstructions of Indian civilization.

The questioning of the theory of Aryan race has arisen both from new evidence and from new methods of analyzing the evidence. The new evidence comes from archaeology and linguistics and the new method is demonstrated in the manner in which caste has been studied in recent years.

The major new discovery in archaeology relates to the Indus Civilization. The chronology of this civilization, the third to early second millennium BC, would place it earlier than the Vedic texts that are generally dated from the mid-second to the mid-first millennium BC. If the texts are dated earlier, as some would like to do, then they would coincide with this civilization. But the societies reconstructed from archaeology and from the texts are strikingly different from each other. Therefore the texts cannot be taken as descriptions of the excavated civilization. The Indus Civilization extended from the Pamirs to northern Maharashtra and from Baluchistan to the Doab with settlements in Oman as well. The early Vedic texts know only the northern part of this extensive area. Familiarity with western India came later. The Indus Civilization was urban, with planned cities built on elevations commanding the plains communicated by written signs that have not as yet been deciphered, had a copper-bronze technology, was unfamiliar with the horse and had extensive trading contacts not only with the upper Oxus region and the borderlands, but also with the Gulf and with Mesopotamia. The Vedic texts depict a society which is pastoral and agrarian but is unfamiliar with urban centres and commerce, knows no script, appears to have used a copper and then an iron technology, gave considerable functional and ritual importance to the horse and the chariot, and its contacts were largely confined to north-eastern Iran and perhaps the Oxus plain, before the migration eastwards into the Ganga plain.

The evidence suggests that the speakers of Aryan languages—whoever they were—migrated into India from the borderlands. The migrations are likely to have been slow and small-scale. If there had been 'an Aryan invasion' it would be reflected in the archaeological evidence, either in the decline of the cities due to attacks, or in large-scale devastation of surrounding settlements. Some decades ago, Mortimer Wheeler maintained that the Indus cities declined because of Aryan invasions, which he summed up in his phrase, 'Indra stands accused'. But the more extensive and detailed evidence now available since the lost fifty years points in an altogether different direction. The theory of invasion has long since been discounted. The decline of cities is no longer attributed to a single cause, since their decline was not simultaneous, those of Gujarat declining somewhat later.

The more likely causes that are under investigation are ecological and environmental—massive flooding at Mohenjo-daro, changing river courses of the Hakra and the Sutlej, deforestation due to agriculture and brick-making resulting in desiccation and a decline in agricultural production on which the cities were dependent, de-urbanization due to a decline in commerce, and possibly some climate change. The falling off of trade with Mesopotamia has been suggested as a factor causing de-urbanization. It is likely that with further analysis the decline of these cities will relate more directly to changes in the political and economic structure as well. Cities do not remain unaltered over a period of a thousand years.

It is equally difficult to argue that the Aryans originated in India and spread to west Asia as this is not supported by archaeological or literary evidence indicating an extensive westerly movement by a specific group of people. One of the archaeological cultures subsequent to the Indus Civilization, known as the Painted Grey Ware, located in northern Rajasthan, Punjab, Haryana and eastern UP, is often regarded as the archaeological counterpart to the later Vedic literature. This does not go westwards much beyond the Indus.

The linguistic evidence does, however, cross borders. There was an affinity in language between the speakers of Vedic Sanskrit and Avestan in Iran, an affinity that was recognized many decades ago. It is possible therefore that small groups of migrants from Iran came into proximity with people settled on the borders of north-western India and through a process of mutual exchange evolved into a variety of communities, among which were the speakers of Indo-Aryan. Such communities can only be identified by speech, using the literature that survives and, therefore, in referring to them the correct form would be not Aryan, but Aryan-speakers, meaning, 'speakers of Indo-Aryan'.

There is a close affinity between the culture and language of the *Avesta* and Old Iranian. Mitra and Varuna occur in both texts, as do *deva* and *asura*/daiva and *ahura* (in Old Iranian), but the meaning is reversed as in other cases as well. The *sapta-sindhu* region of the Indus is referred to as *hapta-hendhu*, and the Haraxvaiti river in south-east Afganistan, would be rendered in Sanskrit as Saraswati, since the 's' sound changes into 'h' in Old Iranian. The relationship of the societies that produced the *Avesta* and the *Rigveda* was clearly close and needs to be investigated in detail. The dates would tally approximately. Further west in northern Syria there is the evidence of a treaty between the two local people, the Hittites and the Mitannis, dated to about 1380 BC which mentions the names of gods that carry names similar to those of some Rigvedic gods. Another text has turns of phrase in training horses that are reminiscent of Indo-Aryan. These pockets of similar languages would date to the late second millennium BC. There are no connections between them so it is thought that those using the language may have originated in the Oxus plain (the Bactria Margiana Archaeological Complex), and migrated from there. There is no survival of Indo-Aryan in the region occupied by the Hittites and the Mitannis.

The debate on the language that might have been spoken by the people of the Indus civilization introduces the evidence of linguistics. The debate as it stands currently is substantially between those who support a possible Dravidian language being used by the Harappans, and those who are in favour of its being an Indo-Aryan language. None of the actual readings in either of these languages has met with acceptance among scholars. If the script remained a pictographic script with little indication of marked evolution and change, it is also possible, as has been suggested, that there was more than a single language spoken but using a common pictographic script.

Recent linguistic analyses ofVedic Sanskrit suggest a rather different picture from the one that prevailed earlier. Non-Aryan vocabulary and syntax are now recognized in the earliest of the *Vedas*, the *Rigveda,* and elements of this increase in the later *Vedas.* For example, the word langala for plough is non-Aryan and it is also known from archaeological evidence that plough agriculture goes back to the period just prior to the Indus civilization. The non-Aryan influence on Vedic Sanskrit could suggest symbiotic relations between speakers of Aryan and non-Aryan languages, possibly even some bilingualism.

That Sanskrit itself, in the course of a few centuries, underwent change is well established. The existence of etymological works in relation to Vedic Sanskrit—contemporary with the Vedic corpus—indicate that the language was changing noticeably. The grammar of Panini, generally dated to the fourth century BC, is another indicator since he distinguishes between what is now referred to as Vedic and Classical Sanskrit. Such changes can be explained by the evolution of the language in use and by non-Sanskrit speakers using the language. Thus even in the process of its spread, Sanskrit as a language was constantly adapting itself to local linguistic forms. This is a normal procedure in the history of a language.

The other important aspect relates to the beginnings of caste. Studies of caste formation have come a long way from the simplistic notions of caste being separate racial entities. The origin of caste in the theory of the four varnas as expounded in the Vedic corpus, appear to have been symbolic explanations of status differentiation to begin with. It is unlikely that a social system as complex as a caste society began with a simple, four-fold division of society into brahmanas, kshatriyas, vaishyas and shudras with the untouchables added on as a fifth category. Possibly the varna system, reflecting social stratification, was nevertheless an idealization of a stratification. Caste looked at as jatis suggests other avenues and emphases in caste society.

Jatis evolve from the intermeshing of a variety of factors such as rules of endogamy and exogamy, location, environment, technology, occupation, access to resources, differences in the patterns of social observances, and the ideology of ritual purity. A caste society consists of hereditary groups so recruitment is by birth; these groups are arranged hierarchically which is actually or notionally associated with occupation among other factors; the hierarchy is important particularly to permissible marriage circles and to rules regarding the inheritance of property particularly in relation to women; and they are often viewed as performing services for each other. The social historian therefore has to trace these factors over time and in relation to historical changes. History provides evidence of the importance of kinship patterns and occupation to caste identities, as well as evidence of the transition from what has been called 'jana to jati' (generally translated as tribe to caste, but perhaps better translated as clan to caste).

Another important aspect is the adaptation to a culture, which has sometimes been called a Sanskritic culture, but would include more than just the language. It would consist of the norms and rituals associated with life cycle rites such as birth, marriage and death. These were generally not uniform across caste in earlier times, although we today tend to think that the upper caste norms applied universally. What is regarded as 'Sanskritic' changes over time, for although on some occasions the Sanskritic assimilates the local non-Sanskritic culture, sometimes the process is reversed and there is more of the non-Sanskritic in the 'Sanskritic' although the veneer of the Sanskritic may be retained. This is particularly apparent in rituals. Some rituals have become relatively uniform and practiced across castes, but many are specific to particular castes. Similarly, practices also change over time and the definition of what constitutes correct behaviour for a particular caste may not be the same what it was in earlier periods. Thus the Vedic corpus makes clear that the good brahmana could consume the flesh of a sacrificed animal even if bovine, and, as part of certain sacrificial rituals he was required to drink soma, which if not an intoxicant was certainly a hallucinogen. Yet, in a later period, from the point of view of the good brahmana, it was regarded as heretical to eat meat and consume intoxicants, even on ritual occasions. Cultural habits constantly change and explaining the change is as important as recording the change if one wishes to understand the change. This is again an area where social history and anthropology can provide helpful explanations. Historically the interesting question is when and why did the prohibition on eating beef become the requirement of a good Hindu.

Asserting the purity of race among upper castes, tracing ancestry back to early times, often came apart given the fact that physically some castes have greater regional affinities than pan-Indian. Nor is this surprising for there was some conversion into castes at local levels with aspirations to higher status and the fitting of these castes into a hierarchy. Regional variations, even in the broader structure of caste, do make it difficult if not impossible to maintain that there was a dissemination of the pure race that retained its purity and its status through time. Today the concept of race as defined in the nineteenth century has been discarded among scientists and scholars. Identities are based on other factors and claims to race are no longer tenable, although the word continues to be used in popular parlance.

The theory of an Aryan race therefore is not supported by historical evidence. What the historian is concerned with is not the spread of a race but the spread of a language. This is a culturally far more enriching and complex subject. We know from many examples all over the world and from many periods of history that it was perfectly feasible for people of different racial origins, brought together through migration, trade, conquest or persecution, to find themselves ultimately using the same language. Despite many attempts the Harappan language has not been read as Indo-Aryan. This would suggest that some other language was in use. Thus the historian of early India has to explain how the two Indo-Aryan based languages, Prakrit and Sanskrit, became current in northern India from the first millennium BC. Those who spoke these languages could well have come from a variety of origins. They are both languages drawing from a common root but becoming diverse in usage. Why was Sanskrit for instance, adopted by the elite in northern India? Was it, to begin with, deliberately kept restricted to the few since it is clear from inscriptions that the commonly spoken language was Prakrit? In the absence of conquest other factors have to be considered. Was the language associated with a superior technology, such as the use of iron and of horses and chariots, which would have attracted elite levels of society? Did those who spoke the language introduce new calendrical knowledge that would have had an impact on the agrarian cycle? There can be many reasons why different social groups use different languages.

There is also the important question of the relationship of Indo-Aryan to other languages, as for example Dravidian, the presence of which is evident in the Vedic corpus. Elements of Munda are also now being traced in the same compositions. This could point to a long period of groups speaking different languages living in close proximity, possibly being bilingual. This would not be the nature of the language if every inhabitant from Harappan times was an 'Aryan' and speaking Sanskrit, as is the claim of one of the theories seeking popular support. This is also suggestive of a slow and graduated migration of some of the Indo-Aryan speakers who, according to the Vedic texts, migrated eastwards into the Ganga plain. We are told that the raja Videga Mathava travelled east to the Sadanira river, carrying Agani in his mouth. On reaching there he and his clan cleared the marshes and settled down. Carrying Agni in his mouth could mean that he burnt the waste land to clear it for cultivation, or that he introduced Indo-Aryan speech into the area. The story also highlights migration as the process of settling in new areas. Migration as a historical and cultural process of change is of course entirely different from an invasion, both in procedure and in result, and the two should not be confused as they often are.

Speaking of the language scene in the first millennium BC, there is still the question-mark of the use of Prakrit, widely attested in inscriptions of the first millennium BC, and how it evolved. If it was a vernacular version of Sanskrit then why were royal inscriptions initially composed in Prakrit rather than in Sanskrit? The inscriptions of Ashoka are in Prakrit, and not in Sanskrit, and he explains that he wants them to be read by or read to, everyone. The Buddhists and Jainas used Pali and Prakrit, and not Sanskrit for the same reason. Prakrit was the language of communication. Did it evolve from the use of more than one language at the time?

The Vedic corpus has many hymns referring to the destruction of the enemy and rituals in praise of the destroyer. The identity of the enemy is however not certain in every case. There are occasions when the enemy is referred to as the dasas or the dasyus, but there are equally many occasions if not more when the enemy is of another clan but of the same culture. Such internecine raids among clans are characteristic of cattle-keeping societies as also of those in the process of clearing and settling land for agriculture, as was the case among the people referred to in the Vedic corpus. Competition over access to resources was intense and did at times benefit from marriage alliances and the intermingling of various groups. Thus, some of the most pre-eminent among these clans, such as that of the Purus who were ancestral to the protagonists of the Mahabharata war, are described in the *Vedas* as being descended from an asura rakshasa and speaking a faulty Sanskrit. They were clearly not 'pure Aryans'.

The empirical evidence, as we have it today, from archaeology, linguistics and various literary sources, does not support the theory of the Aryan race. But this is not merely a matter of interest to the historian. This theory has been used by many others and has come to be seen as fundamental to the understanding of the identity of modern Indians. It is here that its greatest danger lies: the upholding of a theory supposedly explaining our origins, which theory is erroneous. The question of identity is particularly important to the process of change from caste to class, for which purpose the theory was appropriated by the middle-class.

This is, of course, not peculiar to Indian society, for such theories of racial origins and identities have been known to other societies undergoing similar mutations. It has been plausibly argued that the uncertainty of social change and the expansion of the middle class in early twentieth century Germany was one of the root causes of the rise of fascism founded on the Aryan myth. The necessary 'Others' who had to be targeted and destroyed were chosen in part because they were competitors for resources. But perhaps even more than that, the attackers needed an external target to create a bond among themselves. This experience, so close to us in time, should make it obvious that theories of origins and identities have to be handled very carefully else they may explode in a manner which can devastate a society. The historian in these situations has to be alert to the way in which historical ideas can be used or abused in the name of history.

11

DATING THE EPICS

The long-running controversy over the date and historical authenticity of the *Ramayana* and *Mahabharata* (which goes back to over a century) flared up unexpectedly in 1975. It was debated month after month on the front pages of the daily newspapers; enterprising academics cashed in on the public interest by giving their views through a variety of fora. And, any statement on the epics became a matter of priority for publicity. Clearly business is good for those of us in ancient history, archaeology and Indology—as indeed, also for those who are not technically qualified in any of these fields but still feel the urge to pronounce on the subject and enter the debate.

This is all the more surprising in view of the fact that public opinion, educational administration and even researchers in these fields have, by and large, been rather impervious to many of the more important and recent investigations, admittedly less dramatic, pertaining to the ancient past, particularly those which have indicated fundamentally different perspectives on the past from those held before. Such investigations have not percolated to points where they would provide new insights into the popular image of the past.

It would seem that the crux of the controversy in the press did not emerge from the purely academic problems posed. The arguments on the chronology and authenticity of the epics as historical narratives have been current in scholarly circles for the last many decades. The lack of any further incisive analysis at this point at the scholarly level, demonstrates paucity in our understanding of epic traditions and in our handling of the historical method. Although the original controversy stemmed out of an academic debate, the momentum that carried it to the front pages of daily newspapers and the centre pages of innumerable weekly magazines, arose out of a different concern. Some of it may have had to do with the absence of other more 'meaty' debates at that point in time. But there was probably more to it than that. It indicated a point of uncertainty where both a questioning of, and clinging to, what is regarded as a social and cultural tradition becomes enmeshed with social and political change. Attitudes to the tradition then become a pivot for mobilization on other matters: a process which has been repeated throughout history but which has become more pointed in recent times.

Ancient traditions and what are believed to be cultural roots hold a central place in what claims to be cultural nationalism. During the nineteenth and early twentieth centuries, Indian scholarship was as much a party to the inter-connection of contemporary politics and the study of ancient traditions, as scholarship elsewhere in the world. But cultural nationalism has many historical phases. One wonders if the present interest in the epics is not in some ways parallel to the interest in the *Nibelungenlied* in nineteenth century Germany and central Europe, not unconnected with the struggle over identity among various communities. An 'ancient tradition' poses at least two difficult problems for its inheritors. One is the need to identify with it. The other is to either disprove its historical authenticity and dismiss it as valueless for historical information pertaining to person and event, or else to constantly verify its authenticity by testing it with the most recent and, what are claimed to be, the most scientific methods available. The debate over the epics in 1975 suggest the latter.

For those of us professionally involved in these matters, the dating of the *Mahabharata* and the *Ramayana* and the problem of their historical authenticity are hardy perennials. They crop up at every all-India conference of Indologists, Orientalists and 'ancient historians'. They have come to be treated with a slight whiff of indifference. The indifference stems from there not having been in the recent past any strikingly new application of methods of interpretation on this specific subject calling for prolonged discussion, or suggesting new dimensions to tackling the problem. Inevitably, the debate begins with discussing the date of the texts. The traditional date based on the cyclic chronology of the mahayuga, the great cycle or age, refers to the start of the Kaliyuga at the ending of the battle at Kurukshetra in the *Mahabharata*. Others compute the generations from the start of the Kaliyuga, the equivalent date of which is 3102 BC. Some maintain that this is the date for the ending of the war.

It is a sad commentary on the investigation of these problems that it is substantially the old evidence that is juggled back and forth in attempts to suggest a range of dates. The 1975 controversy brought out the array of existing arguments, among which two were recalled repeatedly—the technique of trying to read astronomical data in the texts to work out the date, and the computation of the genealogies listed in the epics and the *Puranas* as a basis for chronological reconstructions. The only relatively new method of investigation was the comparison with archaeological data, which was almost two decades old at that point in time. This posed yet another set of problems. To compare an artifact from an excavation with a description of a similar object from a text is not a matter of a simple equation. The context of each has to be known and has to be similar since the context provides a different kind of validity to the comparison.

Some participants in the debate based their chronological conclusions on what they believed to be references, veiled or direct, to the position of the stars and constellations which they took as readings for astronomical data. The most popular of these were the readings suggested at the time of the death of Bhishma in some versions of the *Mahabharata*. The interrelation of constellations was then calculated back in time for many hundreds of years until a co-relation with the supposed evidence of the text could be made. However, these arguments tend to be highly esoteric and the more serious debate is restricted to a few persons conversant with astronomy. I say 'supposed evidence' not in any derogatory sense but, literally, since in cases where the references to astronomical data are veiled, the interpretation of these statements as symbolic of such data is, after all, a personal matter, and is usually doubted by those wanting precise evidence. It is true that ancient texts are often highly symbolic in content. The cross-check in the interpretation of symbols is that the meaning/interpretation must be uniform within the culture. If on one occasion, rikshas (bears) refers to the Ursa Major constellation, it must do so on all occasions in the same text. The interpretation of symbols having by now become methodologically fairly systematic, this should be the first step in claiming the viability of certain symbols as astronomical data. However, this cannot be a definitive step as the interpretations of symbols often change. Where a text has emerged out of an oral tradition as have the epics, there is always the problem of some passages or even parvans/books being inserted from time to time. Clearly this plays havoc with the dating—unless one agrees with those scholars who argue that the texts were compiled in a short period of time. But even their short period of time is generally a century or two.

Where the reference to astronomical readings were not veiled but direct, as where mention was made of the position of the nakshatras (lunar mansions), these too were subject to investigation. Such references can be interpolations of later editors wishing to give antiquity to the events described by inserting data that belongs to an earlier period. These references can vary from edition to edition, from region to region and some are absent in the Critical Edition of the *Mahabharata,* which is currently accepted as the standard text. For any valid use of such data there would have to be a collection of all such references to astronomical readings and a general agreement on the interpretation of these readings. This would be followed by a careful scrutiny to exclude those that are evidently late interpolations. It would further require a correlation of the remaining readings with the known knowledge of astronomy and mathematics for the period to which the text is being ascribed. The understanding of astronomy is one thing, its application to history is quite another. Possibly it can be facilitated by using the historical Sky Map now available on the internet, as it provides maps of the sky that go back a few millennia.

Others also mathematically inclined, have tried computing the dates of these texts from the genealogical lists which the texts provide. The argument runs that if a mean average can be taken for the lifespan of each generation, then by counting the generations a chronology can be worked out for the events described in the texts. Much time and energy has gone into calculating the average lifespan of a generation in India, particularly with reference to royal families. The dynasties of the medieval period, for whom fairly precise data is available from court chronicles, were used as the primary data to compute the average length of reign of rulers. Other sources on regnal years of dynasties were also consulted. The figures had a large range from fourteen years to twenty-two. Depending on which figures one accepted, it was thought possible to work out the lifespan in epic genealogies.

The way in which this system works is as follows: we are told for example, that a king, Udayin, believed to be a near contemporary of the Buddha, reigned approximately twenty-four generations after the end of the Mahabharata War. Assuming that the Buddha died in 486 or 483 BC, Udayin's reign can be placed at around 500 BC. Taking an average of fourteen years per generation we arrive at the date of 836 BC for the war, as indeed has been suggested recently. But we could as well take twenty-two years per generation as the time span and arrive at a different date of 1028 BC. The choice in either case is arbitrary since there is no reason for choosing fourteen in preference to twenty-two. And, if we accept as some do, 544 BC as the date for the death of the Buddha, we would arrive at a still earlier date for the war. And, since there is no certainty that the generations listed are precise in number, the calculations stand on shaky ground. Not only is the acceptance of a particular figure for a generation highly subjective, but the figure itself is open to question. And besides this, habits of nutrition change over a period of two or three thousand years and these habits together with general ecological changes affect longevity and average life expectancy. Or, for that matter, the chiefs of clan societies or the heroes or the kings of early states would have been living in a different social system from that of the rulers of post-Gupta kingdoms or the Sultans of Delhi; and that this might well have affected life expectancy and therefore the rate of turnover of those in political ascendancy.

Nor has there been much examination of how to read the role of genealogies in various societies, on which there is now a large body of literature, both from historians working on the genealogies of early west Asia and from anthropologists concerned with the function of genealogy as a social tradition in many parts of the world. If this literature is studied, it will soon become apparent that attempting to compute precise chronology on the basis of genealogies can be a negative exercise. Genealogies merely record which persons (and to that extent the events associated with them) came before and which after. Even these can be shuffled in case of need. Time-reckoning is approximate. Further, geneaologies serve an essentially social function as, for example, to allow more recent upstarts to attach themselves to an ancient lineage in order to acquire social status; or to prove the claim of a particular family to rights over land. At most, some information on the system of succession and the geographical location of a lineage can with difficulty be milked out of a genealogical record.

The genealogists had little compunction about either conflating the number of generations or of reducing them should they be desirous of fitting the lineage into a politically expedient pattern. The variants in the genealogies listing the lineage of Rama or of the Pandavas and Kauravas are almost as many as there are recensions of the texts. The purpose of the genealogy has much more to do with the time at which it was compiled than with the early ancestors whom it claims to be listing. And ancient Indian genealogical material is no exception to this.

In the last few decades the attempted chronology for the Indian epics has turned to archaeology as a possible source of information. This has resulted from the exploration and excavation of modern sites bearing place-names or associations occurring in the epics, the classic example being Hastinapur, the city associated with the Kauravas. The situation is analogous with the excavation of Troy to prove the correctness of the Homeric epics. The discussion is virtually limited to the *Mahabharata* since only a few sites associated with the *Ramayana* have been excavated or have yet to be excavated, or the excavation reports of those sections that have been excavated at Ayodhya have yet to be made publicly available. Until the legal controversy over the Ramjanmabhoomi is settled, these reports will presumably remain in judicial custody.

Up until now the simplest way of using archaeological data was that if the contribution of an archaeological culture is found to roughly coincide with the geographical locale of the epic, a co-relation is suggested. However, even this can be deceptive since the geographical reach of the epic can undoubtedly expand as the geographical knowledge of its editors/redactors increases from century to century. Thus, the geographical locale of the epic can only refer to the time of the most recent redaction of the text. Nevertheless, it has been argued that the archaeological culture called the Painted Grey Ware, distributed in the main over Punjab, Haryana, northwestern Rajasthan and western Uttar Pradesh, and dating to the early first millennium BC may be associated with the *Mahabharata,* since this is broadly the geographical area to which the text relates. On the assumption of this association and the genealogical exercise to which reference has been made above, we have been given the precise date of 836 BC for the war.

To calculate such pinpointed chronology from archaeological evidence is almost to deny the validity of the evidence. One of the joys of using archaeological evidence for those of us who are non-mathematically inclined is precisely that it shifts the focus from the historian's obsession with chronology, to the wider implications of aspects of the society under consideration. Thus, apart from the geographical co-relation, the more important investigation is whether the material culture excavated from the site(s) conforms to that described in the epic. Such an analysis would be of immense value but is virtually impossible to do at the moment since hardly any of the major sites associated with either of the epics has as yet been excavated horizontally over a sizeable area, to reveal the nature of the culture at any given point in time. Since the excavations are generally vertical, cutting a slice through the mound, the evidence on material culture is limited. The recent excavation in Ayodhya at the site of the Babri Masjid seems not to have yielded what those who asked for the excavation were hoping for.

It is here that we come up against the core of the problem. Only a few isolated attempts have been made to examine the social contexts of the epics. In the main, the texts are taken as 'a given' and are cherry-picked by researchers. The epic is searched and the relevant evidence is picked out. Yet, the compilation of an epic is a study in itself. In origin it is often a collection of bardic poetry describing heroic exploits, and uses folk-tales, narrative episodes, fragments of genealogies, gobbets of customary law, myths and segments of religious cults, ethical theories and even philosophical speculation. The time-dimension of all these various nuggets ranges over a few centuries and refers to a variety of social forms and situations. Whereas myths involve deities and humans, epics focus more on the humans and are assumed to contain some trace of an historical kernel. But this does not mean that all the events are historically accurate or that even the historically proved event is accurately described in the epic. Epic literature based on bardic fragments is by definition a collection of many social traditions, generally referring back to the twilight period of clan societies and the dawn of early kingdoms. The bard evokes nostalgia for the heroic age and imbues it with a utopian gloss to which future generations look back with envy.

Epic literature therefore cannot be precisely dated for events merge into events and narrative slowly gets welded with commentary. The *Mahabharata* is a clear example of this as has been shown by scholars who have discussed the many accretions and interpolations over equally many centuries. Even the interpolations are not of a single date. The *Bhagvad Gita* for example, has been shown to have its own interpolations, apart from what went into the *Mahabharata*. The purpose of such accretions was both to bring the text up-to-date with contemporary changes as well as to use it to legitimize new ideas and new ethics. The *Ramayana* carries fewer traces of the early epic tradition and is evidently of the more developed literary form of court poetry, hence its description as a kavya. Although even in this text the composition is not uniform in style and time.

Any archaeological co-relation therefore would be complicated, to say the least, as it would require the sorting out of the stratification of the text, before such a co-relation could be attempted. At most, some period of occupation of a particular site could be connected with textual references. To try and identify an entire epic with an archaeological culture is virtually to attempt the impossible. What archaeology can be used for is the co-relating of items of material culture with literary descriptions from the epics and this would indicate the technology, perhaps the socio-economic background and possibly an approximate time-context for that particular episode. But as I have said earlier the context of each has to be ascertained.

The stratification of the text creates problems for easy co-relations with archeological data. We have all in the past tried to co-relate the Painted Grey Ware culture as the archaeological counterpart to the *Mahabharata* and to the Vedic corpus. But the question is which part of the text can we co-relate with which section of the archaeological data? If an unusual or striking object shows up and its counterpart can be found in the text then a comparison can be made. But by and large the descriptions have to be of a general kind. Archaeological evidence can sometimes be a useful corrective. Those who take as literal the descriptions of the wealth and splendour of the court at Hastinapur, or the stunning palace associated with the magic of Asura Maya at Indraprastha, are in for a rude shock, since the archaeological evidence indicates a rather simple, pastoral-cum-agricultural, pre-urban society living in wattle-and-daub huts. Archaeological evidence can sometimes juxtapose the reality with the richly poetic imagination that infuses the epic compositions.

The concern for dating the central event of the epic in the light of existing evidence becomes something of an exercise in futility since the reflections that surface in the epic change with each new skin that the epic acquires over time. A question posed a few decades ago still has relevance, namely, was there only a single Bharata war or was there an earlier one whose memory alone lingered, and that the one referred to in the present text is a more recent conflict which got accreted on to an earlier epic? There are a number of inexplicable discrepancies such as that the two protagonists, the Pandavas and the Kauravas are not related by blood to the lineage whose rights over territory and government they are claiming to inherit. The kinship link with the lineage is based on a series of fictions. This is a puzzling situation for a society where kinship links were fundamental and extended to rights over property.

Many of us now work with the assumption that both epics were given their present shape, from the initial composition to later redactions and interpolations, during the period from about 400 BC to the early centuries AD. This then precludes a specific epic age. The epics were in a sense garnered from the oral tradition and composed alongside other literatures. Whereas the *Mahabharata* is concerned largely with narratives of clan societies, the *Ramayana* suggests that it may be a trifle later as it focuses on the conflict between the kingdom and clan society. As such the *Ramayana* would have played a significant ideological role in the mutation of clan societies into kingdoms, and in establishing the authority of the incipient kingdom. The relatively egalitarian society of clans was gradually converted into the hierarchical society of caste and kings.

There has also been some discussion on the question of why the two epics have survived in India, and have also been accepted in other parts of Asia, especially Indonesia, Thailand and Cambodia, as part of their tradition, whereas in Greece the *Iliad* and the *Odyssey* are not nearly so prominent. It is largely only scholars that know about *Beowulf* in England. Much the same would have happened to the *Nibelungenlied* in Germany and the *Kalevala* in Finland, but for the fact that they were revived as part of nationalism.

It has been suggested that the ethical values of the texts and the negation of the finality of death were among the reasons for the survival of the epics in India. These reasons would apply to any epic literature since its creation links it to situations of changing values, and epics try to comment on these in an ethical strain. The didactic thread is always present though possibly more emphasized in the Indian epics. Bardic poetry, since it sets out to immortalize the exploits of the hero is, in a sense, a negation of death as finality. Bhishma's lengthy discourse on life and death as he lay dying on a bed of arrows at the battlefield, which is what is often quoted in support of the argument, is quite clearly extraneous to the original epic and was introduced by later redactors who were manipulating the epic for other functions, as for example, to glorify kingship and caste society.

There are of course more obvious reasons for the continuity of the epic in India. In epic literature, generally, the distinction between gods and heroes is clearly demarcated. The gods participate in events but strictly as gods. The heroes may be close to the gods but are essentially human heroes. In the Indian epics, some of the heroes have a divine parent, but Rama and Krishna born of humans are incarnations of Vishnu. The epic began as part of a secular, folk tradition as is evident from the variant versions of the narratives in Buddhist and Jaina texts, where they are not directly associated with deities. The source for some of the narratives of the two epics may have been in the stories in the Buddhist *Jataka* collection. The intention in collecting these stories was that they were supposed to narrate the previous births of the Buddha and his associates. This idea may perhaps have triggered off the notion of treating epic characters as incarnations of deities. At some point the epics were converted into sacred literature. This did not happen to the ancient epics of Europe. For example, in the Mediterranean, the new religion, Christianity, dispelled the earlier gods; in India the new religion, Vaishnavism, devoid of any notions of paganism, introduced the idea of incarnations of Vishnu and used the epics for proselytizing. The continuity of the epics in India was in part because they remained inclusive cultural idioms.

Apart from this, social groups moving up the social scale and acquiring kshatriya status sought and were given a connection with the two traditional genealogies, the Suryavamsha or Solar Lineage and the Chandravamsha or Lunar Lineage, each of which form the genealogical core of the *Ramayana* and the *Mahabharata* respectively. Newly arrived elites therefore helped popularize the epics, which they projected as the story of the ancestors, with whom they had claimed connections. Some inscriptions of the late first millennium AD make this link in passing.

Traders, and those who settled in new lands in various parts of Asia, carried the epic stories with them, accompanied by monks and priests who possibly took texts with them to strengthen the diffusion. Where it became the literature of those in power it was also accepted by others. But it would be as well to remember that it is not necessarily the Valmiki *Ramayana* or the *Mahabharata* ascribed to Vyasa that is being discussed in a pan-Asian context, or for that matter even often in a pan-Indian context. The local version of what was created from the bare bones of the story was of greater significance, and these variations on the original theme need to be analyzed.

It comes as a surprise to many people that there are many versions of the story of Rama, from folk literature, to drama, to narratives comprised from particular perspectives. The story was picked up and refashioned in the most creative literary forms drawing from a variety of cultural idioms. This was done not only in India but virtually all over Asia and especially so in Southeast Asia. What is important is not just that the story occurs in a Buddhist or Jaina context as well, or that it is used for preaching a distinctly Buddhist, Jaina or other ethic on the impermanence of life and the inevitability of death, but that it is given a particular focus which may have been unacceptable to Valmiki, but which is consistent with the symbolic framework of thought at that time, and would therefore have been quite acceptable to the larger public of that period. The same process occurs in greater or lesser degree in various versions of the narratives of both epics. It would be more worthwhile to try and understand how and why these stories were incorporated into the tradition of a culture or society and the function that they performed as the media of ideologies (both religious and secular), values and social concerns, rather than to merely reiterate *ad infinitum,* the pan-Asian reach of the stories. What is worse is when attempts are made to annul all but one version from the Indian consciousness, which is happening with greater frequency these days.

The *Ramayana* in particular became the metaphor of kingship in areas where the state had newly arrived and kings had to claim status and a respectable past. Newly established kingdoms required the state to appropriate the metaphor. Royal temples in Indonesia and Cambodia for example demonstrate the acquisition of a past by appropriating the two epics and giving them a local gloss. It would seem, therefore, that the necessary groundwork on the epic tradition still awaits completion before we can enter meaningfully into a discussion on its historical authenticity, let alone the date of the events described. This will require not only a sifting of the strata and 'skins' of the epics and an analysis of the changing function and purpose of the literature from age to age and region to region, but also a rigorous questioning of the methodology of analysis. The 1975 controversy on variants of the story of Rama emerges partially out of the wish to determine the accuracy of the tradition, but more one suspects, out of the fear of attack on the bastion of tradition, as well as the desire to prove it right. This would appear so from the fact that the controversy has focused on statement and counter-statement rather than examining the methods used to arrive at the statements. Such a focus always carries the danger that what is being sought to be proven right is not the actual tradition, but what we today would like to interpret as the tradition, and this has to do with contemporary culture eliciting legitimacy from the idiom of the past.

12

THE EPIC OF THE BHARATAS

The *Mahabharata* calls itself itihasam-puratanam literally, thus indeed it was in times past. This is not a Rankean statement with definitive claims to historicity of persons and events in the narrative. However, there is a hint that some of the narrative may have been an attempt to cull from the remembered tradition, that which may have happened, even if what is culled is disordered in the retelling. The *Ramayana*, however, is most often described as a kavya, a poetic composition, in fact the adikavya, the earliest, suggesting a distinction between the two.

There have been many commentaries in Sanskrit on the epics from the eleventh to the seventeenth century examining their meaning and intention. An analysis of these could tell us about how the epic was perceived in periods prior to ours and by scholars whose intellectual roots would have differed somewhat from ours in many ways. One wonders, for instance, whether historicity as we understand it today, was of concern to the authors and to the audience of past times. Undoubtedly among the more attractive features of the epic, although historically tantalizing, are its many enigmas. Some however suggest the occasional facet of the historical past. The attempt in this essay is to point to these and indicate the problems they raise.

Epic as a genre uses narrative to represent situations from the past. It looks back nostalgically from the point in time when it is being composed and being given form, which is its present. The nostalgia is for a past age of heroes and the clans to which they belonged. This slowly gave way to the present where the heroes are less important, as now it is a society governed by kings and the code of caste. The nature of authority is more focused and therefore different in kingship, and the determining of status and social attitudes by reference to caste gradually becomes predictable.

Given that it spans more than one kind of society, re-examining the concepts we use in interpreting the epic becomes essential. Some are inflected by the translations we may use, since translation reflects the culture of the translator as encapsulated in the language. But knowing the two languages is in itself not a sufficient qualification. It is equally important to know the historical and cultural context of the text being translated. The context of the epic was that of clan societies and small-scale kingdoms. It is as well to remember that the term 'raja' did not in origin mean a king, but referred simply to 'the one who shines', an appropriate title for a chief. As such it is likely to have been continued when the system changed to kingship, although the nature of the authority of the raja had changed. To project the *Mahabharata* as a conflict among kings, together with the conventional definition that we give to kingship, is to give altogether different colour to the epic. To translate samrat as 'imperial monarch' is to impose a later meaning on an earlier term. A more accurate meaning might refer to the one 'who has authority over the many'. The context of the term can illumine its meaning.

Part of the transition from clan to kingdom also lay in the evolving form that was being given to varna and jati. The structure of clan societies did not require that they follow the rules of the *Dharmashastras* but a king ruling a kingdom generally had to uphold caste. There were of course exceptions such as Ashoka who does not mention caste in his edicts, although he refers to clans, but this was doubtless due to his heterodox thinking. There would certainly have been castes by the time of the Mauryas although possibly not as clearly defined as later in Manu's *Dharmashastra*.

The transition from clan to kingdom is vividly etched in the different nuances of how the clans functioned. The Vrishnis in Dvaraka in western India with their eighteen kulas, extended families or clans, conform to a distinctive way of functioning, reminiscent of chiefships. The Kauravas and the Pandavas battling for territory in the Doab and the western Ganga plain, still observe the rules of clan ethics and codes of kin relationships, but are seen to be slowly succumbing to the rules of kingship and the codes of caste, the pattern emerging in the easterly region of Magadha.

Authorship of the *Mahabharata* is attributed to Krishna Dvaipayana Vyasa, a brahmana of uncertain antecedents, born of the sage Parashara and a fisherwoman, and who is also said to have sired Dhritrashtra and Pandu. Authorship and fatherhood are coalesced and in effect Vyasa is narrating the lives of his own sons and grandsons. They in turn have no blood connection with the lineage of the Bharatas although they are constantly referred to as 'bull of the Bharatas'. The blood connection actually ended with Bhishma, unless of course his being called pitamaha—the paternal grandfather—is taken literally, despite his vow, in which case the story would have been different.

Genealogies can be accurate over a few generations but are also useful to those who wish to fabricate connections and latch on to a respectable ancestry. This fragment of the lineage has an equally ambiguous end since the lineage continues through Parikshit, who is stillborn but revived by Krishna—a termination that is converted into continuity. Possibly the invented connection was necessary since in the Vedic corpus the epithets used for the ancestor Puru, are not the most complimentary: his speech is described as mridhra-vach, impure, and he has an asura-rakshasa ancestry.

The epic recitation had two beginnings a generation apart. It was first recited by the brahmana Vaishampayana at the snake sacrifice of the kshatriya raja, Janamejaya (the son of Parikshit). A generation later it is recited at a sattra, a sacrificial ritual usually intended for, and performed by, brahmanas, although the recitation this time is by the bard Ugrashravas. A brahmana recites it to the kshatriyas and a non-brahmana to the brahmanas, an inversion that is curious. The epic as we know it was in origin the bard's memorization of what he had heard from the brahmana's recital, and there is an insistence that both renderings are exactly as composed originally by Vyasa. One is immediately suspicious about changes and interpolations. The interleaving of brahmana and bard as authors or the likelihood of bardic origins is not unexpected.

Some modern scholars have argued that the dasharajna, the battle of the ten rajas, described in the *Rigveda* was the seminal event that later gave rise to the idea of the battle at Kurukshetra. Some of the clans from the Vedic corpus such as the Bharatas, Purus, Yadus and Kuru-Pancalas reappear in the *Mahabharata* as lineage ancestors of the epic protagonists, but not necessarily in the same situations. Panini in the fourth century BC refers indirectly to grammatical constructions associated with words such as mahabharata, yudhishthira, arjuna and vasudeva.

Epic personalities have parallels in the Buddhist *Jataka* stories where persons with the same names occur in events that are often dissimilar to the epics. The secreting away of Krishna as a baby, his hostility as a young man to his uncle Kamsa at Mathura and the migration of his clan to Dvaraka, are part of the narrative of his clan, the Andhaka-Venhu/ Vrishni. Its end came through a drunken massacre, a story repeated in the Vaishnava texts. Neither Krishna nor his clan come off well in these stories. But as a contrast to this, stories of the descendants of Yudhishthira ruling the Kuru realm from Indraprastha and being advised by the minister Vidura-pandita are characterized by what is called Kuru righteousness, particularly noted for its virtue. Whether these variant versions were taken from the epic or contributed to the making of the epic, remains a debated subject. The ideological underpinning also differs.

The stories are not identical but may go back to a common source. The boxing-in of stories as in the epic is also a technique of adding to a narrative. Subsequently, when they were given an ideological gloss they served the needs of Buddhist ethics and later of Jaina versions, or the sectarian beliefs of Vaishnava Bhagavatism, each in disagreement with the other. The diversity of these initial fragments seems to be echoed in the varied regional versions and recensions of the epic, a process that continued through the centuries. This multiplicity makes it necessary sometimes to identify the version one is referring to.

The composition was doubtless in the nature of a slow accretion as is characteristic of the early epic genre virtually anywhere. Nevertheless at some point it was brought together. Tradition has it that a small text, the *Jaya*, became larger, as the *Bharata*, and the larger became still larger, as the *Mahabharata*. It is, therefore, virtually impossible to calculate a date for the events and to define an 'epic period' in ancient history as was once done.

This would also be one reason for the difficulty in identifying a particular archaeological site as the archaeological equivalent of a location in the epic. Excavations have been conducted at locations that are called Hastinapur and Indraprastha. These could be ancient sites although we know that place names also travel, especially with migrant populations. Distances on the ground do not always tally with the text. In today's identifications these two places were a considerable journey away from the present-day site of Kurukshetra, the possible location of the battlefield. Equating a site with a text can raise problems of reconciling material culture with evocations of poetic licence. Will we ever find the fantasy palace of the Pandavas built by the magic of Asura Maya even if we believe it existed and dig up the whole of Indraprastha? Homer's epic met with similar problems after the extensive excavations at Troy and other sites.

The epic maintains that the battle at Kurukshetra took place on the cusp of the Kaliyuga. The latter has been dated as equivalent to 3102 BC. Dates calculated on the basis of the genealogical lists of kshatriya lineages in the *Puranas* generally work out to between 1200-1000 BC. There is archaeological evidence of a heavy silt deposit at the site of Haṣtinapur dating to about 800 BC. This has been linked to the epic's reference to a flood after the war. Mention of Yavanas, Shakas, Hunas, would be interpolations in the late BCs and early centuries AD.

V.S. Sukthankar, to whom the Critical Edition of the epic owes much, argued that the epic's composition ranged from 400 BC to AD 400. More recently other scholars have suggested that the oral epic was put together as a text in about 150 BC and that this may have taken a century or so. Attempts have been made to correlate readings in astronomy with references to planetary configurations in the epic. These differ and would relate not to the text as a whole but to particular segments carrying the reference. Diversity in dates also makes it problematic to attribute authorship to a single author. The meaning of Vyasa is interestingly, one who edits and arranges.

To add to the complexity it has been argued that the epic had two intentions. The earliest narrative was constructed out of fragmentary stories of the heroic: tales of combats, marriages, games of dice, exile in the forest—and were probably formulaic on occasion. The same process has been noticed in the Homeric epics. For the bard, exile comes in handy as it can be stretched with add-ons heightening the reach of the imagination. Heroic exploits can be enlarged with every recitation, whether the hero is wandering across the 'wine-dark seas' of the Mediterranean as in the *Odyssey* or in the tangled forests of northern India as in the *Mahabharata*. Exile to the forest in India reinforced the dichotomy of grama—settlement, and aranya—forest, central to cultural perceptions.

It was probably the immense popularity of the epic, both as a linear narrative of the heroic as well as in the embroidered intricacies of the stories, that led to the second intention and reformulation—its conversion into a Bhagavata text. Sukthankar argued that this was done by the

Bhrigu brahmanas who also 'Bhriguised' the *Ramayana*. Both Krishna and Rama became avataras of Vishnu and this changed the character of the epic. It is worth noting that on the second occasion of its recitation the bard was required to proclaim the descent of the Bhrigu Lineage, perhaps to legitimize the Bhrigus and their appropriation of the epic.

The Bhrigus, were often linked to the Angirasa brahmanas, associated with the *Atharva Veda* and among other things, regarded as the practitioners of sorcery and magic. Neither group was the most highly respected among learned brahmanas. The Bhrigus were called brahma-kshatra, as they married kshatriya women. Their learning extended into knowledge and custom beyond the conventional, and in addition they were said to know niti and dharma, the codes of conduct and ethics.

The question could be asked that if the Bhrigus were not pre-eminent brahmanas why were they permitted to reformulate the epic. Epic origins lay in popular compositions not in divine revelation; therefore they were not as sacred as the *Vedas*. The Bhrigus may have wished to convert the epic into a Bhagavata sectarian text, if they were associated with early Bhagavatism. The didactic section was the palatable way of preaching the various brahmanical dharmas. The *Mahabharata* can be viewed as a civilizational text not because it reflects the propagation of a particular view of these dharmas but because, among other things, it speaks to the debate on social ethics, especially between the brahmanical perspective and those that question it—a debate that has continued over many centuries.

The Bhagavata religion was not identical with the Vedic even if the *Mahabharata* is referred to as the fifth *Veda*—as indeed was the itihasa-purana itself, and many other bodies of knowledge. The Bhrigu brahmanas may have had associations with pre-Vedic and non-Vedic ideas as has been suggested. In one *Upanishad* the Bhrigu-Angirasas are linked to the itihasa-purana. This would, up to a point, make them appropriate editors of texts pertaining to the past. Nevertheless the controversy on 'Bhriguisation' continues.

Why the Bhagavata reformulation was necessary needs an explanation. Perhaps the realization that the Buddhist gloss on popular stories was a successful way of propagating sectarian belief may have encouraged the Bhagavatas to do the same. Buddhism was subordinating the worship of clan deities to the higher ideal of the ethic of dharma as defined by the Buddha. Bhagavatism required the worship of Vishnu as the supreme deity and the varna dharma, the code of caste, was its social ethic, both of which incidentally reinforced the requirements of kingship. This subsequent addition has left a heavy imprint on the *Mahabharata* and the epic genre of the text has tended to be subordinated. It is to this genre that I would like to give more space.

The first few books narrate the epic of the Kauravas and the Pandavas and take the story, together with whatever is tagged onto the narrative, to the point where war is imminent. The description of person and event veers towards the functioning of a clan-based society. It conforms in the main to the pattern of lineages functioning as segments of an extensive network. The *Puranas* a little later called it the Chandravamsha, the Lunar Lineage. This was one of the two lineages into which kshatriya clans of early times were divided. The other was, predictably, the Suryavamsha or Solar Lineage. The *Ramayana* is the epic of the Solar Lineage. Identity is through being born into a clan, kinship controls relationships and social functions, governance is through an assembly of the heads of families, and status is relatively egalitarian within the clan.

Agro-pastoralism is the major source of income with an emphasis on cattle herding as also cattle-raids, mentioned in the epic. The *Vedas* also refer to the Kuru-Pancala clans going out in 'the dewy season' to raid cattle. The more spectacular sacrificial rituals asserting the political authority of the patron, such as the rajasuya performed by Yudhishthira, are occasions for bringing in the tribute and the gifts. These are largely in the form of the produce of hunting and herding, and of weaving textiles. Wealth is measured in gold and gemstones and in numbers of domestic slaves—mainly women. Agricultural activity is of course a necessity but tends to be low key. Dependence on agriculture increases in the later parts of the text. Items of wealth initially placed as stakes in the game of dice are as listed above but of larger amounts. Ultimately, Yudhishthira stakes the town, the territory and himself and then Draupadi.

The listing of wealth is in substantial if not exaggerated terms. Such occasions have been thought to be rituals but also gift-giving ceremonies, characteristic functions of heads of clans. On special occasions, the chief collects, consumes, distributes and if need be, even destroys what remains of his wealth. The ritual of the rajasuya sacrifice was one such occasion with inevitable consequences. The intention to assert status leads in turn to a competition among clan chiefs, each trying to outdo the other. Therefore gift-giving is not a one-way process. It assumes that the holding of these ceremonies turn by turn by important chiefs of clans ensures the circulation of whatever wealth is produced. This prevents one among them from acquiring excessive power through accumulating enormous wealth. Should this happen conflict may be unavoidable. The items brought to the yajna, the ritual of sacrifice, come as gifts and tribute and not as tax. There is also an exchange between the one who holds the ritual, the patron referred to as the yajamana, and the ritual specialist, the brahmanas who perform the ritual. The ritual legitimizes the status of the chief, and the priests receive substantial material wealth in the form of dana (gifts) and dakshina, (the fee). The exchange involves tangible wealth for the one and an intangible gain for the other.

The clans were described as kshatriyas, their status dependent not on caste but on the hierarchy among the clans. Identity came from the clan. Hence the emphasis on genealogies, all of which may or may not have been taken literally, the social forms reflected in their structure also being significant. Breaks in the genealogy can be indicators of change.

That the rules of caste were not strictly observed would explain why three disparate systems of marriage are adopted over two consecutive generations in the family of Pandu. In Pandu's marriage to Madri it would seem that a bride-price was involved, even if not in material goods, that is, that some concession had to be given by the husband to his wife or her family. Some manner of exchange was involved. This made it an asura form of marriage according to the *Dharmashastras*. The fraternal polyandry of the five Pandavas marrying Draupadi is outside any *Dharmashastra* scheme and is discussed at some length in the epic before it is accepted. Draupadi questioning Yudhishthira's right to stake her in the dicing match is not the kind of statement that conforms to the patriarchal values advised for wifely behaviour in the social codes. The three women who command the narrative are Draupadi who poses the question of the legality of Yudhishthira's right over her, Kunti who chooses the deities she wants as surrogate husbands, and Gandhari who insists on being permanently blindfolded after her marriage to a blind husband.

The third variant form, and quite legal, was that of Arjuna's marriage to Subhadra. It was a cross-cousin marriage generally associated with the south in the caste codes. Arjuna's marriage involved abducting Subhadra, and this goes by the name of a rakshasa form according to the *Dharmashastras.* The Vrishnis are literally up in arms at this and Krishna has to calm them down. The lineage continues through their still-born grandson, Parikshit, who was revived by Krishna. Such flexible social practices suggest societies undergoing immense change where alien practices and custom could be incorporated to accommodate a new situation.

Krishna's clan, the Andhaka-Vrishni, had a lower status than the Kurus. Political functioning among them lay in the sangha or assembly where the senior kinsmen of the eighteen kulas, extended families, sat to take decisions and were the effective decision-makers. In kingdoms, the assembly was reduced to an advisory body whose views were not binding on the king. The concentration of power required in kingship perhaps accounts in part for the hostility of the Vrishni clans towards Magadha. The kingdom of Magadha was a challenge to the gana-sanghas, the clans conforming to chiefships and opposed to kingship as a form of political functioning. Eventually the clan confederacy of Vaishali was destroyed by the kingdom of Magadha through devious means leading to the consolidation of kingship as a political system.

Beyond the clans was the non-caste 'Other', treated by the heroes as virtually bereft of human value, as is apparent at various points of the narrative. These were the people of the forest such as the Nishada and the Shabara, and the excluded and impure mleccha and therefore dispensable. The episode that has been commented on is that of Eklavya, who, surpassing Arjuna in archery but being a Nishada, what we would call a tribal, had to give his thumb as a fee to the brahmana guru, thus terminating his skill as an archer. But equally traumatic is the reference to how a Nishada woman and her five sons were left in the house of lac, which was set on fire to mislead the Kauravas about the presence of the Pandavas. As a comment on clan society this requires explanation, unless it can be argued that such episodes were introduced later when the mleccha were treated as less than human.

The battle at Kurukshetra forms a substantial section of the epic. As a time-marker it touches many dimensions. It marks the end of clan societies. Krishna's comment is telling: *sarvam kshatram kshayam gatam*—

literally, all the kshatra (constituted of kshatriyas) has been destroyed. It is said that the end of the war marked the end of the Dvapara age—the third of the four ages—and the start of the fourth and final, Kaliyuga—the present age. The theory of the four yugas is referred to in various texts of the post-Mauryan period and was probably not in the early epic. It seems to have been a later reflection on a substantial historical change expressed literally as the coming of a new age. As with exile, war is another occasion for the bard-poet to show his skill, so the narrative extends over many parvans, books, of the epic. Despite references to formations of standing armies familiar with warfare in later periods, the battle was essentially heroic warfare and often single combat—thus allowing for some of the dubious manoeuvres attributed to Krishna's advice.

That the war was pushed by Draupadi's demand for revenge is an epic-heroic feature. So too was the fact that the succession was contested by the absence of unchallenged primogeniture, both brothers being physically disabled. It was probably in origin a clan conflict involving those that had claims on the territory and their friends or enemies. Enlarged into a massive eighteen-day event it was said to have involved clans from all over. That this was an exaggeration is suggested by Arjuna arguing about the futility of war prior to the event and Yudhishthira doing so after the event. Validating violence becomes a necessity. The simile of the battle being a yajana, a ritual of sacrifice, is also introduced in support of war.

Although the *Bhagvad Gita* is placed in the narrative just before the start of the war, its teaching seems more appropriate to the society that emerged after the war. Arjuna, dismayed by the thought that he would have to kill his close kinsmen, questions the ethics of such an act. The killing of kinsmen seems to have been more heinous in a society where kinship was a primary identity than in a society where kin ties were subsumed in caste. Krishna speaking from the perspective of a caste society explains to Arjuna that as a kshatriya it is his svadharma, the social obligation required of members of a caste, to fight against evil even if it means killing kinsmen. Is the moral dilemma being subordinated to caste duty?

As has been pointed out in some recent studies the urgency of this discourse most likely had to do with the debate then current on ahimsa, provoked by Buddhist and Jaina teaching, and by the alternative ideal of kingship propagated by Ashoka. In the latter the social ethic is not dependent on caste but on the quality of human behaviour as encapsulated in the definition of dhamma—righteousness, virtue. This may have been the context to Yudhishthira questioning the model of kingship and Bhishma having to defend it in the rajadharma discourse. Judging by inscriptional evidence, support for Buddhism and Jainism at all levels of society was extensive in the post-Mauryan period and there would doubtless have been at least ideological confrontations with the code of the *Dharmashastras*. Is the Shantiparvan then a polemic in the debate with the heterodoxy? Yet as has been argued there is also the play on Yudhishthira being the son of the deity Dharma and that should have enhanced his sensitivity to the question of ethics.

The later part of the epic, sometimes described as the didactic sections, although these were scattered briefly elsewhere as well, begins effectively after the end of the war and consists substantially of the much-quoted Shantiparvan and Anushasanaparvan. These are important in themselves but in some ways represent a discourse outside the epic. To discuss the epic largely on the basis of these sections as is sometimes done is to do it an injustice.

Bhishma wounded in the war and lying on his bed of arrows holds forth on the benefits of kingship. His long peroration on various categories of dharma and even on situations where it fails, is significant in these political transitions. Kingship as a political form is viewed implicitly as superior to what existed before or what continued as an alternate system. Yudhishthira, appalled by the violence of war, is reluctant to assume kingship and wishes to retreat to the forest, but is eventually persuaded not to renounce kingship. The discourse by Bhishma is almost certainly a later interpolation of the time when the gana-rajyas, chiefships, had declined—but not disappeared—and in many places had been replaced by kingdoms.

The discussions on rajadharma—the code for kingship and administration—on punishment, on times of distress, run parallel to themes in texts such as Kautilya's *Arthashastra* and Manu's *Dharmashastra*; not to mention the continuing memory of the Mauryan state. Kautilya's list of what constitutes a state system assumes a kingdom ruled by a king with decision-making powers, through an administration manned by non-kinsmen, located in a capital city to which the revenue comes via taxes, and where the kingdom is identified by demarcated territory, defended by a regular standing army and where other kings are allies or enemies. The didactic sections where these features are taken as normal were in a sense looking back at the epic past, but were legitimizing the coming change to kingdoms. The change was not linear nor was it clearly determined. It was somewhat meandering with various offshoots. In some cases earlier forms may have continued, as we know that they did historically until much later. But that such a change was represented in the eventual version seems apparent. What I am suggesting is not a dichotomy between clan-society and the kingdom, nor a textbook version of each, but the difference in societies with more of one and less of the other.

This essay is only one passing historical perspective of the *Mahabharata*. Even from historians there are many more. And beyond them the perspectives multiply still further. The narrative of the epic is sequential, set in a frame of linear chronology, nevertheless there are substratum layers of structures, order, legitimation, and claims that seem extraneous to the narrative but are insightful. What is perhaps being indicated in all this is that historicity should not be sought for only in person and event, for it may lie at a deeper level.

In the interface of the two kinds of societies that I have sketched, partially sequential and partially concurrent, there lies what might be seen as a historical tradition—the tradition of a later society remembering and reconstructing what it believes to be the earlier one—where the reconstruction becomes the perceived past. Perhaps it is because of this that the *Mahabharata* can call itself itihasam puratanam.

13

THE RAMAYANA SYNDROME

The opinions that were gathered by newspapers when Ramanand Sagar's TV serial on the *Ramayana* ended revealed what an extraordinary media success it had been. The show's popularity reached out across religions, castes, occupations, languages. Was this because it was an emotion-filled story narrated in the style of TV serials; or the enactment of a religious belief in a new idiom associated with modern life? Is there an intrinsic attraction in fantasies on good vs. evil that have a particular appeal if they claim to represent past times? It was stated that its popularity resulted from its being a part of the collective unconscious; that among adults it evoked memories of childhood stories and among children it paralleled the exploits of a hero like Superman; that it was an embodiment of higher values and laid out the quest for dharma in a simple, narrative form; that it projected the ideal woman in Sita; that it appeased the apprehensions and insecurities of a society transitioning to modernity; that it gave visual form to the spiritual fountainhead of Hinduism. Those who were unhappy with the rendering complained of the absence of poetry and meaning. It was also described as a folk genre, a small town Ramlila that managed to hit the big lights by being broadcast on television.

Only a few seemed concerned about the long-term effects of such a serial. Were we perhaps witnessing an attempt to project what the new culture of the country should be, an attempt to expunge diversities and present a homogenized view of what the *Ramayana* was and is? Could the serial be seen as part of an increasing trend of treating the state as the arch patron of culture, of state patronage requiring a uniform culture with the state determining the manifestations of culture, whether it be the festivals, the media or the aims behind the cultural zones? The state defines culture, finances culture, is the final arbiter and as the patron bestows recognition on those whom it regards as creative and worthy. Private initiative cannot compete with the financial outlay and the public reach that the state can provide, and there is not enough public initiative to provide alternate avenues to support innovatory forms. Would private initiative support innovation or would it encourage the conventional and the conservative?

The state prefers to endorse a uniform, homogenized culture, as such a culture would be simple to identify and easy to control. To concede that a nation's culture may be constituted of a variety of cultural systems would require that the functionaries of the state be sensitive to these multiple cultural systems and respond to their political implications. Where culture is taken over by the state as the major patron, there the politics of culture is inevitably heightened. It is therefore often easier for the state as patron to adopt a particular cultural stream as the mainstream: a cultural hegemony that frequently coincides with the culture of the dominant social group.

Some would see this new extension of patronage by the state as legitimate, for the state is now expected to provide for everything. But others would see this as a threat to creativity. The relationship between the patron and the one who creates, is delicate, where, although the patron controls finance and recognition, the patron is at best merely the agency for the act of creativity. In earlier times acts of creativity had an audience but could do without a patron, although the more elaborate arts and literature required a patron. That creativity today is far more dependent on patronage, requiring the patron to be particularly careful about the representation of culture, particularly where culture is being represented through the authoritative state-controlled media. I would like to illustrate this by reference to the *Ramayana*.

The *Ramayana* does not belong to any one moment in history for it has its own history which lies embedded in the many versions which were woven around the theme at different times and places, even within its own history in the Indian subcontinent. The Indian epics were never frozen as were the compositions of Homer when they changed from an oral to a literate form. Professional reciters, kathakaras, recited the written versions with their own commentary and frequently adjusted the story to contemporary norms. The appropriation of the story by a multiplicity of groups meant a multiplicity of versions through which the social aspirations and ideological concerns of each group were articulated. The story in these versions included significant variations that changed the conceptualization of character, event and meaning.

Even within the literate tradition there are substantial differences. Scholars working on the *Ramayana* argue that the now non-existent original ramakatha was perhaps worked over and added to by Valmiki. This version may then have been changed by the Bhargava brahmana redactors who introduced the concept of Rama being an avatara of Vishnu, thus transforming the epic into sacred literature, a transformation that in the past captured popular literature for didactic purposes. Parallel to this was the Buddhist rendering in some of the *Jatakas,* whereas in the *Dasaratha Jataka,* Sita is the sister of Rama which change in the kinship pattern is reflected in Buddhist origin myths and carries its own meaning.

A Jaina version, the *Paumacharyam,* claims to be the sole authentic version of the story and maintains this unequivocally. The treatment of Ravana in this text is much more sympathetic. Lanka is as important if not more so than Ayodhya and the events are coloured by Jaina ethics. Thus Dasharatha and Rama end up as Jaina munis and Sita gets herself to a nunnery. The earliest Tamil version by Kampan changes the treatment of Ravana who is here the tragic hero rather than the villainous demon. The religious importance of the story increased in the early second millennium AD with the spread of the Ramanandin sect that worshipped Vishnu in his incarnation as Rama and their most popular sacred literature was the sixteenth century work of Tulasidasa, the *Ramacharitamanas.*

Even within the literate tradition the significance of these variations is not ignored. The differences highlight the varying perceptions of many aspects of the story, more than are underlined in any one of the various versions, such as notions of ethical behaviour, whether it be the ideal of the kshatriya in the brahmanical version or the ideal of the Jaina ascetic in the *Paumacharyam*; or the idea of historicity, where the Jaina version claims it, but the brahmanical one ignores it; or of the depiction of Ravana as the personification of evil or as a tragic hero; or of the embodiment of women where the role of Sita varies. These were not simply variations in the story to add flavour to the narrative. They were conscious attempts at taking up a well-known theme and using it to present a new point of view arising out of ideological and social differences of perspective.

These were acts of deliberate innovation, where the creator of the form, felt free to experiment with the story even after the story had been given a sacred character by brahmana redactors. These variants were not hidden in some obscure treatise. They took the form of popular narratives, recited and written in Pali and Prakrit and later in regional languages, and therefore available to large numbers of people. If we are to be aware of at least this strand of our cultural tradition then the debate and the dialectic embedded in these various versions should be more openly discussed.

What would happen today if an attempt were made to project on TV a different version of the story. It is likely that Doordarshan or any other channel would not allow it, arguing that it would hurt the religious sensibilities of the majority community. Even if an attempt were to be made to put it not on the media, but only as a play, the self-appointed guardians of Hinduism, such as the Shiv Sena, VHP, RSS, Bajrang Dal and similar organizations, would prevent its being staged. The assault of the Shiv Sena on a theatre in Bombay and the beating up of the playwright, where a play was to be performed on the interlocking theme of Rama and Sita and Romeo and Juliet, is an indication of what would happen. Unfortunately, public protest has been too ineffectual to counteract such attitudes. But if the state or whomsoever else claims to be the major patron of culture, such incidents require at least a statement from the patron.

If the state as the main patron of culture withdraws from innovations in creativity on the grounds that it will hurt the sentiments of a 'religious community', culture will tend to be reduced to the lowest common denominator. The interface between religion, politics and culture becomes a central issue in this situation. Religious sects of various beliefs in India—Hindu, Muslim, Sikh, Christian, Animist—are characterized by a relative absence of the equivalent of the fiat from the Vatican. Who then speaks for that nebulous mass which is referred to as a 'religious community'? Those that force the issue on the state taking action on cultural or intellectual items are not always the religious functionaries of a community, but often the political spokesmen of some group claiming to represent a religious community.

Thus the Shiv Sena can once again object to the government of Maharashtra reprinting a chapter of Dr Ambedkar's book because it questions the authenticity of the brahmanical version of the *Ramayana* among other things, and the government bends. It may not even be a question of objecting to the suppression of the views of Ambedkar *per se,* but of allowing various readings of a cultural tradition. Or another person demands the banning of Salman Rushdie's book *The Satanic Verses*, and again the government accedes to this demand. Predictably the next step is that the government anticipates a demand from some Christian groups to ban *The Last Temptation of Christ* and yet once more it caves in under pressure and bans the film. Are we going to be left then with laundered strips of culture because the patron, the state or whatever the agency of authority cannot distinguish between claims to religious sensibilities and cultural articulation?

Our politics are being increasingly conditioned by appeals to the sentiments of various religious communities enhancing the politicizing of religion. But at the same time we insist that religion is sacrosanct and cannot therefore be treated as a political ideology despite its having become a political ideology in association with the communalism of various religious groups. How long will we continue to use this political blackmail, of a threat that something will hurt or hurts the religious sensibilities of a community, in order to keep religion as a convenient ploy with which to play politics? This is all the more objectionable in a society that has traditionally been open to intellectual and cultural discourse even where it is conducted through religious texts.

A statement repeated ad nauseum is that of tolerance being a value characteristic of Indian civilization. There has been little attempt to analyze the nature of this tolerance. It assumed a segmented society in which each caste functioned in accordance with its own dharma and the totality was juxtaposed and co-existed. Intolerance was effective within each caste but by and large other castes were left alone to do and believe as they pleased. All of course except those that were treated as outside caste—those whom we now call tribals and Dalits. They had a permanent rank at the bottom. Polemics were in fact an essential part of ideology and belief. Now that we are moving away from a segmented society, we have to consciously acquire a concern for tolerance that includes the entire society. We can retain tolerance only if we refrain from rushing to censorship of all kinds.

Tolerance does not grow with banning what is thought to be unpalatable; it grows with arguing and talking about it; for that which is unpalatable gets discarded. Before a book or a film or an exhibition is banned there should at least be a debate about why it is necessary to do so. There was no attempt to discuss what had actually been said in *The Satanic Verses* and the issues involved. Those who demanded the ban blatantly stated that they had not read the book. Those who rushed to ban it had not read it either. To demand the immediate banning of the book was shrewd as it also pre-empted any discussion, even among Muslims, on the issues raised in the book. Such a discussion might have revealed differences of opinion, differences indicating that not every Indian wanted the book banned and there were many that wanted it discussed to ascertain what exactly was being attacked in the book. And such discussions are imperative even for those who have a strong religious identity of any kind, if, as a society, we are to break the siege of communalism.

Let me return to the *Ramayana* and its different versions. The authorship included bards, brahmanas, monks, local storytellers. Change in authorship and social setting introduced new features. Even those aspects that are regarded as intrinsic to the story, such as the birth of Sita from the furrow, and the ten heads of Ravana, were at one point, innovations. So too were other events, as for example, the notion of the shadow Sita—that the real Sita was not the one who went through the agni pariksha, the fire ordeal, but an illusory or shadow Sita, for the real Sita returned to Rama. This innovation has been explained as deriving from the advaita-vedanta philosophy and the doctrine of maya. Possibly a more immediate reason was the influence of the Shakti cults, where a woman was viewed as an embodiment of power and the indignity of a fire ordeal to prove chastity may not have been easily accepted. This episode might even reflect the debate on sati that was prevalent at the time, since the self-immolation of a widow, was supposed to lead to reunion with her husband and the sati was regarded as a symbol of chastity.

The gradual diffusion of the story influenced the folk genres and the result was something very different from the literary tradition of upper caste culture. One of the major areas of difference focused on the depiction of Sita. I have recently been informed that in one tribal version, the fire ordeal is performed not by Sita or a shadow Sita; but by another woman substituted for the purpose, the tribal Shabari.

This speaks volumes for the way in which a tribal society perceives its relationship with the mainstream culture.

Tamil speaking societies derive their version from Kampan or from a variety of local forms, which were earlier recited but during this century have come to be published and are now read. A recent discussion on this genre focuses on the *Catakantaravana-katai,* or the story of the ten-headed Ravana. Here it is Sita who, with Rama as her charioteer, goes into battle against Ravana. In single combat she is the one who kills Ravana. Clearly the imprint of the powerful, assertive, goddess figure overrides the more accommodating and submissive image of the Sanskrit and Hindi texts. These are not marginal traditions for they are central to the societies from which they emerge. If it is claimed that Indian culture, as being propagated by the state, is representative of the Indian people and not just of a small segment of Indian society, then these variants must also find a place.

The question then is that of whose version of the story are we propagating? What was shown on TV and has now become the received version was essentially a mix of the Valmiki *Ramayana* and the *Ramacharitamanas* of Tulasidasa. The choice of this version must have a reason: perhaps because it is best known among Hindi speakers and is therefore familiar to north Indians? Epic-type compositions need not be religious documents in origin. But some versions of an epic story can be transformed into religious statements as happened with the later version of the Valmiki *Ramayana.*

The TV version is not a folk genre. It borrows from the films of the 1940s and 1950s, the 'mythologicals', and it borrows from the Ramlilas. The latter are again prevalent in the region where Hindi is spoken, for in other parts of the country, these festivals associated with Rama have other connotations and rituals, such as the widespread Durga puja. But what is absent from the TV version is the incorporation of the folksiness and the comedy of the Ramlilas. Local issues and local commentary gave a flavour and vibrancy to these performances. If the literary version in Sanskrit attempted to freeze the rendering of earlier centuries, the TV version may now have the same effect on future Ramlilas. Curiously and perhaps as a consequence of the TV version, local Ramlilas and their audiences from the neighbouring mohallas, seem to have declined especially in the larger cities. Yet these multiple and connecting versions had and still have legitimacy since they are statements of a social condition and a historical moment. Received versions deny the legitimacy of others as also the idea that a society does not have a single culture but is a collation of cultures.

Culture is not an object. It is among other things a way of conducting social relationships expressed in various idioms. State patronage and direction of culture tends to look for a single 'national culture'. It tends to take on the perspective of the dominant group and the culture of this group is projected as the mainstream national culture. This happens where the state may not be the main patron of culture. The media for instance envisages the cultural ideal as that adopted by the middle class and it aspires to appropriate and project that culture. Cultural hegemony requires the marginalizing or ironing out of other cultural expressions. Those who complain against this hegemony and argue that to treat Ramanand Sagar's version as the received version is to display poverty in understanding Indian culture, are for some strange reason described as deracinated, westernized Indians, out of touch with the culture of the masses. They are dismissed as 'elitists' seeking to dictate cultural norms, forgetting of course that in the system described, choice is anyway restricted and the so-called 'elitists' are in fact supporting a more extensive choice. What is also surprising in this context is that no comment is made on some of the more glaring examples of deracination and elitism seeking to influence cultural choices, namely, the majority of the advertisements that precede and follow the sponsored programmes on TV.

The enthusiasm of the masses has been repeatedly invoked in justifying the TV version as an expression of national culture. Which masses are we invoking? Those below the poverty line who are unable to come within watching distance of a TV set? Or are we referring to the urban underclass who have access to a neighbourhood set? Even if it is the latter, one wonders what they make of the commentary spoken by Ashok Kumar, who, like the bard of older times, introduces after each episode, parallels with contemporary life. When the young princes of Ayodhya are sent at a tender age to the gurukula for training, and their mothers are saddened by their departure, Ashok Kumar introduces the parallel of young children today going to boarding school—hardly an experience with which the masses would be familiar.

When supernatural weapons, the brahma-astras, swirl and zig-zag across the screen, the commentator compares them to the weapons in *Star Wars*—perhaps a subtle appeal to the wishful thought that Indian civilization once might have had space-age weapons, and certainly an endorsement of such weaponry. The depiction of the demons who threaten the noble rishis and whom Rama and Lakshmana are fetched to destroy, are so evidently the physical type associated with tribal peoples that the message of their being alien and evil hardly needs stating in words. If the TV version is fulfilling the live role of the storyteller in the life of the young child, then what are the nuances that it portrays? Comics drawing on these stories and the TV version are part of an urban child's fantasy. The versions that had a universal appeal also had a different kind of message. Are we really talking about an appeal to the masses or are we talking about the expanding middle class and other aspirants to the same status?

Tulasi's *Ramacharitamanas* did have an appeal for caste Hindus. The upsetting of caste hierarchies and the rise of low castes to positions of status did not auger well especially in the Kali age. A return to a rama-rajya would set society on the right course. If each man functions according to his allotted caste then all is right with the world. The notion of rama-rajya does have a widespread appeal. It is a generalized millennarian dream that envisages the well-being of all. It does not go into the question of social inequities. To romanticize hierarchy is one way of supporting it and the message means different things to those at the upper levels and to those down below. The appeal to the latter is the religious message. The religious wrapping around the past tended to hide the political message. But it could not altogether hide the political message when the actor cast as Rama campaigned on behalf of the Congress-I in the Allahabad election in the early 1990s and his role on TV was constantly referred to. If religion is reduced to a vote-catching mechanism then the consequences can only be very different from the avowed goals of either the state or the religion.

The religious message of the Tulasidasa version is stated in no uncertain terms. Tulasidasa repeats that the only thing of supreme importance is Rama-bhakti—unqualified devotion to Rama as the incarnation of Vishnu, to which his text is dedicated. Clearly this rendering of the *Ramayana* theme has to be differentiated from the many others which either identify with other religions and ideologies or else are genuine folk genres where such identities are subordinated or are at any rate less sectarian. The very specific identity of the Tulasidasa version cannot be extended to include the picking up of the theme and its alteration in other religious traditions (including incidentally Islamic features in Indonesian and Malaysian versions).

There have been statements by the public, commenting on the serial in defence of the right of the Hindus to see their religious literature on TV. It is said that the majority of Indians are Hindus and therefore a public broadcasting system and television has a duty to bow to the tastes and preferences of the majority. This is a statement that may be seen as impinging on the government's policy towards programmes on the audio-visual media and would require a response from a secular government. If the media had been autonomous, as has often been urged by various government appointed committees, then the onus would not be on the government. But since the media are government controlled, the government is responsible for the categories of programmes it is supporting and the influence of these programmes on public issues, not to mention concepts of culture. If the state is anxious to be the patron par excellence, one assumes that it is aware of what it is patronizing.

Of course the Ramanand Sagar version has a popular appeal. It is the world of Indian middle-class fantasy, in which problems arise but are miraculously solved. Its presentation through spectacular sets, glittering costumes and ham acting, matches up to these fantasies. And we all need fantasies, ranging from those who have avidly watched the serial every Sunday, to those who play Dungeons and Dragons with the computer, or others like me who read science fiction.

One's anxieties about the *Ramayana* syndrome arise from other causes: that the fantasy of one social group should not be projected as the fantasy of the entire society, for the essence of cultural renewal is the freedom to innovate and to use changing idioms even for themes regarded as traditional or sacred—as indeed was done in the past; that culture be treated not as a single, homogenized, national package, but as free intersecting cultural systems reflecting the assumptions of all the constituents of Indian society; and lastly, the question of whether the state realizes that behind every fantasy there lies a reality and the fantasies of some can be in conflict with those of others. Is the state aware of the reality behind this particular fantasy?

14

IN DEFENCE OF THE VARIANT

In the 1988 Annual Number of *Seminar* (353), I had written about the variant versions of the ramakatha and expressed my fears that the television version as well as the politics of the Ramjanmabhoomi would drive out all versions of the story that did not conform to those of Valmiki or Tulasidasa. I had mentioned specifically that it was unlikely now, that a Buddhist version as narrated in the *Dasaratha Jataka* would be permitted a public performance, given the facility with which the Sangh Parivar has set itself up as the arbiter in matters relating to the sentiments of all Hindus. The validity of this view was demonstrated in the reaction to a brief mention of this version in one of the panels of an exhibition on Ayodhya organized by Sahmat: the *Dasaratha Jataka* has become a cause celebre. More recently there was opposition to the variant versions of the story and this time it came unexpectedly from the Delhi University. It would seem that most academics are as ignorant of the Indian past as are most politicians. The incident began with student members of the ABVP (Akhand Bharatiya Vidyarthi Parishad), the student wing of the BJP, arriving at the History Department, and demanding the removal of an essay by AK Ramanujan—the much respected literary critic and poet—on the many versions of the Ramayana story prescribed for reading as part of the History syllabus. They then proceeded to vandalize the office and assault the then head of the department, Professor Jaffri. Having informed various TV channels in advance, the proceedings were filmed and shown in the news later that day. A PIL (Public-Interest Ligitation) was then filed in the court making the same demand and giving the same reason (that it hurt Hindu religious sentiments). The History Department put up a fight against the demand, drawing attention to why the essay was regarded as excellent and was necessary to the syllabus. A committee of four historians was appointed to give a verdict on the matter of which three were in agreement with the department and the fourth was somewhat ambivalent. Soon after, at a meeting of the Academic Council the matter came up for discussion. Neither the Vice-Chancellor nor many of those who opposed the stand of the History Department appeared to have read the essay since they kept referring to it as a book. The Academic Council by an almost unanimous vote decided that the essay should be withdrawn from the syllabus.

The collapse of the Academic Council of the Delhi University was pathetic given that a university is precisely a place where students are expected to discuss variants and alternative readings, and to understand how statements of various kinds are to be evaluated. If variant versions are going to be objected to, then we will be left with just a single, received version. The richness of the theme and the ways in which it has captured the cultural imagination of the people of India through the centuries and why, are no longer legitimate subjects of research.

What was startling about the earlier denunciation of the brief statement of the Sahmat exhibition was that the entire political spectrum went down like a row of nine-pins. Not a single politician enquired into what this version was and its meaning, but rather they all rushed to join in the denunciation, so as to share in what the Sangh Parivar saw was the ignorance about the *Jataka* stories, about their Buddhist connection and meaning. This from people who preach to us ad nauseum about preserving our cultural heritage and the wisdom of the ancient texts. Some referred to the *Jataka* as 'some old book'; another wanted to know what the Rama story had to do with Jakarta, but he was not referring to the Indonesian versions of the story.

The *Jataka* was a collection of popular stories intended for an audience of common people and therefore frequently borrowed themes from stories familiar to the general public. The stories were originally part of an oral tradition and were incorporated into texts at a later date. As an oral tradition they had common currency and were obviously well-liked or else they would not have been incorporated into the texts. They were not exclusive stories meant for a limited audience. The themes were used in many narratives and changed according to need and some of these went into the making of the *Ramayana* and the *Mahabharata*.

Epics often draw on the oral tradition of stories and frequently fragmentary narratives are strung together. There is also the use of formulaic descriptions. Epic stories, therefore, are constructed, albeit in a loose manner. The Valmiki *Ramayana* is a construct, as are other narratives that pick up segments of stories. Some *Jataka* stories refer to characters and events from the ramakatha, believed to be the original oral story but now extant. Examples of these would be Kaushalya's grief at Rama going into exile, or Sita's insistence on accompanying Rama. Some of the place-names are similar: thus Mithila is a very prosperous city and Dandaka is a forest. Others have similar narrative themes such as the story of the *Sama Jataka*, of the young ascetic who takes care of his blind parents and is accidentally killed, or the princess going into exile with her husband and being courted by a rakshasa which leads her husband to doubt her chastity as narrated in the *Sambula Jataka,* or the role of the hunch-backed maid in the *Kusa Jataka.*

The *Jataka* stories were eventually collated and included in the corpus of the Buddhist Pali Canon. The *Dasaratha Jataka* has been widely commented upon during the last hundred years in the extensive discussion on whether it was prior to the Valmiki *Ramayana* or subsequent to it, or as is more likely that both drew from the same source but treated the story differently. Was the essentially Buddhist reformulation of the story incidental or was it making a statement in relation to the other versions? It is again the stories from the *Jatakas* that are depicted in large numbers on the railings and gateways of stupas such as at Sanchi, Bharhut and Amaravati. Both the narrative and the precept were part of the folk tradition of villagers and townsmen visiting the stupa. Some of the themes of these tales are generic and recur in later collections of stories as well, irrespective of religious affiliations.

The *Jataka* stories refer to a previous life of the Buddha. It is claimed that they were narrated by the Buddha supposedly at the Jetavana monastery and each is adapted to Buddhist purposes and is used to explain and illustrate an ethical precept; hence their inclusion in the religious texts. Many of the stories that carry parallels to those familiar from the *Ramayana,* gloss the *Jataka* version by a strong moralistic tone conforming to Buddhist ethics. In the story of the young ascetic who is killed by mistake while tending to his blind parents, he is later revived because of the faith of his parents. This function of the *Jataka* stories was continued into later times, and can be seen in many parts of the Buddhist world. In Southeast Asia for example, where the *Dasaratha Jataka* is both popular and highly regarded, the emphasis in its popular presentations has always been on its illustrating the need to be distanced from the illusions of mortal existence, and to be concerned with the impermanence of mortal life.

The *Dasaratha Jataka* belongs to a distinct group of stories that indicate the Buddha's concern with the allaying of sorrow. It is said that the Buddha told the story to a householder, to console him on the death of his father. The Buddha was explaining the impermanence of life through the following story:

In times past, Dasaratha was the maharaja of Banaras and from his chief queen he had two sons, Rama-pandita and Lakkhana, and one daughter, Sita. The queen died and Dasaratha grieved for her but eventually raised another to her status. The second queen bore him one son, Bharata. After this she asked repeatedly of Dasaratha that he declare her son the successor. Dasaratha, fearing that she might harm the older children, suggested that they go away to the forest and return to claim the kingdom on his death, which had been predicted for twelve years later. The three travelled to the Himalayas where they built a small hermitage. Rama-pandita became an ascetic and Lakkhana and Sita looked after his needs.

Meanwhile, Dasaratha grieving for his children died after only nine years. When the queen tried to raise the royal umbrella over Bharata, the ministers objected and said that the rightful successor was in the forest. Bharata went to fetch Rama and seeing him in the hermitage fell at his feet weeping and informed him of their father's death. Lakkhana and Sita were uncontrollably upset to hear the news but Rama-pandita sat quietly. He comforted his brother and sister. When Bharata asked him why he wasn't mourning, Rama preached to him on the impermanence of life and the uselessness of sorrow to those who have acquired wisdom. A mortal dies alone and the wise can see beyond this world to the next.

Bharata then asked him to accept the kingship which Rama refused saying that he would wait until twelve years had been completed in accordance with his father's wishes. He did, however, give his sandals to Bharata saying that they would signal him on whether his decisions were correct or not. After three years, Rama-pandita, Lakkhana and Sita returned to Banaras. The ministers anointed Rama as king and he and Sita ruled for sixteen thousand years.

The Buddha is said to have explained that the various persons in the story were those connected with him who had taken birth as the characters of the epic. Thus Rama-pandita was the Buddha himself, Lakkhana and Bharata were his disciples Sariputta and Ananda, Dasaratha was Suddhodana and Sita was the mother of Rahula. Of all these, Rama-pandita was the most highly respected.

This myth raises interesting questions about the role of mythology in ancient societies. Buddhist origin myths where they relate the story of an important clan begin with sibling ancestry. This is as true of the Shakyas, the clan to which the Buddha belonged, of the Koliyas and others who play an important role in the events of the Buddha's life as told in the Pali Canon. These myths are also narrated in Chinese texts recording Buddhist mythology. Even the ancestory of Vijaya, who established the first kingdom in Sri Lanka, goes back to sibling parentage as described in the famous chronicle of Sri Lanka, the *Mahavamsa*.

As mythology these narratives are intended to be taken metaphorically. Origin myths of this kind are what might be called 'cultural codes', encapsulating extensive concepts symbolically but perfectly understood by the audience. If these stories are taken as cultural codes, then we have to ask what they are stating. Such narratives clearly are emphasizing the legitimacy of a clan, a territory or a kingdom, and such legitimacy is linked to the appropriate descent group. Origin myths, even when not taken literally, give priority to purity of lineage and reinforce claims to high status. The myth is a form of social demarcation. High status groups can deviate from the norm. The notion then becomes the symbol of origin of a royal or near-royal family.

For an audience familiar with Buddhist origin myths and their cultural codes, the story in the *Dasaratha Jataka* would not have posed a problem, since they would have recognized it as a pointer to the high status of the family. There was also the association of both the Buddha and Rama belonging to the same descent group since both families were descended from Ikshvaku, an association that is made even in the *Puranas*.

There is however more to the *Dasaratha Jataka* than merely a matter of understanding a single story embedded in the Buddhist tradition. Throughout history various groups have appropriated the ramakatha and used it to project their own ideological concerns and social aspirations. Some of the versions therefore become dissenting versions. Others are assertions of self-perception and projections of what is culturally significant to a particular segment of society. Still others introduce their own social norms and the story becomes an agency of legitimation.

There is also the very interesting Jaina version of the ramakatha, the *Paumachariyam*, written by Vimalasuri in the early centuries AD. The ambience and the protagonists of the story are Jainas. It is a remarkably rational version of the story. Thus Ravana does not have ten heads but wears a necklace of nine large gemstones each of which reflects his head, so he comes to be called ten-headed. He is not a rakshasa but on the contrary, a respectable member of the Meghavahana clan. This identity, by the way, is also given to a king of Kalinga, Kharavela, in his Hathigumpha inscription in Odisha dated to the first century BC. The Meghavahana clan was linked to the famous Chedis who are much praised in the *Vedas* and also play a role in the *Mahabharata*. For the historian this version of the story is both crucial and illuminating in terms of contributing to the historical discussion. Again, in the *Paumachariyam*, the battle between Rama and Ravana is predestined and it is Lakshmana who actually kills Ravana. At the end of the story Sita becomes a nun. Both the Buddhist and the Jaina version even of they differ from the Valmiki version have the highest respect for Rama, Lakshmana and Sita, who are spoken of with much admiration. This then becomes a form of further elevating the story and opening it to an even more expansive vision for potential worshippers of Rama.

If the variants are disallowed, the strength of the ramakatha tradition will wither and result in the imposition of the single version. As an intelligentsia we are already impoverished in terms of familiarity with the essentials of what we call our cultural heritage. If only a single version is to prevail then we are cutting the ground from under the feet of our own cultural past. The denial of other versions is a mechanism by which other voices are silenced. Do we still have a right in public places to refer to other versions or are we now expected to live with the lie that there is only one version?

It is curious that for many centuries now the alternate versions of the ramakatha have been known and accepted without objections from Hindus and others. The notion of blasphemy was alien. Suddenly one morning it is stated that other versions are hurtful to Hindu sentiment. Until now, variants were seen merely as an appropriation of the ramakatha by others. This surely indicates that the hue and cry was part of a political agenda and had little to do with the sentiments of the Hindu community. The espousal by the Left parties of the condemnation of the variant can only be explained by their general confusion over the question of the role of religion in contemporary Indian life.

The existence of the variants and their acceptance by Hindus was possible (and may continue to be possible surreptitiously), because for the true rama-bhakta, the version is unimportant as long as Rama is the focus of Bhakti and supports an ethical message. From this perspective the *Dasaratha Jataka* cannot be faulted, since its focus is on the wisdom and perceptiveness of Rama and the belief that he was a bodhisattva. What will become increasingly impossible will be the other uses of the story as articulating dissent.

The objection to the *Dasaratha Jataka* or the *Paumachariyam* for that matter, is not just a matter of objecting to a particular version of the ramakatha that some people may regard as too different from the Valmiki version. It does raise the wider question of the closing of the mind. There was a time when the complex symbolism of such stories was recognized, but today we are shearing them of their richness of form and meaning and replacing it with a narrative that lacks the nuances pointing to diverse ideas. A shorn narrative can only point in one direction. On each occasion when a ban is imposed, be it on *The Satanic Verses* or on the Sahmat exhibition, or on the scholarly analyses of Sikh scriptural texts, or a book by Taslima Nasrin it is invariably argued, by a small, politically motivated group of people that the larger community will find it offensive. Is there any mechanism for asking the larger community if this is really so? And are such matters really only limited to one community: do they not have wider repercussions across communities, on society in general?

In these situations the media plays a crucial role. The politics of the ban can be played up, to a point where the ban is projected as inevitable. This also raises the issue of who takes the decision. Is it always the state that has to judge and intervene or is it the community in whose name the decision is being taken? If all such decisions are relegated to the state without an open discussion on the issue, then we are in fact placing more power in the hands of the state than is necessary. And the state has shown itself to be partisan to particular views. Today it is the banning of a book or the tearing down of a panel at an exhibition and these may seem marginal; tomorrow it is the dogmatism of substituting knowledge by political slogans in school textbooks which works towards stunting the mind; and by the day after it will be the assertion of control over what citizens are allowed to think which can seriously impinge negatively on the quality of our lives.

15

HISTORICAL MEMORY WITHOUT HISTORY

Faith and history have been brought into conflict once again by being forced to jointly occupy public space in contemporary India. In effect there should be no conflict if it is recognized that the two are irreconcilable and that they cannot be fused together. They are independent of each other. Their premises, their methods of enquiry and their formulations are dissimilar. So instead of trying to conflate them it might be better to concede the difference and maintain the distance.

When historians speak of the historicity of person, place or event, they require evidence—singular or plural—that proves the existence of any of these and this evidence is based on data relating to space and time. The two important spaces in the Valmiki *Ramayana* are Ayodhya and Lanka. The location of both is uncertain.

It has been argued that the present-day location of Ayodhya may not have been the same as in early times. Buddhist sources locate it on the Ganga and some argue for a different Ayodhya on the Sarayu. When excavations at Ayodhya were started as part of the project on 'Ramayana Archaeology' in the late 1970s this question was raised and there was some discussion among archaeologists. Was it confusion on the part of the authors? Could it have been another place with the same name? Site names are often relocated in history sometimes as a wish to retain a memory and sometimes to legitimize a new settlement. Or even sometimes when it is ecologically necessary to move elsewhere and the name accompanies the migration. This difference in locating Ayodhya was pointed out by historians at the time of the Ramjanmabhoomi movement, but it was dismissed by stating as usual that it was the distortion of Marxist historians! One does not have to be a Marxist to see common sense.

The location of Lanka has been disputed by scholars for the past century and remains unidentified with any certainty. For a variety of reasons many scholars such as Hiralal, Raikrishandas, Paramasiva Iyer,

U.P. Shah and H.D. Sankalia, locate the Lanka of the Valimi *Ramayana* in the Vindhyas—in Amarkantak or in Chhota Nagpur—and others locate it in the lower Mahanadi valley in Odisha. The identification with present-day Sri Lanka is problematic—as has often been pointed out—since Lanka was not the earliest name for Ceylon.

One of the chronicles of the island, the *Mahavamsa,* written in the mid-first millennium AD lists a number of early names, associated with previous Buddhas and therefore possibly imaginary, such as Ojadipa, Varadipa, Mandadipa. But the names more commonly used in a variety of other sources are different. The earliest name of the island judging by Sanskrit, Prakrit, Greek and Latin references of the Mauryan and post-Mauryan period was Tamraparni/Tambapanni, (in Sanskrit and Prakrit) and Taprobane (in Greek). Ashoka in the third century BC in one of his edicts mentions Tamraparni as being at the frontier. Most scholars have identified this with Ceylon as it comes together with a reference to the Cholas, Pandyas and Keralaputtas of south India. A few have suggested that it might refer to the river Tamraparni in the extreme south.

Subsequent to this, comes the name Ilam, and in Pali sources, it is Sinhala or Sinhala-dvipa, rendered in Greco-Latin sources as Silam or Sieledib. The island is also frequently referred to in these texts as Palai Simoundou, the derivation of which is unclear. These references continue into the first millennium AD. At this early stage the name Lanka seems not to be associated with Ceylon. In the mid-first millennium AD it is used in the Ceylon chronicles. It appears to have been a later name.

This is puzzling for the historian. If Valmiki was referring to Ceylon then the name should be the one by which the island was known at the time of the composition of the text, that is, either Tamraparni or Sinhala-dvipa. Since the name used is Lanka which at this time appears not to have been the name for Ceylon, it could mean that Lanka was located elsewhere. In that case the location of the Ramasetu has also to be reconsidered. This has been suggested by some of the above-mentioned scholars. Some have argued that the setu was more likely located in a small expanse of water in central India or linked to an island in the Mahanadi delta and not located in the sea of the Palk Straits. Another view holds that the focus on the setu grew in the time of the Cholas when they were developing their naval power and conquered a part of northern Ceylon. Nor is the setu mentioned in every version of the narrative. There are other ways of reaching Lanka, described in other versions of the story, some of which are quite fanciful.

If Lanka in the text is a reference to Ceylon, then the date of the composition of the Valmiki poem would have to be reconsidered. It would date to a period when the island came to be called Lanka, which was later than the date popularly accepted for the text. The chronology of the currency of the name Lanka becomes a significant question. All this is quite apart from the technical viability of building a bridge or even a causeway across a wide stretch of fifty-three kilometres of sea, in the centuries BC.

It is said that the Ramasetu is a cultural heritage and therefore cannot be destroyed even if it is a natural geological formation. More likely it is the idea of such a structure that has become a heritage. To search for a non-existent man-made structure takes away from the imaginative leap of a fantasy in which it might have originated and denies the fascinating layering of folklore. It would be more appropriate to recognize the undersea formations of the Palk Straits as a part of our natural heritage and protect the relevant areas. We pay no attention to the fact that such marine parks are as important to our ecological future as those visible on the landscape.

Questions of identifying location and chronology do bother archaeologists and historians, but they need not be of consequence to those whose concern is only with faith, and the distinction has to be reiterated.

Keeping the distance might help in defending historical research. The notion of questioning what is believed is not alien to Indian tradition. When we assess our cultural heritage we often tend to forget or we downplay the fact that rationality and scepticism were very much a part of early Indian thought. This was not limited to the Carvaka/Lokayata thinkers but is also clear from some other schools of philosophy, as indeed it is noticeable in Buddhist and Jaina thought. We have inherited a tradition of questioning, which was not limited to philosophical thought but is apparent in popular literature as well. It would be as well to nurture that tradition.

The description of Ayodhya in the Valmiki *Ramayana* as an opulent, well-developed, extensive urban centre would suggest to the historian a comparison with the urban centres of the Ganga plain in about the fifth centuries BC, or later, known from texts and from archaeology. The extensive excavations at Ayodhya carried out on different occasions in the last forty or so years make it clear that Ayodhya as a city cannot go back much earlier than the mid-first millennium BC. Unlike the textual description, the archaeological evidence does not suggest opulence. This contrast is apparent at more than one location at Ayodhya. But allowance has to be made for poetic licence in a text that is acclaimed, and rightly so, as the adi-kavya, the first of the great poems. The first urban experience of settlements in the Ganga plain doubtless evoked a new vision of the world, certainly one that brought in ideas and activities very different from the previous village settlements. Why poets exaggerated this experience has to be understood. Other kinds of pre-urban habitation in the area go back by a few centuries, but do not reflect the urban life of the Ayodhya of the text.

The existence of habitation by itself is not enough to argue that such locations, occupied by hunter-gatherers, pastoralists and peasants, is evidence enough to identify the site with a city-centre of an epic, even allowing for the normal fantasies of epic poetry. There has to be some substantial co-relation between the textual description and what is excavated—although many archaeologists and historians would still hesitate to accept this as the basis for identification. The co-relation can only be clinched when inscribed objects are found that were common to both textual and archaeological sources. This is one reason why, despite extensive excavation, some of Homer still remains uncertain.

That Rama is central to variant versions of the story is, in itself, not evidence of historicity. There can be infinite variants some of which are way beyond the horizon of any original location and chronology, such as the Javanese and Malaysian versions. If the variants contradict each other as they do even in the Indian versions, this may create problems for those who believe that only one of the variants is true. But multiple variants enrich the interest in historical and comparative analyses and in assessing thereby the degree to which each approximates, if at all, the historical past, or for that matter what the divergence signifies.

The Buddhist version of the story in the *Dasaratha Jataka* is entirely different and differences are also registered in the Jaina version. This assumes that there was freedom to reformulate the projection of Rama in accordance with local needs. Such a range of diverse presentations may not be conducive to defining a historical person or even insisting on a single belief.

This does not happen with the biographies of those who were known to be historical figures and who founded belief systems: the Buddha, Jesus Christ, Muhammad, Guru Nanak. Their biographies adhere largely to an accepted story line and this helps to endorse the 'official' narratives of their lives. Their existence is recorded in other historical sources as well that are not just narratives of their lives but have diverse associations. The historicity of the Buddha, for example, is established, among other things, by the fact that a couple of centuries or less after he died, the emperor Ashoka visited Lumbini, as recorded on a pillar erected to commemorate the Buddha's place of birth. In celebration of this the emperor reduced the taxes due from the village. Roman historians of the first two centuries AD refer to the teaching of Christ and comment on the reaction to it by both the people and the administration. Arab historians from the eighth century onwards narrate the life of Muhammad and comment on his teaching and its reception among his peers.

If the recent debate on the Ramasetu had grown from a genuine sense of enquiry, historians might have participated. But it is only too evident that the issue is a matter of political strategy on the part of those who are mobilizing in the name of faith, and those who are reacting politically to the mobilization. Thus, from the point of view of archaeology and history, the Archaeological Survey of India was correct in stating that there is to-date no conclusive evidence to prove the historicity of Rama. The later annulling of this statement was a political act. But this lack of historical evidence is relevant to history and the historical construction of the past; it is hardly relevant to belief and faith. Reliably proven evidence is of the utmost significance to history, but not to faith. Accepting the existence of an avatara is a matter of faith, it cannot by definition be a matter of history. Doubting historicity is not blasphemy. The historian may not question the legitimacy of a particular faith adhering to a religion, but the historian does have to explain the historical context of the person and the event, if it is thought to carry historicity, and why, in a particular space and time, a particular faith acquires a following.

If there is a strong faith—faith in the religious sense—among millions of people then it does not require to be protected through massive demonstrations, violence and the killing of innocent persons, all geared towards political mobilization. Nor do archaeology and history have to be inducted to keep that faith intact. Faith finds its own place and function, as do archaeology and history. And the place and function of each is separate.

Those in India that claim to speak in the name of faith in order to confront and beat down knowledge, have so far been careful not to tangle with scientists. Scientific knowledge is beyond the ken of politicians. Yet scientists in their work do confront issues tied to questions of faith. Where does Indian society stand in relation to these confrontations? Other times and other places have seen fierce conflict as for example, between the Catholic Church and Galileo, or the opposition to Darwin's idea of evolution since the nineteenth century and even now in the USA. Political lobbies elsewhere do oppose scientists. The lobbies have been and are extremely powerful, but nevertheless they do fall short of seriously damaging scientific knowledge, through seeking the sanction of the state to oppose this knowledge. Part of the reason for this can be attributed to some societies allowing the relative independence of knowledge systems, be it archaeology, history or astrophysics. That this does not seem to be so in India is a qualitative disadvantage.

To say that the partial removal of an underwater formation in the Palk Straits is going to hurt the faith of millions, is not giving faith its due. Is faith so fragile that it requires the support of an underwater formation believed to have been constructed by a supernatural power? At the same time, formulating faith as a political issue in order to win elections is surely offensive to faith? Pitting it against history feeds the formulation. The intention is doubtless to make both faith and history helpless pawns in political chess.

Setting up a confrontation between faith and knowledge has at least two purposes. One is to convert the confrontation into a mechanism to help with political mobilization and this is always useful just prior to elections. The pattern and objectives are familiar from the past. The other purpose is to permit a deviation from the essential questions that need to be addressed in ascertaining the viability of what is now called the Ramasetu project, apart from diverting attention from more essential concerns that should be occupying us.

Even within the definition of the project, what is at issue is not whether Rama existed or not, or whether the underwater formation or a part of it was originally a bridge constructed at his behest, but a different and crucial set of questions that require neither faith nor archaeology. They require far greater discussion involving intelligent expertise if we are to understand what the project might achieve and what it might destroy. Will the removal of a part of the natural formation eventually cause immense ecological damage and leave the coasts of south India and Sri Lanka open to catastrophes, to potential tsunamis in the future? Or can it be so planned that such a potentiality can be avoided?

Some detailed discussion is necessary as to what would be the economic benefits of such a scheme in enhancing communication and exchange. Such benefits should also be seen in terms of the future of local livelihoods in case they are negatively affected. Are there plans for the occupational relocation of local communities that may be ultimately at a disadvantage? We have become a society so impressed with figures and graphs that we tend to forget that each number is actually a human being. The benefits are mentioned by politicians and the media but rarely explained in terms of the nitty-gritty. Equally important, one would like to know precisely what role will be played by the multinational corporations and their associates in India. Who will finance and control the various segments of such an immense project? It is only when such details are made transparent that we will also get some clues to the subterranean activities that are doubtless already simmering.

16

THE MANY NARRATIVES OF SOMANATHA

The history of Somanatha has been dominated by a single narrative woven around the events that took place there at a particular point in history. Those of us who have examined other sources that also narrate events relating to Somanatha, feel that the single narrative does not tell us very much. So, when speaking on Somanatha, I would like to discuss three different categories of sources that give us three different narratives, that do seem to get integrated at the end. This is what some historians call the many voices of history. What we mean by this is that history should not be written only on the basis of one source of evidence, for, if there are other narratives about the event, the place, or the person, or are related to either of these, they have all to be examined. This is not because we think that only one narrative is giving a true description, but because we are interested in observing how various people saw the event. We maintain that by looking at the perhaps contradictory versions of the same event, it may be possible to understand more fully what might have happened, and how it was viewed both at the time and subsequently. It is worth looking at these various voices, because their narratives tell us about how a variety of people, depending on their interests, continued to perceive the event, or else had forgotten about it, and also why these perceptions sometimes differed. The context therefore is of central importance: who is narrating the story of the event and why; who constitutes the audience or the readership that the narrative is addressed to, and what is the purpose and meaning of the narrative.

This also becomes a demonstration of the change that has taken place in historical research in the last fifty years. We have moved from being concerned only with political and dynastic history to examining the broader dimensions of social, economic, religious and cultural history—and more particularly with how all these aspects interact with each other. This gives us a much richer and more detailed picture of the past.

The data I am using are not new. But I am juxtaposing whatever diverse historical information we have and seeing them in relation to each other. This is new. I am addressing three questions. What is the manner in which historians today assess the event and the sources, and how has this changed from fifty years ago, when the history of Somanatha was narrated in textbooks and later became a political slogan? Did the Turkish raid on a Hindu temple create a trauma among the Hindus as a reaction, as has been maintained by earlier historians, resulting in a permanent hostility between Hindus and Muslims? How did a supposed memory constructed about an event of a thousand years ago, become an issue in present-day politics?

We know that Mahmud, the Sultan of Ghazni, a principality in Afghanistan, conducted frequent raids into northwestern India partly to conquer territory but more than that to loot temples. In 1026 he raided the temple of Somanatha in Gujarat and broke the idol. Reference is made to this specific action in many Turkish and Persian sources, and some of the references contradict each other. Other sources lead historians to asking new questions that were not thought about earlier. Asking new questions is, as we all know, essential to the advance of knowledge. An event or a person in history can be treated differently from century to century, either because there is new evidence or because the evidence is being questioned in new ways. This changes how we look at the event. As historians, therefore, we have to be aware not just of the how we assess a past event in our times, but also the ways in which the event was interpreted through intervening centuries.

Many texts refer to the historical context of that period in Gujarat and its neighbourhood, but three categories of sources refer specifically to the Somanatha temple. These three representations differ as narratives and add to the interest and puzzle of the problem. They are accounts from Turko-Persian texts, some contemporary and some later; from Jaina texts of the period; and from Sanskrit inscriptions of the time. They date from the eleventh to fourteenth centuries. Once I have examined these historical sources, I will analyse the debate on Somanatha in the British Parliament in the nineteenth century, and finally look into how the subject was treated soon after Independence in the twentieth century.

▪

The original temple dedicated to Shiva, dated to about the ninth-tenth century AD, was located at the port town of Veraval in Saurashtra. Many small rajas were ruling in Saurashtra and were subordinate to the major dynasty—that of the Chaulukyas or Solankis—who were powerful during the eleventh to thirteenth centuries AD.

It was a period of much prosperity in the region, the wealth coming from trade, particularly maritime trade, with ports along the Gulf and the Arabian Peninsula. Veraval or Somanatha was one of the three major ports of Gujarat. The trade between Gujarat and West Asia across the Arabian Sea and up the Persian Gulf went back many centuries to Harappan times. Arab traders and shippers from the eighth century AD onwards settled along the west coast of India, and some worked as officers for the Rashtrakuta dynasty in the western Deccan. Those that settled in the coastal areas, married locally and founded many communities that today continue to thrive—such as the Khojas and Bohras in western India, and the Navayatas and Mappilas further south. Indian merchants were equally adventurous and set up businesses in Hormuz in Persia and in Ghazni in Afghanistan. They remained prosperous even after the eleventh century when there were raids and campaigns in the area.

The trade focused mainly on the importing of horses from west Asia and exporting metal, textiles, gemstones and spices, although other items were also exchanged. Investments in the trade came from individual merchants, from temple treasuries and from local administration. A large sum of money was also collected by the local administration at Somanatha as pilgrim tax from those who came on pilgrimages to Saurashtra. Some local rajas looted the pilgrims of their donations intended for the temples. Prosperity unfortunately leads to piracy. Judging by the inscriptions, the Chaulukya administration spent time and energy policing these attacks on pilgrims and traders.

Despite this, trade flourished. Gujarat in this period experienced what can perhaps be called a renaissance culture of the mercantile community. Rich merchant families were in political office, controlled state finances, were patrons of culture, were scholars of the highest order, were liberal donors to the Jaina sangha, and had temples built for various sectarian persuasions. Temples became the repositories of wealth. This wealth came as donations from patrons and pilgrims as also from the estates owned by the temples and from the commercial activities that they conducted.

This was the scene at the time of Mahmud's raid on the Somanatha temple in 1026. The prosperity of Gujarat was an attractive target as were the temples with their treasures. There are many accounts claiming to describe the raid, some sober and some very fanciful. There is one sober contemporary reference and this comes from Al-Biruni, a central Asian scholar of the early eleventh century. Mahmud exiled him to India because he was critical of Mahmud's activities, arguing that his raids caused economic turmoil and the kind of disruption that results from any such raid. Al-Biruni spent many years in India, was deeply interested in the country and its culture, and left an incisive account of what he saw and learnt during this time. According to him the temple at Somanatha was renowned for its lingam that many came to worship. It was located by the seashore and built within a stone fortress, presumably to safeguard its wealth. Al-Biruni dates the temple to a hundred years before Mahmud, to the tenth century AD. The temple and its image were particularly important to sailors and to merchants, he writes, some of whom had contacts with places as distant as Zanzibar and China.

The accounts written in Turkish and Persian by those attached to the courts of the Delhi Sultans and other courts, make entertaining reading as they are exaggerated and often contradict each other. Let me relate some of their stories. A major poet of the Islamic world, Farrukhi Sistani, who claims that he accompanied Mahmud to Somanatha, provides a fascinating explanation for the breaking of the idol. According to him the idol at Somanatha was not of a Hindu deity but of Manat, a pre-Islamic Arabian goddess, and that the name Somnat was actually Su-manat, the place of Manat. We know from the Qur'an that Lat, Uzza and Manat were three pre-Islamic goddesses widely worshipped, and it was said that the Prophet Muhammad ordered the destruction of their shrines and images. Legend has it that the image of Manat was secreted away, presumably by a trader to Gujarat, and installed in a place of worship. Manat, in some accounts, is said to have been just a block of black stone so the form could be vaguely similar to a lingam; others say she had a female form. Some took this story seriously, others however denied it and insisted that the icon was of a Hindu deity.

We may well ask why this story of Manat was linked to the raid of Mahmud. The answer seems obvious. It gave greater prestige to

Mahmud who in destroying Manat was carrying out what were said to be the wishes of the Prophet. He was therefore a champion of Islam. Although he raided many other temples, the raid on Somanatha received special attention in the accounts of his activities. It was also said that Mahmud wrote to the Caliph and boasted of his great deeds as a protector of Islam, and in return grandiose titles were bestowed on him. This established his legitimacy in the politics of the Islamic world which was his primary ambition, the raids on India being largely to acquire the wherewithal for this ambition. This is a dimension that is overlooked by those historians who see his activities only in the context of northern India. And we have to remember that, as was common to all large empires, the empire of the Arabs also went through periodic crises. Such crises became points of intervention for the likes of Mahmud.

But Mahmud's legitimacy also derives from the fact that he was a Sunni Muslim, and therefore attacked the Shi'as as heretics. He desecrated their mosques at Multan and at Mansura in Sind. He claims to have killed 50,000 kafirs (infidels), and this claim is matched by similar claims to his having killed 50,000 Shi'as who were regarded as heretics. The figure appears to be notional as it is frequently repeated in various contexts. Mahmud's attacks on Hindus and Shi'as, was undoubtedly a religious crusade against them. But let us also remember that many of the places that he attacked, such as the Shi'a mosques in Multan and Mansura, were located in cities where traders were involved in the very profitable horse trade with the Arabs and the Gulf, as also with Central Asia. Both the Muslim heretics of Multan and the Hindu traders of Somanatha had substantial commercial investments with the Arabs. An inscription in Sanskrit from Peheva in Haryana records brahmanas trading in horses and making donations to temples from their profits of such large amounts that these could be recorded with pride. The historian therefore has to ask the question whether Mahmud, in addition to religious iconoclasm, was also trying to terminate the import of horses from Arabia into India via the western coast? This becomes a relevant question when we realize that the horse trade with central Asia went through Afghanistan and northwestern India, which was crucial to the wealth of the kingdom of Ghazni. Was Mahmud combining iconoclasm with trying to ensure a commercial advantage? As we know from history, rulers have always kept an eye on every possible chance of combining political and economic aggrandizement and have acted to enhance this.

In the subsequent and multiple Persian accounts—and there are many in each century—there is no agreement on the form of the image. Some say that the image was a lingam, other accounts contradict this and say that the image had a human form. This would also be important to determining whether it was the icon of Manat, a female goddess, or of Shiva, a male god.

The human form of the image leads to other stories. It is said that when the belly of the image was pierced, jewels poured forth. But then one wonders how does one pierce the belly of a stone image? Attar states that the image contained twenty mann of jewels, one mann weighing several kilograms; Ibn Zafir's account says that a gold chain weighing two hundred mann kept the image in place. Al-Qazwini has a more interesting description. He says that the image was made of iron and a magnet was placed above it, so it got suspended in space, which would certainly have been an awesome sight. But then again one wonders if a magnet would be able to raise such a large iron image? This link between an iron image and a magnet seems to have been popular at the time. In the *Rajatarangini,* Kalhana describes the same thing—an image of metal in a temple, suspended by the force of a magnet. So perhaps the chronicler took the idea from Kalhana. What is historically interesting is the manner in which the idea of a magnet and metal is employed in the context of an image in a temple. The age of the temple is taken back 30,000 years, to give it greater prestige, and thereby greater prestige for Mahmud as well. All these contradictions suggest that none of these writers really knew what the image was, and seem to have given descriptions based on rumour. And, as with all rumours, the fantasy increases with each retelling of the story.

More purposive writings of the fourteenth century are the chronicles of Barani and Isami. Both were associated with courts in India, one in the Delhi Sultanate and the other with the Bahmani kingdom in the Deccan. Both projected Mahmud as the ideal Muslim hero but somewhat differently. For Barani religion and kingship are twins, and the ruler needs to know the religious ideals of kingship, if he claims to be ruling on behalf of God. Sultans must protect Islam through observing the rules of the shar'ia and destroy both infidels and heretics such as the Shi'as. Mahmud who did both was said to be the ideal ruler.

Isami composed what he regarded as an epic poem on the Muslim rulers of India. This was in imitation of the famous Persian poet Firdausi's earlier epic on Persian kings, the *Shah Nameh*. Isami argued that kingship descended from God, first to the pre-Islamic rulers of Persia—in which he includes Alexander of Macedon and the Sassanid kings—and subsequently to the Sultans of India, with Mahmud establishing Muslim rule in India. Interestingly the Arabs, who had both a political and economic presence in the subcontinent prior to Mahmud, hardly figure in this history since the focus was on Turkish Sultans. There is a difference of perception in these narratives as compared to the earlier ones. These perceptions need to be studied more carefully as they are a comment on the attitudes of the chroniclers.

Historians have to remember that court chroniclers often exaggerate or even twist descriptions of the activities of rulers in order to make a political point. Earlier, historians tended to take many such descriptions at face value, but today we are more ready to question the texts, and compare them with other contemporary sources. We are interested in asking questions such as why the events are being presented in particular ways, and why the presentations differ.

With the establishments of the Sultanates in Delhi and the Deccan, the representation of the role of Mahmud was also undergoing change. He was now not just someone who raided temples but was the one who showed the way to political power, and more particularly to the founding of an Islamic state in India. This is not historically accurate, for he did not found an Islamic state in India, but that was the view of the chroniclers. Pre-Islamic Persian rulers were also brought into the narrative in order to make the Sultanates legitimate. We must keep in mind that the Sultans in India were ruling over a society that was substantially non-Muslim. This may have made them less confident of their rule that in turn had to be covered up by narratives of their greatness. If they were not fully confident of the loyalty of their subjects, their courtiers would have to project them as great statesmen and praise their activities. This was common to politics at all times and was particularly so in cases where coming to power was through violent means. Violent deeds had to be justified, or whitewashed or forgotten, so as to make the perpetrators into heroes. History has many such examples, going back to pre-Islamic rulers. This gives the historian much to think about in terms of how violence is used in acquiring power, as well as the way in which court chroniclers justify it or disguise it.

Narratives of the event continue with still greater embellishments. Of the actual temple at Somanatha, the impression created is that it never recovered from the initial raid and ceased to be important as a temple. Yet every now and then some Sultan or other is said to have attacked the Somanatha temple and converted it into a mosque. Logically therefore, after the first of these attacks, the later Sultans in these many accounts, would be attacking a mosque. In a sense the claim ceases to be history and becomes rhetoric. Nor does this stop Sanskrit inscriptions and texts from continuing to refer to it as a sacred, powerful and prosperous temple, up to at least the fifteenth century.

I have this far only referred to the Turkish and Persian chronicles, because up till now modern historians have largely used these texts in reconstructing the events at Somanatha. But the evidence that we have from Sanskrit sources of various kinds—such as Jaina histories of Gujarat and biographies of kings, or from Sanskrit inscriptions of brahmana priests, traders from Persia, and local kings—paint an altogether different picture.

An eleventh century Jaina poet, Dhanapala, mentions in passing Mahmud's campaign in Gujarat and his raids on various places including Somanatha. His boast is that Mahmud was unable to damage the icons of Mahavira in the Jaina temples because the icons were imbued with immense power, or as he expresses it: snakes (Mahmud) cannot swallow Garuda (Mahavira). This for him is proof of the superior power of Jaina images as compared to the Shaiva.

In the late twelfth century, a hundred and fifty years after the raid, during the reign of the famous Chaulukya king, Kumarapala, there is much activity around the Somanatha temple. Among the ministers of Kumarapala was Hemachandra—a respected and erudite scholar of Jaina religious history and of Sanskrit and Prakrit grammar. There seems to have been some rivalry between him and Bhava Brihaspati, the Shaiva Pashupata chief priest of the Somanatha temple. There is therefore a discrepancy between the statements attributed to the minister and to the chief priest.

A dynastic history of Gujarat, the *Prabandha Chintamani*, written by Merutunga in the fourteenth century, refers in some detail to the reign of Kumarapala the Chaulukya king, and his minister Hemachandra. We are told that Kumarapala wished to be immortalized. So Hemachandra suggested that the king replace the dilapidated temple at Somanatha with a new one. He says quite specifically that the temple had fallen into disrepair because it was located on the seashore and was damaged by sea spray. This is confirmed by many sculptures now housed in a museum near the site. Some show marks of the stone having been hacked but many are just worn out by weathering, and sea spray would have worn them out faster. When the new temple was being consecrated, Hemachandra accompanied the king into the sanctum and wishing to impress the king with the powers of a Jaina acharya, requested the deity of the temple, Shiva, to manifest himself. Shiva did so. Kumarapala was so impressed that he converted to the Jaina faith. The focus is again on the superior power of Jainism over its rival Shaivism. It does seem curious that these activities that focused on the Somanatha temple, a couple of centuries after the raid, make no mention of Mahmud, nor is he linked to the dilapidated state of the temple. The miracle of the appearance of Shiva is the central point in the connection with Somanatha.

Some hints of raids come from another Jaina text of a different kind. In an anthology of stories, one story refers to the wealthy merchant Javadi, who went to the land called Gajjana, evidently Ghazna, looking for an icon. The ruler of Gajjana was a Yavana—a term by now used for those coming from the west. He allowed Javadi to search for the icon and when it was found, gave him permission to take it back. Not only that, but the Yavana ruler even worshipped the icon prior to its departure.

This is a story of reconciliation, and reconciliation therefore becomes the Jaina ethic that dominates the relationship. The Jaina sources underline their own ideology and argue that this accounts for the survival of Jaina temples. Attacks are to be expected in the Kaliyuga—the present age of evil. Wealthy patrons will restore temples and icons.

The third category of major narratives is the collection of inscriptions in Sanskrit from Somanatha itself, focusing on the temple and its vicinity. These again give us a very different perspective of Somanatha from that of the earlier two sources. Inscriptions of the twelfth century inform us that the king Kumarapala, appointed a governor to protect Somanatha. The protection was required to safeguard it against the piracy and against looting by local rajas. In the thirteenth century the temple and its vicinity had to be protected from attacks by the Malwa rajas. Yet the chronicles of the Sultans were claiming that it had been damaged by Mahmud and subsequently converted into a mosque.

In 1169 an inscription refers to the appointment of the chief priest of the Somanatha temple, Bhava Brihaspati. He was a Shaiva, hailing from Kanavj, and, as the inscriptions show, established a succession of powerful priests at the Somanatha temple. He claims to have been sent by the deity Shiva himself, to rehabilitate the temple. According to the chief priest this rehabilitation was required because it was an old structure, much neglected by wicked and greedy officers, and also because in the age of Kaliyuga, temples tend to fall into disrepair. Again no mention is made of Mahmud or later attacks on the temple and its conversion into a mosque.

Perhaps looting temples was not such a big deal. As we have seen in an earlier essay, Kalhana in the *Rajatarangini* records the looting and devastation of temples by a series of Hindu kings of Kashmir between the eighth and eleventh centuries who were trying to acquire financial resources. One of these, Harshadeva appointed a special category of officers, the devotapatananayaka—officers for the uprooting of gods—to supervise the looting of temples. In Gujarat, Bhava Bhrihaspati insists that it was he who persuaded the king to replace the older temple, thus contradicting the statement of Hemachandra having done so in the account of Merutunga.

In 1264, two and a half centuries after the raid, a long, legal document was issued in the form of an inscription with both a Sanskrit and an Arabic version and located in Gujarat. The document written by Nuruddin Firuz, a trader from Hormuz in Persia, records his acquiring land at Somanatha, to build a mosque. It begins with invoking Vishvanatha, a name for Shiva, but possibly also the Sanskrit for Allah, the lord of the universe. This juxtaposition of Hindu and Islamic elements is noticeable throughout the inscription. Was it a form of cultural translation? The document states that Nuruddin Firuz, the owner of a ship and a respected trader, acquired land in Mahajanapali in the town of Somanatha, to build a mosque. This is referred to as a dharmasthana, a sacred space. The land was acquired from the local raja, Shri Chada, son of Nanasimha, and reference is also made to the governor of Saurashtra, Maladeva, and to the Chaulukya-Vaghela king, Arjunadeva.

The acquisition of this land has the approval of the panchakula of the town of Somanatha. The panchakulas were powerful administrative committees established locally in various places and consisting of recognized authorities such as priests, officers, merchants and dignitaries. This particular panchakula was headed by the chief priest of the Somanatha temple, Virabhadra, and included the gentry of the town. The witnesses to this agreement of granting land for building a mosque are mentioned by name and described as the brihat-purusha, literally the 'big men'. They were the Thakkuras, Ranakas, Rajas—titles of the landed intermediaries, and merchants from the Mahajanapali section of the city. Some of these dignitaries were functionaries of the estates of the Somanatha and other temples. The land given for the mosque in Mahajanapali was part of these temple estates.

The document lists the endowments for the mosque. These included two large measures of land which were part of the temple property from adjoining temples situated in the town of Somanatha; land from a matha or Shaiva monastery; income from two shops in the vicinity; and an oil-mill. The measures of land were bought from the chief priests of the temples and the men of rank attested the sales. The shops and the oil-mill were purchased from local people. One of these chief priests, Tripurantaka, appears again, twenty-three years later, in a number of inscriptions as a wealthy and powerful priest who built many temples in the neighbourhood. As with many Sanskrit votive inscriptions, this inscription too ends with the hope that the terms and conditions of the agreement may last as long as the moon and sun endure. The Arabic version of this inscription concludes with the hope that the local people will take to Islam, a sentiment that is tactfully omitted in the Sanskrit version!

The tone and sentiment of the inscription of Nuruddin are amicable and the settlement had been agreed to on all sides. The building of a mosque in association with some of the properties of the Somanatha temple, not by a conqueror but by a trader through purchase and a legal agreement, was obviously not objected to, neither by the local governor and dignitaries nor by the priests, all of whom were party to the decision. The mosque is thus closely linked to the erstwhile properties and the functionaries of the Somanatha temple.

This raises many questions. Did this transaction, two hundred or so years after the raid of Mahmud, not interfere with the remembrance of the raid if it was remembered by the priests and the 'big men'? Were memories short or was Mahmud's raid unimportant? These transactions would hardly support the idea of the local Hindus having been traumatized by the raid of Mahmud, leave alone this happening with all Hindus.

Perhaps the local people made a distinction between Arabs and Persians who came as traders, which made them acceptable, and the Turks or Turushkas as they are called in Sanskrit, who came as conquerors, which made them less acceptable. The Arabs who had come earlier as conquerors were limited to Sind and subsequently became more familiar as traders who settled along the western coast and gave rise to a number of local communities of mixed Arab and Indian descent and religion. Clearly they were not all homogenized and identified as 'Muslims', as we would do today. We need to separate the responses of particular groups of people as determined by their needs. Hormuz was crucial to the horse trade therefore Nuruddin was welcomed. Did the profits of trade, with investments by traders, administrators and temple authorities overrule other considerations?

The Delhi Sultans were anxious to conquer Gujarat for its mercantile wealth and therefore there were battles. There is one very moving inscription dating to the fourteenth century, and in Sanskrit, which is from Somanatha itself. It begins with the Islamic blessing—bismillah-rahman-i-rahim. We are told that the town of Somanatha was attacked by the Turks. One of the townsmen, Farid who was a Bohra, and was the son of Bohra Muhammad, joined in defending the town, fighting against the Turks and on behalf of the local Hindu ruler, Brahmadeva. Farid was killed in the fighting and the inscription is a memorial to him.

To return to historical assessments of Somanatha, the popular view is that events such as Mahmud's raid created a permanent antagonism between Hindus and Muslims. This statement needs to be re-examined, because such statements are based on partial evidence. Obviously at the time of the raid there must have been much antagonism. But in the period after it, there were other voices that tell a different story. These voices have remained unheard by those writing on this subject.

How then have we arrived today at the theory that the raid of Mahmud created a trauma in the Hindu consciousness which has been at the root of Hindu-Muslim hostility ever since? Or to put it in the words of K.M. Munshi, writing in 1951, 'For a thousand years Mahmud's destruction of the shrine has been burnt into the collective subconscious of the [Hindu] race as an unforgettable national disaster.'

As we have seen earlier in this book, the first mention of the 'Hindu trauma', as it has been called, does not come from any Indian source, but from the debate in the House of Commons in London in 1843, that is, eight hundred years after the event. The debate was on the question of the gates of the Somanatha temple. In 1842, Lord Ellenborough, the Governor-General of India, issued his famous 'Proclamation of the Gates' in which he ordered the commander of the British army in Afghanistan, to bring back to India the sandalwood gates from the tomb of Mahmud at Ghazni, believed to have been looted by Mahmud from Somanatha.

The proclamation raised a storm in the British Parliament and became a major issue between the Government and the Opposition. The reference to the gates was puzzling since no one had ever mentioned them in earlier accounts. Many wondered if Ellenborough had made a mistake. Some of those who participated in the debate asked if Ellenborough was catering to religious prejudices? Others asked if there had been a trauma among Hindus after the raid which Ellenborough was trying to assuage? This seems to have been the germ of the idea—that there was a Hindu collective memory of the raid that resulted in regarding the Muslim as the enemy.

The chronicles written at the courts of the Sultans and the Mughals were taken to be reliable history by British writers, without any questioning of their ideological perspectives. However, such questioning is necessary to any reconstruction of history based on any chronicle, whether it is written in Persian, or Sanskrit, or Latin, or in any other language from any court; or for that matter the questioning of the agenda of any source is essential to its being used as historical evidence. Chronicles of that period are like state reports and often ideologically committed to praising those in power and who are patrons of the chroniclers. Furthermore, the colonial scholars who read these chronicles used them to support colonial policy in India. Among these policies were British attempts to insist that there had been, and continued to be, hostility between Hindus and Muslims since the coming of Muslims to India. Colonial rulers are known to have often resorted to this policy of creating hostility between the communities among their colonial subjects, as is evident from the history of many colonies in Asia and Africa. Creating and emphasizing antagonistic identities among colonial subjects, made it easier to control them. In propagating the greatness of Muslim rulers, the chronicles dramatized the power that these rulers had had over their subjects. Such exaggeration is also in part a style of writing in courtly literature. In Sanskrit inscriptions the portions praising the dynasty or the ruler are referred to as the prashasti or eulogy. Because it is a stylistic convention, the historian has to be cautious about accepting the veracity of the statement.

The account of the chronicler Ferishta, written in the seventeenth century, six hundred years after the event, describes the attack on Somanatha in so exaggerated a manner as to be almost implausible. Nevertheless, it was repeated by British writers in their accounts of the event written in the nineteenth century; moreover, they added the idea of a trauma. From there it went into the textbooks and came to be accepted as accurate history. The antagonism between Hindu and Muslim was also emphasized in the periodization of Indian history by James Mill. This periodization was strictly adhered to. So the convention was to use Sanskrit texts for writing Hindu history and Persian texts for writing the history of the Islamic period after AD 1000. That would explain in part why inscriptions in Sanskrit were not widely consulted for the history of Somanatha since it was mainly a history from after AD 1000. As for the texts in Sanskrit, because they came from Jaina authors, they were not given the primary importance that they deserved. Yet, inscriptions and texts continued to be written in Sanskrit well after this period.

As we have seen, such a periodization is completely unacceptable to historians today. Change in history is registered on a far more extensive scale, involving the entire society, and does not refer to merely the religion of rulers. So it has been discontinued in current historical writing. Mill's book, *The History of British India*, was read extensively in the nineteenth century, not only in the universities but also by those who entered government service. It was again other British historians such as Eliot and Dowson, who propagated the idea that there was an innate hostility between Hindu and Muslim, and that there was a tyranny of the Muslim over the Hindu. To this was added the idea that the Hindu should be grateful to the British for conquering India and thus removing the tyranny of the Muslim. But tyrannical rulers, although infrequent, were known from all periods of Indian history. Tyranny was not limited to Muslim rule. Nor indeed was good government limited to any particular group of rulers.

This was the background to the discussion on the Proclamation of the Gates in the British Parliament. The gates were uprooted from Ghazni and brought back in triumph by the British army. However, on arrival they were found to be of Egyptian origin and had nothing to do with India.

But from this point on, Mahmud's raid was made into a central point in Hindu-Muslim relations. K.M. Munshi, as minister in the first independent government of India in 1947, led the demand for the rebuilding of the Somanatha temple. Having written a novel on the subject in 1937, entitled *Jaya Somanatha*, he wished to restore what he thought were the glories of Hindu history, but unfortunately his knowledge of the subject remained superficial. The novel was nothing more than an entertaining story. Like many of us he enjoyed reading the historical novels of Walter Scott and Alexander Dumas, which of course are not history but are fiction set in a historical period. He was also deeply influenced by Bankim Chandra Chatterjee's novel, *Anandamatha*. On this, it is worth remembering the words of the historian R.C. Majumdar, who argued that Bankim Chandra's nationalism was Hindu rather than Indian, with passionate outbursts against the subjugation of India by the Muslims.

Munshi insisted that despite the temple still standing, although in a dilapidated condition, a new temple had to be built on the site. This led in 1950 to uprooting the remains of the earlier temple to clear the ground for the new temple. A small segment of one corner was left to show that the new temple was built on the site of the old. What was removed from the site was quite substantial. It is now stored in neighbouring sheds that are called a museum. This shows neither respect nor concern for the ancient temple that had both religious and historical importance. The anxiety was merely to get rid of it and put up a new building at the site. The motive seems to have been more political than religious.

This action was against the policy of the Archaeological Survey of India that disallowed protected monuments to be removed. But Munshi was a minister so the policy was overruled. The remains of the old temple show some signs of desecration which may have resulted from Mahmud's raid, or from much later times, but there is as much damage through the effect of weathering, most likely from the sea spray. The early temple was replaced in about the twelfth century with a more elaborate structure. This may have been the rebuilding of the temple by Kumarapala. There is little evidence of later structures or major reconstructions. A rather nondescript dome of a subsequent period remained as part of the dilapidated temple, possibly as an attempt to convert it into a mosque.

On the rebuilding of the Somanatha temple in 1951, Munshi had this to say: '... the collective sub-conscious of India today is happier with the scheme of reconstruction of Somanatha, sponsored by the Government of India, than with many other things we have done so far.' The claim to sponsorship of the new building by the Government of India is wholly untrue, although many politicians today repeat this incorrect statement. It is on record that the Prime Minister, Jawaharlal Nehru, and some others, objected to the Government of India being associated with the project by Munshi, arguing that the Indian state was a secular state and could not therefore either finance or be the patron of the building of a temple. They had insisted on the temple being restored entirely as a private venture. Therefore a private trust was established that collected donations that were used to finance the building of the present temple. This introduces a further dimension to the reading of the event, involving the secular credentials of the state.

▪

What I have tried to show is, that even monuments have their own history, wrapped in narrative. This may vary according to who is viewing the monument and reading the narrative, and what is the nature of the event associated with it. I have referred to three categories of texts that deal specifically with the history of what happened to the temple at Somanatha. There are other texts that tell us about the persons who might have had distant associations with it, such as references in medieval epics or in the folk traditions of Rajasthan and the western Ganga plain. They are all written at different periods of time and refer to persons and events that have an indirect connection with the main story, but provide vignettes of other ways of looking at it. And I have also tried to show that each view can be quite different if not contrary to the other. In such a situation it is difficult to accept only one view as the accurate view. There has to be a critical assessment of all categories of evidence and an analysis of each, in order to understand the social and cultural dimensions of the past.

The plea that some views are based on memory, or the accumulated memory of many generations over a thousand years does not help us either. We all know that memories are constructed. We choose to remember certain things and forget others. We choose to remember fragments of the past in particular ways and imbue them with meaning that is often only pertinent to the present. And we have reasons for narrating a supposed memory which may not be what actually happened, but is what we would like to think might have happened. This is familiar to us in our individual lives. Memory for example seldom matches a photograph taken a few decades ago. And when we are speaking of a collective memory of a society, of many thousands of people, and of an event that happened a thousand years ago, it is even more unlikely to match the reality from the past and to tell us of what actually happened. In the case of Somanatha, the supposedly collective memory and the 'trauma' was constructed by the British debate in the House of Commons, and subsequently adopted by colonial historians as well as a variety of Indians to serve various political purposes.

Historians therefore have to be very cautious when reconstructing the past and more so when claiming that it derives from collective memory. Every tiny piece of evidence has to be fitted in like a jigsaw puzzle. And sometimes these bits of evidence come in a strange manner from unexpected places. Ultimately, the historian is providing as complete a picture as is possible, on the basis of the evidence available at any one time; and is not claiming to be omniscient, but is at best presenting an understanding of the past, and of what might have happened. That even such an understanding is invaluable stems from the fact that we are all products of our pasts. We have therefore to do our utmost to understand the past as well and as fully as we can, and be sensitive to its nuances and its complexities. It is this that distinguishes the maker of myths from the historian.

IV

OUR WOMEN—THEN AND NOW

Religion and caste have been taken as central aspects of the social ethic. But even more crucial to its practice is the way our society treats its women. This awareness is of recent vintage in societies everywhere, but the mindset that directs attitudes towards women has also been a presence in societies that have been viewed as advanced or less so. The mindset varies from that of groups that live off the given environment to those that attempt to bring the environment under their control in a variety of ways. In the former the subservience of women seems to be less marked, but gradually as conditions in the latter are strengthened, the gender status becomes more demarcated until patriarchy begins to determine the social codes. The kind of subservience and the degree to which it is required varies from groups in power and authority to subordinate ones. Women of upper caste royal families live well but can flout the social code only up to a point, whereas those some rungs down the social ladder can do so if the consequences are not too severe. The relative freedom at the lower levels and lack of it at the upper, is compensated by the wealthy life-style at the upper levels, denied to those lower down. But those at the still lower rungs of the social ladder had neither the wealth nor the freedom to choose the kind of life they wanted to live. In assessing the position of women, then and now, caste and wealth are indicators even where they do not necessarily coincide. Some social activities and institutions were open to women to express their independence but these activities and institutions, specifically for women, remained marginal to the society as a whole. Nevertheless, a small possibility did exist.

It is true that the women of the elite were indulged and lived well. However, this good life has to be juxtaposed with the fact that even symbolically, they had an inferior status, encapsulated in their speaking Prakrit in the literature of high culture whereas the men spoke Sanskrit (barring the companion to the king). Those of middle status were the wives, the ideal wives or pativratas, and remained subordinate to the men. Those of the lowest status were household servants and slaves, or women working in artisan and peasant families, counted like chattel in numbers suggesting that they were treated with contempt by the upper castes. The occasional woman philosopher such as Gargi, who is often quoted to prove the high status of women in ancient times, is actually the proverbial swallow and does not make a summer.

Women had few options other than becoming housewives and this was not unusual in other ancient societies as well. But the other options were two: a young woman could be trained as a skilled professional in the arts and in literature in preparation for becoming a respected courtesan; or else she could renounce being a housewife and take orders as a nun. Interestingly, sexuality in the first instance was enhanced and in the second it was denied. Patriarchy ensured that two options were open to a miniscule number of women. Perhaps, this was a safety-valve, since otherwise the need to observe the caste codes in arranging a marriage was a mechanism of the caste patriarchs controlling women, even if the control was tyrannical: a pattern that continues in many parts of the country. Caste and patriarchy are intertwined and patriarchy can survive if it can control caste—that means in effect if it can control the code of marriage connections within or outside a pattern of caste. 'Honour' becomes a euphemism for this control, frequently involving extreme violence against women. Yet the irony is that women are the only ones who know the true paternity of the child. And the mitochondrial DNA is also from the woman.

In gender-biased societies like ours where women are treated as inferior, established religions do not demand gender equality. There is no condemnation of those organizations that pride themselves in murdering their women members who seek to be equal to men and take independent decisions about their marriage lives. If the shar'ia required that a woman suspected of adultery should be stoned to death, the *Bhagvad Gita* establishes a mindset by referring to women and low castes as sinfully born, and khap panchayats do the rest. In a recent diktat they required women to cover themselves from top to toe—virtually the same as wearing a burkha. The model of the mullahs is unmistakable. This is, they say, to prevent the male gaze from resting on revealingly tight jeans and churidars. Would it not be simpler to do something about the male gaze?

In the past, there was a debate as to whether a woman of status should immolate herself on her husband's funeral pyre in order to demonstrate the status of the family as well as her dedication to her husband. And, incidentally, it ensured the removal of at least one possible claimant to the inheritance of property. Some women who were better established or of a higher caste, were required to become satis. But even in the past this was a subject of debate with many disapproving of this requirement of women.

In our times many women were set on fire if they brought an inadequate dowry. One could well ask if there is some subconscious link in the patriarchal mind between the agni-pariksha, fire-ordeal of Sita; the encouraging of women to become satis, the practice of entering the fire jointly in a jauhar when a Rajput raja was defeated in a campaign; and the frequency of dowry deaths in recent times. And it is not even curious that it is always the woman who has to burn; it is always the woman who has to burn to prove her chastity; it is always the woman who has to burn in order to protect the male honour of her husband. The violence and the brutality inherent in demanding that these acts be performed seems now to be diverted into the appalling number of rapes that are becoming apparent every day.

When will there be real concern in practice, about our social ethic towards women? Perhaps this will come when women are given equal rights over property and inheritance, setting aside the Hindu Code Bill and the Muslim Personal Law; when there are no caste barriers to marriage and when claims to tradition and customary law do not determine the rules of marriage; and when the mindset of Indians, particularly of the men, accepts gender equality with its corollary of equal respect for men and women.

17

WOMEN IN THE INDIAN PAST

Events of the nineteenth century reflected a disjuncture in Indian society in several ways. Colonization implied domination and subordination as evident in the relationship between the colonial power and the colonized. This also extended to relationships within the colonized. The existing dominance of the upper castes was underlined as was the subordination of lower castes. The middle-class that emerged in this period was initially largely drawn from the upper castes. This condition affected many aspects of living and thinking and the study of the past was no exception. The reconstruction of social and cultural history by colonial scholars, also gave direction to the identity of the emerging middle-class. It determined how we understood the past in what we regard as our tradition and inheritance, and this perception continues to this day.

Colonial scholarship had defined Indian society as having been a static society registering no change, governed by despotic rulers and ground down into poverty. This depiction was rightly questioned. Indian historians, influenced by Indian nationalism, responded to these theories. However, the response was not questioning enough as some colonial interpretations were accepted. Despotism was opposed but Mill's periodization was effectively continued. Historians influenced by nationalism contradicted the negative aspects of the colonial view. For example, they argued against the notion that all Indian rulers were despots or that the ordinary people lived in extreme poverty, and instead they maintained that the wealth of India was drained away to finance British industrial development. Such questioning advanced the discipline of history as it introduced a necessary debate.

Nationalisms all over the world draw on a golden age of the past. The further back in time it can go the better so that it cannot be closely questioned. Some Indian nationalist historians did the same. Instead of continuing to analyse the data from the past they tended to project an idyllic and prosperous society for the ancient period. Ancient India became the utopian foundation of Indian civilization.

It was thought that Indian society functioned as stated in the normative texts, the *Dharmashastras*. The social codes and obligations of the four varnas were observed according to these texts. This was viewed as a system by which everyone knew his or her place in society and abided by it. Indian scholars working on social history initially saw it as an acceptable way of organizing society. There was some, but not nearly enough discussion, on the inequities of a system that resulted in gross inequalities. The intention was primarily to contradict the negative features presented in colonial writing, and portray Indian society in a positive manner. Possibly part of the reason for this was that many historians of that period were themselves from the upper castes and for them the inequalities were normal to social functioning.

Because social inequalities received less attention there were three groups whose actual social conditions remained vague. They were kept at the margins of history. These were, first, women at all levels of society; secondly, the lower castes—the shudras and Dalits and those not part of mainstream society; and thirdly, the 'tribal societies' who were mainly forest-dwellers.

The neglect of these groups was augmented by the relative lack of texts written in ancient times by women and by authors from the lower castes. Such sections of society were not required to be literate and the contrast with the literate shows up when this lack is compared to the many by upper caste men authors. Early histories of any part of the world are generally constructed from the writings of elite groups, and an effort has to be made to look for sources from other groups or read the history of such groups from existing sources. Even more important, most historians themselves did not think it necessary to write the history of those regarded as socially inferior. The demand from feminists and Dalits that their history also be written was yet to come.

On the subject of women in the Indian past the standard text was the well-known study with which we are all familiar, A.S. Altekar's *The Position of Women in Hindu Civilisation,* published in 1956. This summed up the way in which the subject was thought of up to that point. References to the activities of women were collected from the texts and put together in an attempt to suggest that women were uniformly respected members of society. It could not be otherwise, it was said, since those were the times of Vedic civilization in which women were venerated. Implicit in these descriptions was that the ideal woman, the pativrata—the one devoted to her husband—acted in accordance with the *Dharmasastras.* There was little attempt to investigate what women were doing and saying and what the reality of their lives was.

This had to wait for two events. One was the advent of research and writing on social and economic history. Historians interacted with other social sciences and investigated theories of historical explanation, all of which were asking a different set of questions. The second change came with the beginnings of what is now called feminist history. The consciousness of this history came from societies in various parts of the world, and began to consider the centrality of women in both past and present societies. In India the movement began in the 1960s and gathered momentum in the 1980s with studies analysing this perspective in the Indian context.

Historians began collecting data from various sources to try and fill out the picture of the social role of women, but it should be said here that the realization had by now dawned upon them than the accumulation of data in itself was not sufficient. New questions had to be asked of the data. A major change was that women were no longer treated as a single category defined by gender with little differentiation between women of different social classes and castes. Earlier generalizations had been made from the evidence of women of the elite and applied universally. This was misleading. In some texts there is adulation for women, in others contempt and they are referred to as a single category. The *Gita,* for example, speaks of shudras, vaishyas and women as one category, all being papa-yoni, born of sinful wombs. Other texts refer to only one group of women among many others. These references have to be differentiated. Regional variations, crucial in terms of kin-relations, tended to be papered over especially when it came to rights over property and inheritance. Customary law was sometimes contrary to the normative codes, yet was observed. And then there is the question of hidden patriarchy that continues to control society to this day, even where it is seemingly less visible. All these questions are inter-connected. Attitudes towards women were obviously conditioned by the social level of the women being discussed. In the past, as in the present, this varied according to their social and economic level. It is now recognised that when generalizations are made about women, their precise location in society should be indicated.

The initial representation of women by historians was generally that women had a high status, going back to Vedic times of around 1000 BC. Much is made of the reference to Gargi, who debated with a leading philosopher of those times, Yajnavalkya, as recorded in an *Upanishad*. She is said to have asked many tough questions and differed from him. So much so that when her questions became really sophisticated and he probably could not answer them, he told her to stop asking them lest her head should split. This was a technique of ending the discussion.

Such incidents need to be juxtaposed with others that speak of a different condition. Some women were educated but this was not expected of them. The hesitation to their being educated in Sanskrit is taken to such an extreme that in classical Sanskrit dramas, the women characters irrespective of whether their status was high or low, uniformly spoke the commonly used Prakrit, whilst the men spoke Sanskrit—the language of the educated. Quite evidently it was meant to be a putting down of the woman. The exception of course was the curious anomaly of the brahmana vidushaka, companion to the king, who spoke Prakrit.

Despite this, there were queens who made substantial religious grants or held administrative office, or even ruled. One of the edicts of the Mauryan emperor Ashoka of the third century BC, states that all the grants made by the queen Karuvaki, the mother of Tivara, are to be recorded. This is an unusual document as kings seldom proclaim the donations of their queens. Possibly this was because the ambience at this time was Buddhist and Buddhism made more concessions to accepting the right of women to express themselves.

There are other instances of queens making grants when they were politically in authority as individuals and therefore the need for endorsement by male rulers was not required. The daughter of Chandragupta II, Prabhavati Gupta, was married into the Vakataka family in the fourth century AD. She issued inscriptions and made grants when she was ruling as regent for her minor son after the passing away of her husband. Another regent and one of the most colourful of royal women, was the Kashmiri queen Didda in the tenth century. She was regent for her son and grandson and governed as a full-fledged Queen for twenty-three years. Her success lay in playing off the various political factions at the court, pitching one against the other.

Some royal women were associated with making grants to religious sects, and to institutions such as monasteries and temples and later to brahmanas. The grants are frequently of villages and land. Such grants would have involved a clearance from the state administration, since the financing of the grants would have come from the royal treasury. This in turn would have involved assessing the grant in terms of the loss of revenue to the state, and balancing the loss against political gain to the king from the supporters of those receiving the grant. This would be particularly important to sects competing for royal patronage, which was a significant source of finance and status. Such substantial grants cannot be viewed solely as an exercise in religious charity. The activities that followed from the grant would have had wider implications. One may ask whether large religious donations were a sign of the intervention of royal women in the politics of the court, where patronage in some situations was a political statement in addition to being a religious activity.

An interesting case of differentiation in patronage within the same royal family is that of the Ikshvaku royal women who made donations to the Buddhists at Nagarjunakonda, whereas the men were patrons of Vedic sacrifices. These were sects known to be often hostile to each other. This pattern of distribution of largesse to different religious groups suggests that some political calculation also went into determining patronage apart from religious sentiments. At the level of patronage, donations sometimes become an act of asserting choice within the limited independence on the part of women. Where they made the choice in opposition to prevailing patriarchy, such women have to be given credit, even if they represented a small minority.

Women who belonged to the upper castes and to families of status had also to contend with another practice, that of having to become a sati, requiring them to immolate themselves on the funeral pyre of their husband. This was forbidden initially to brahmana wives and there are few if any references to lower caste women doing so. Possibly in many cases it was an assertion of higher caste status conveniently requiring only the women to burn. Because it occurred more often among those who owned property it may also have been a way of reducing the number of legal claimants to inheritance.

The ritual has been traced to Vedic sources that associate it with a form of levirate. The widow could lie briefly on the pyre, but would then be married to her husband's brother. Having been marked with the identity of the family on her first marriage, she as property, remained within the family. Views on immolation are controversial in many early texts such as the *Mahabharata* and Bana's *Kadambari*. The earliest recorded case dates to a sixth century AD inscription. Memorials to satis, the sati-stones, often occur together with the hero-stone that commemorates the hero defending the village cattle in a raid. By modern times, the context changes as does its meaning.

Gargi became the popular icon among those writing on the position of women in early India. But we should remember that she was exceptional, as she was individually gifted but was also from the more privileged section of society, and did not represent the majority of women. Similarly, the royal women who made grants were a small minority. The larger number among the better off were the wives of grihapatis, householders, and this determined their status. The concession to their role was that in most Vedic rituals the wife of the yajamana, patron of the sacrificial ritual, had to be present and participate in some of the ritual.

It is difficult to provide data on the vast majority of women of early times, the women who were working partners in small households. These were peasant women and those that assisted their artisan-husbands in their professions. References to them are occasional and suggest that their aspirations were limited by their low shudra status. They are shadowy figures in the brahmanical narratives but more assertive in the Buddhist *Jataka* stories. They were not included in the category of the pativratas of the better-off households, but this in a sense encouraged the possibility for them of a greater degree of freedom.

The substantial number of women were dasis, whose condition was unenviable. Until recently historians gave little attention to these women, as has been so eloquently pointed out by Uma Chakravarti, a contemporary feminist historian. This was the other side of the picture. Initially the term referred to the women of the dasa community, the community of the Other, to whom the arya was opposed. But gradually, it changed to meaning the women who were enslaved and worked in the households. These were the women who were treated as inferior, and who could be gifted as an item of property. Not only in the danastuti hymns but also in the *Mahabharata* when Yudhisthira gambles away his wealth, mention is made of large numbers of dasis as part of this wealth. Dasis were the main prop of every reasonably well-off household.

The dasi was owned as property and therefore had no rights. Her status was the lowest but her work was the heaviest, and her wage was generally minimal. She had no authority over anyone. Quite the contrary, she had to submit to anyone who came her way, male or female. There was little recognition that there were some who protested against their role and did so out of a wish for independence from the social code. Some resented the labour they had to put in as part of household tasks. The poems of the women who became Buddhist nuns, the *Therigatha*, provide descriptions of the chores involved for women in running a household, even if they were not always dasis.

That dasis were treated with scant respect is evident. For example, the story is narrated of Jabala in one of the *Upanishads*. He was a young man anxious to be taught by the rishis. When asked about his caste he said he did not know what it was. His mother had told him that she worked as a dasi in a household and men came and went, and she did not know who his father might have been. The teachers decided that since Jabala had told them the truth, his father must have been a brahmana, and accepted him as a student. Dasis were the polar opposite of the pativrata, the ideal being applied only to a higher social category.

This is not altogether unconnected with a curious category of brahmanas, whom we have encountered earlier in this volume, the dasiputra brahmanas, almost an oxymoron, as its literal meaning is 'brahmanas who are the sons of dasis'. At first they were despised because of their parentage, but when it was seen that the gods approved of them, they were accepted as ritual priests. Some of the more renowned Vedic rishis were of this mixed category. Among the better-known ones was said to be Kakshivant, the son of the priest of the Bharatas who married a dasi, Usij.

The wife who was expected to be devoted to her husband and the household, needed to act according to the rules of the *dharmashastras* as laid down for women, rules that envisaged little else than patriarchy. This is only too evident in the verse quoted so often from Manu, that a woman is under the surveillance of her father when unmarried, of her husband when married and finally of her son when widowed.

Where identity is determined by birth and is crucial as in caste, it is essential to know the parentage. In order to maintain the rules of caste it is essential to keep women under control. This is obvious because ultimately only a woman knows the biological father of her child. Caste and patriarchy are therefore inseparable. We see a demonstration of this in our own times in the so-called 'honour killings', where young women who break away from the caste laws of marriage, are brutally murdered in the name of maintaining caste purity, on the orders of the male elders of the caste.

But there were other less obvious ways in which patriarchy was exercised. Among these were the diverse forms of marriage permitted in the *Dharmashastras*, some familiar and some strange. The explanation for the diversity may lie in wanting to include various ways in which women were exchanged and acquired, ways linked to caste practices.

The *Mahabharata* has a fund of contradictory stories about these patterns of exchange. In the Pandava family itself, three consecutive generations observe three entirely different forms of family relations, a situation which would never occur now. These three are: endogamy—marriage within defined circles but excluding blood relations, as in the case of Pandu marrying Kunti and Madri; fraternal polyandry where one woman, Draupadi, is married to all five Pandava brothers; and the cross-cousin marriage of Arjun marrying his mother's brother's daughter, Subhadra. Polyandry and cross-cousin marriage are not included in the marriage forms discussed in the *dharmashastras*. Nevertheless, they are otherwise legitimate because they reflect the variations among the societies portrayed in the epic. This becomes a codification outside the *dharmashastras* that was doubtless legitimized as customary law.

The legally acceptable forms of marriage, as in Manu, are supportive of the subordination of women. Whereas the social codes are particular about caste boundaries, there are nevertheless contradictions within the texts and between the texts. Eight forms of marriage are regarded as legal. In the much-lauded kanya-dana, the father with full patriarchal rights appropriate to the upper castes, gifts his daughter. As the recipient of a gift that does not call for a return gift, the groom's family asserts superiority and can make further demands. We have seen this carried to an unacceptable extreme in the hundreds of dowry deaths where the bride is murdered, often burnt to death for not being able to provide more and more consumer commodities as part of the dowry. Husbands and in-laws are frequently held guilty of the death. The asura form involved a bride-price, where the value of the woman and the marriage alliance was weighed in terms of the wealth paid by the family of the man. The rakshasa form required the abduction of the bride by the groom and his family, as in the case of Arjuna marrying Subhadra in the *Mahabharata,* with Krishna having to cool the anger of the Vrishnis.

The gandharva marriage is by mutual consent and motivated, Manu informs us, primarily by sexual desire, doubtless appropriate to the roving eye of kings. The context more frequently is when a king finds himself face-to-face with a desirable woman, as for instance Dushyanta and Shakuntala. The woman's caste is of less concern although Dushyanta is relieved to hear that Shakuntala is of a high caste. The woman in such marriages is often an apsara, a semi-celestial being, so she is allowed to exercise her choice freely. When included in the genealogies of lineages such marriages become a device to give status to a new lineage or to plaster over a break in succession. The apsara was a liberated woman, coming and going as she pleased and not as ordered by the hero. The prototype is the famous Urvashi, who jettisoned the distraught Pururavas and agreed to visit him only once a year, and after each visit bore him a son.

Myths are of interest to historians, not because they narrate events that have actually happened, but because they encapsulate the hidden assumptions of a society. They provide clues for instance, as to how a community disguises the breaking of normative rules. Deities and semi-celestial beings do not observe the norms. The apsara for example, contradicts the behaviour of the ideal human woman, but she is not condemned for doing so. Instead, she is the personification of the freedom of women. Was she a concession to the aspirations of those women who wanted greater freedom, or was she the fantasy of the upper caste male? Does she mark the demarcation between the liberated semi-celestial woman, and the limitations on the earthly woman who had no such freedom. Even if semi-mythical she could be claimed as an ancestress by families of considerable status.

The apsara is more visible in the *Mahabharata* and the legends narrated in the *Puranas* pertaining to the past. In these narratives women tend to be outspoken and more independent, perhaps because patriarchy and caste rules were still flexible in the earlier period. Their actions are not invariably in conformity with the codes of caste behaviour. The women are the truly heroic figures and the motivators of events but not as the 'tigers among men', as the heroes were called. At every crucial point in the narrative it is the initiative of a woman that is pivotal. Kunti is the effective patriarch of the Pandavas, both in arranging for their birth from the gods and in their polyandrous marriage; Gandhari mothers a hundred sons providing the counterpoint of evil so essential to an epic narrative; and Draupadi questions the legality of her being staked in the dicing match and instigates revenge and war. Interestingly these are not the women usually held up as the role model in the society of today. The preference is for the more submissive Sita.

A decline in the importance of apsaras, when clan society also declined, seemed to coincide with goddesses emerging as more powerful figures than before. But there is sometimes an overlap between the two that needs investigation. The worship of goddesses has been a substratum religion in India for a longer period than any other. Goddess figurines of terracotta go back to at least the Indus cities. These have continued to be made and worshipped to the present day, which gives them a history of five thousand years. Insistence on the subservience of women did not dull male ardour in worshipping female deities, encapsulating the quintessential female force. The goddesses were made the consorts of the major gods, or worshipped in their own right, but curiously despite their being icons of fertility, few bore children.

By the mid-first millennium AD, some goddesses continued to symbolize fertility, others were associated with destructive force. A couple of centuries later, Shakti worship became more visible at all levels of society. Temples to the yoginis began to be constructed, many observing a circular architectural form, deliberately it would seem, to differentiate them from temples dedicated to male deities with or without consorts.

With the emergence of Puranic Hinduism and Bhakti, devotional worship, taking the form that it did, there were women who were peripatetic singers of hymns to Shiva and Vishnu, who enhanced the Bhakti tradition and wandered through town and countryside, joined by large followings. From Lalla in Kashmir to Mira in Rajasthan to Andal in Tamil Nadu, they all wandered, singing and propagating the bhakti form of worship. These were women who broke away from the *dharmashastra* code on how women should live and behave. In the case of Mira, the legends about her life in the oral tradition, are fully aware of the tension in controverting the code.

Another category of women partially reflect the freedom of the apsaras. These were the courtesans. But unlike the apsaras who made their appearance in forest habitats, the courtesans were part of the urban scene. The profession of the courtesan, ganika, was distinctly different from that of the prostitute, veshya, and the two should not be confused, as we often do today.

The prostitute was an established institution of urban life in Kautilya's *Arthashastra* and prostitution was recognized by the state as a profession. The prostitute was registered and paid a tax on her earnings, there being no qualms on collecting such a tax. There was awareness that she could be abused therefore she is said to have some degree of state protection. There is also a concern about rape victims and the degrees of punishments for various categories of rape are listed. These include physically branding the rapist. This suggests a greater degree of condemnation of the act, than is often forthcoming in our times. It is recommended that prostitutes be used in obtaining information from various sources and in state espionage.

The woman who chose to be a courtesan was of a different category. She was not a professional sex-worker. She was more in the nature of a pleasurable companion for members of the elite and an accomplished performer in the arts. She could choose her clients and was therefore herself the patron. She had to undergo a rigorous training in music, dance, poetry and the arts. The profession was regarded as quite respectable and most courtesans lived well and were a recognised part of the urban scene. The more accomplished could be attached to the royal court and could become the concubines of kings. If they bore children to the king, such children or their descendants could be claimants to the throne. Such a descent was associated in one source with Kumarapala the pre-eminent Caulukya king of Gujarat. A much-respected courtesan, Ambapalli, gave substantial donations to the Buddhist Sangha, and was regarded as so special that she was treated as an icon of the city of Vaishali. In literary texts such as the *Mricchakatika,* the courtesan is highly accomplished and helpful to the family of the hero. Perhaps the absence of the notion of Satan and of 'original sin' in Indian mythology of pre-modern times, allowed there to be a sane attitude to sexuality as one of the components of a balanced life. The internalization of Victorian mores in the nineteenth century helped to unsettle this sanity.

There is a tenuous link between courtesans and the later institution of devadasis, who were also well-trained in the arts but dedicated to the temple. This group was recruited through daughters being gifted to the temple, a better proposition than what is done today through female infanticide, and from the daughters of those devadasis who remained attached to the temple but could, in effect, be concubines of priest and patron. Free in theory, they were effectively subservient to various authorities, primarily those in charge of the temple. Justification of this system was sought by maintaining, ironically, that they were serving the gods!

These various categories of women chose a profession but one that was conditioned by, and dependent on, the world of men. Nevertheless, in the articulation of their professional accomplishments they did shape the form of music and dance in ways that could be innovative and could advance the form. So much of our appreciation and enjoyment of these art forms today derives from the creativity of the ganikas and devadasis, and their successors in later times. These women were not required to maintain the boundaries of caste nor was it essential to their own identity. As women they could deny the centrality of procreation, not observe monogamy and have an independent income. Thus they opposed Manu's rules regarding the subservience of women to fathers, husbands and sons. In addition, their profession drew on sexuality—enhanced, extensive, and breaking caste boundaries—the very thing that patriarchy wished to prevent through its control over women. In a sense, the courtesan could oppose patriarchy because she was well-connected to the life of the royal court and the urban rich. If such opposition is a response to power then the courtesan's freedom lay in her access to power, although the access differed from the usual. But the courtesan was regarded essentially as someone who had opted out of observing the social norms required for the women of the household. Nevertheless, her freedom was circumscribed by a certain degree of social mores.

There was another category of women, altogether different, that also asserted its relative independence. These were the women who became Buddhist and Jaina nuns and thereby broke the rules of the

Dharmasastras. These women moved away from their role of being wives and mothers in perpetuity. Some did so out of a wish to lead a life dedicated to worship, but others probably just wanted to get away from the chores of a mundane existence. As a nun, the woman was required to live with other women of various castes, from shudras to brahmanas. In living off alms as food she had to eat food collected from people of diverse castes, some lower than her own. As a nun she negated caste. Judging by the votive inscriptions at Buddhist stupa sites, she could as a nun, make a donation to the Buddhist Sangha, so she retained some rights to income.

These votive inscriptions carry information about women, some of whom became nuns, but made donations. Other women who did not become nuns, also make donations. They identify themselves by their kinsfolk—as daughter, wife, mother, sister, niece, and such like. They mention the occupation of the family, such as small-scale landowners, merchants, artisans, and the location from where they came, but seldom their caste. This information is interestingly complemented by the views expressed by some Buddhist nuns in the *Therigatha*.

Initially, many nuns were from the upper castes, as were the monks, but gradually this changed with members of the lower castes also joining monasteries and convents. Nuns on entering the Order were asked a series of questions that related to their station in life. Did they have a sponsor if they were working somewhere, and if they were young then the consent of their parents was necessary, or presumably their husband if alive. In some cases where the husband was a member of a guild, permission was required from the guild. They had to establish that they were free of debt since the convent did not wish to be pursued by creditors. That the nun's independence was relative was because she had to conform to the rules of the establishment, and of course the monk was always held in greater respect than a nun. Nevertheless it did in a sense reflect the woman's freedom to choose an alternate life-style. This was an area where patriarchy had a more limited reach. The rules were broken but the affect of this on society was contained. Contrary to the courtesan, the nun had to deny her sexuality.

Nuns, where they had some personal control over property, were allowed to use it to make votive gifts. The question has been asked whether these gifts were made from their stri-dhana—their personal wealth gifted to them from either the family into which they were born, or their mother. Or, did the wealth come to them from an inheritance? Or like the monks did they also invest in trade? That monks and nuns continued to have some personal income has been the basis of much recent discussion on the role of the Buddhist monastery as an institution, with links to commerce and land-ownership, and therefore not characterized by social isolation. Nuns as managers of the property donated to a convent, would have involved their having a status that goes with holding office, wielding power in a recognized institution—that of the convent. This brings in the wider question related to the rights of women to property where both law and custom had regional variations.

In generalizing about patriarchy in pre-modern India it is as well to keep in mind that there were some pockets of matrilineal systems that continued for centuries. They even reformulated caste rules to accommodate the customary law and practices of the region. An example of this was the Marumakkathayam in Kerala and also that which prevailed among the Khasis of Northeastern India. What the effect of these systems has been on current society would be worth exploring further. A major initial difference in these societies related to inheritance and control over property. The rights of women although not absolute did concede more than their almost incidental rights to their own wealth, the stri-dhana, in the patriarchal system.

The question of stri-dhana as exclusive to women is also tied to property rights among women of propertied classes. Stri-dhana was wealth over which women had exclusive rights and which they could pass on to their daughters. The question raised was whether this was a gift or an inheritance, in the context of women's rights to property. The debate on these rights became controversial from the early second millennium. Some commentators on property law argue that stri-dhana disqualifies a woman from a share in the patrimony, particularly of immovable property, which was generally inherited in the male line. It is thought therefore that a woman's personal wealth would have been largely movable items.

Some tension is apparent between the son's exclusive right to the patrimony or his having to share it with his mother and sisters, a question that continues in present-day litigation on this issue in many well-to-do families. The definition of sapinda, belonging to the same ancestry, became crucial in the context of inheritance, but there was a debate on the definition. These concerns applied to the well-off, since most families as even now, had little to inherit in the way of property.

The social codes seem to vary according to the scheme of caste and of social custom of a region. Therefore the study of the customary law in various regions is important for the understanding of variations in the *Dharmashastras* dealing with inheritance, laws of ownership and partition of property.

Women in the history of Indian society cannot be seen as a uniform group all conditioned in the same way and observing the regulations as laid down in the normative texts. They are from different castes and social classes therefore their activities are diverse, as are their aspirations. Some conformed to the social codes. Some observed customary law that was more pliable to meeting change. Yet others, not unexpectedly of a smaller number, sought alternative paths of self-fulfilment, given to pursuits of prevalent religions or of pleasure, or various combinations of both.

There was a tendency among earlier historians to focus only on what was said in the normative texts and the evidence that we have of women conforming to this. Occasional deviations were noted. But now we have to consider other questions. Was there really such a strong conformity with the codes and if so, then why? The continued insistence that the code be observed, raises suspicion that perhaps it was not so meticulously observed. And how do we explain the many deviations and in varying contexts? As has been rightly said, where women resisted the norms, their resistance has to be recognized, else it would have been in vain. However much the orthodox social codes may have wanted to iron out and straitjacket their lives, there were women who questioned the codes, some to a greater and some to a lesser degree. As a consequence such women lived multi-faceted lives. We have to illumine these facets if we are to understand the women of the past.

18

BECOMING A SATI—THE PROBLEMATIC WIDOW

P.V. Kane in his monumental work, *History of Dharmasastra*, dating to 1958, starts his brief chapter on sati with what can only be described now as a quotable quote. He states: 'This subject is now of academic interest in India since for over a hundred years (i.e. from 1829) self-immolation of widows has been prohibited by law in British India and has been declared to be a crime.' However, as we know only too well passing a law is one thing but having it universally implemented is another. Incidents linked to women becoming satis have declined and hopefully stopped, but there's no certainty at all that there will not be another. The last one was when a woman was required to immolate herself on the funeral pyre of her husband at Deorala in 1987. This led to a considerable debate on sati, both as religious belief and as social ethic. The debate is not of recent origin as it has been a controversial subject since early times. There continues to be among some people a mindset that almost condones the act as a demonstration of the freedom of choice that a woman can exercise and as a demonstration of loyalty to her husband and a wish to follow the most extreme diktats of her religion. But those that became satis in the past rarely did so out of choice.

What is of significance today is not just the incidence of widows becoming satis even in the last century, but the attempt to justify the custom by arguing that its prevelance in the past gives it historical legitimacy as a tradition. This overlooks the fact that even in the past it involved more than merely a funereal custom. It symbolizes an attitude towards women as a definition of what is regarded as 'tradition.' It has been defended as being a symbol of traditional values, especially those concerning the ideal relationship between husband and wife. It feeds into the cast of mind still current that women are inferior and vulnerable and therefore are assumed to be unreliable. They have to continually prove their devotion to their husbands even in ways that can only be called extreme. A prevalent view is that it was necessitated by the 'Muslim invasions' when upper-caste Hindu women had to defend their honour from Muslim marauders, a view that began to be propagated in the nineteenth century. But the historically recorded incidents of sati predate not only the arrival of Islam in India but even the emergence of Islam.

The fact that there was a debate on the subject even from early times speaks of its not being a universally accepted custom. It was generally restricted to the families of the dominant castes where it became symbolic of status and that too not in all dominant castes. The woman through immolating herself established the status of the family. Today we require other ways of establishing status, so sati has become expendable. That some cannot bring themselves to condemn it outright, is curious. Is it an attempt to justify what are thought to be the preservation of Hindu values even if many Hindus opposed it in the past? Incidentally, it should be pointed out that a woman who thus immolates herself or is forced to do so, is not committing sati, but it is through the act, becoming a sati—a faithful wife, a virtuous woman.

It is easy enough to take the stand that those who do not accept sati as part of the Hindu tradition are westernized Indians deracinated from the mainsprings of the Hindu ethos. They are therefore unable to understand either the concept of honour among those that approved of the act, or to appreciate the idealized relationship between a Hindu husband and wife, such, that it is sought to be perpetuated to eternity through sati; or to see that sati is a pure act of the ultimate in sacrifice (even if such an act is reduced to a public spectacle with a variety of entrepreneurs literally cashing in on it). Such arguments deny a discussion on the subject and the latter is necessary if we are to attempt an understanding of our traditions. Traditions in any case often arise out of contemporary needs but seek legitimation from the past by claims to antiquity. Therefore the past has to be brought into play where such legitimation is sought.

There is no simple explanation for the origin of the custom of burning widows on the funeral pyres of their dead husbands. The Rajput connection is only of the last few centuries whereas references to the custom go back many centuries. References to the practice are scattered in various parts of the subcontinent. It would be helpful if these could be mapped to provide evidence of regions more prone to the practice as well as its chronological spread. It is said to be a symbol of aristocratic status associated with some early societies such as those of the Greeks and the Scythians. There is however no other society where it was practiced by variant social groups for different reasons at various points in time, and where the controversy over whether or not it should be practised was so clearly articulated over many centuries since early times. Because of this, in India it underwent changes in its meaning arising out of the reasons for its observance as well as the degree to which it was accepted.

Its origin is generally traced to the subordination of women in patriarchal society. But in searching for origins, other factors might also be considered. If a woman is purchased as a bride, the logical termination may have been the requirement of her dying together with her husband, although this is not associated with such purchase. Perhaps a more acceptable explanation may relate to societies changing their systems of kinship and inheritance. In some circumstances the wife would be an alien who would have to be debarred from claiming an inheritance. A further reason could be that it demonstrated control over female sexuality. The practice may have originated among societies in flux and become customary among those holding property such as the families of chiefs and kshatriyas. Once it became established as a custom associated with the kshatriyas it was to continue to be so among all those claiming kshatriya status.

The earliest hint of a ritual that might have been similar to sati comes from the *Rigveda* of the late second millennium BC. But it takes a different turn. The Vedic texts on the contrary endorse the system of niyoga or levirate where a widow is permitted to marry her husband's brother if she has not borne a son to her husband. In the *Rigveda* the act was only a mimetic ceremony. The widow lay beside her dead husband on the funeral pyre but was raised up by a male relative of the deceased. Elsewhere there is mention of her being married to his brother. If she was lying on the pyre it would be just short of a sati ritual, but if she was subsequently married to the brother it became a niyoga. This would keep her identity tied to the family. The property of her husband remained intact within the family. Attempts were made in later times to seek Vedic sanction for the immolation by changing the word agre, to go forth, into agneh, to the fire, in the specific verse. But where the widow is not meant to immolate herself this change is spurious. The Vedic ritual, referring to families of high status, may represent the termination of an earlier practice when the woman had to immolate herself, or else, it could also have been symbolic of the death of the wife on the death of her husband.

In some ways the idea of niyoga is the counterpoint to sati. Whereas sati requires the death of the wife, niyoga ensures her remaining alive and bearing children until she has a son, and being looked after by her husband's family even as a widow. An impotent husband can allow his wife to have a son by another man, preferably his brother, which son is regarded as the son of the husband. But niyoga refers to the widow conceiving a son from her deceased husband's brother. The necessity for a male child is to ensure that a son performs the ancestral rites, which enable the father to be saved from hell. This was an entirely acceptable custom discussed in the social codes as a practice or else described in narratives. Not that everybody resorted to niyoga but should it be required it was a possible solution. The choice between the two was of course not in the hands of the woman, but was dependent on the status of the family.

The act of immolation is first described in Greek texts, quoting from earlier accounts referring to incidents of the fourth century BC. Widows are burnt on the funeral pyres of their dead husbands among the Katheae (Kshatriya or khattiya) in the Punjab. Unable to explain this practice the author remarks that it was an attempt to prevent wives from poisoning their husbands! According to the same sources bride-price was the prevalent custom in the Punjab. If bride-price was a factor then one would expect it to encourage the legitimacy of sati in other parts of India as well—wherever the kshatriya ethos combined with this form of marriage. But such references are absent. In the early *dharmashastras*, bride-price is not regarded as being on par with the giving of a dowry, required in the kanya-dana or gifting-a-daughter form of marriage, the latter being the favoured practice.

The *Mahabharata* refers to some widows becoming satis such as Madri the wife of Pandu. On the death of Pandu there is a discussion on which of his two wives, Kunti or Madri, should become a sati. This is a partial reflection of the controversy over the observance of the custom, a controversy that continued throughout the centuries. The custom is not associated with the wives of those Kauravas who died in the battle at Kurukshetra. It was obviously not required of all kshatriyas. It has been argued that these references to sati are later interpolations. Madri however was from the Punjab. Abducting a woman to become a bride or paying a bride-price were ranked as legal forms of marriage and listed as such in the *dharmashastras.*

The *dharmashastras* seem to hold contradictory views on sati. The Manu *Dharmashastra* dating to the turn of the Christian era, requires the widow to live a chaste life. However, if she has no son then she is permitted to try for one through niyoga. The later Vishnu *Dharmashastra* allows an option to the widow: she can either be celibate and live like an ascetic or else can become a sati. Medhatithi, the major commentator on Manu, writing in about the tenth century AD, is strongly opposed to widows becoming satis. He argues that the practice is adharma and ashastriya, against the laws of dharma and not conceded by the shastras. He maintains that it amounts to suicide and this is forbidden, since each person must live his/her allotted span of life. He even urges that in some situations a widow should be permitted to remarry. Medhatithi's position was not unique and the discussion was controversial and continued to be so over the centuries. That Medhatithi felt it necessary to comment forcefully on sati unlike Manu, may indicate its wider prevalence during the post-Gupta period of the latter part of the first millennium AD. Nevertheless, there are also inscriptions from these times that record widows from royal families donating property to religious beneficiaries.

More precisely dateable evidence comes from inscriptions. An inscription of AD 510 at Eran in central India refers to the wife of Goparaja who immolated herself when her husband died in battle. The practice was by now known in this area. Similar inscriptions from Rajasthan and Nepal date to the seventh and eighth centuries AD. Banabhatta writing the *Harshacharita* in the early seventh century AD does not condemn the mother of king Harshavardhana of Kanauj for becoming a sati, perhaps because the book was an official biography. But in his other work, the *Kadambari,* he objects strongly to the practice and lists many women of high status who did not become satis. This change is reflected in other sources as well. The *Hitopadesha,* a collection of stories, glorifies the act of becoming a sati, the argument being that it ensures for the wife and the husband an eternity of living together after death. The act is described in various texts as sahamarana (dying together), sahagamana (going together) and anuvarohana (ascending the pyre). This belief would contradict the notion of reincarnation since nowhere is it argued that the couple would be constantly reincarnated as husband and wife in every birth.

Inscriptions from the peninsula refer to women becoming satis when their husbands died in battles fought between and among Hindu rulers such as the Chaulukyas, Yadavas and Hoysalas, in the period from the tenth to the fourteenth centuries AD. Many of these inscriptions are located in Maharashtra and Karnataka. The peak period of sati was prior to the invasion of these areas by armies of the Sultanates so 'Muslim invasions' were not the cause. Later, when faced by Sultanate armies from the end of the thirteenth century, the requirement or not of widow immolation would have been as prevalent or not, as in earlier times.

The other interesting feature is that most of these late first millennium inscriptions refer either to families of kshatriya status or those seeking the same or an equivalent status. One oft-quoted inscription of the eleventh century refers to a shudra woman whose husband died in battle against the Ganga ruler and who, despite opposition from her parents, became a sati. Her husband held a high military position. Her insistence may have been occasioned, among other things, by the wish to establish status. Were members of lower castes who happened occasionally to hold a reasonably high position emulating the style of the kshatriyas?

Another indication of the existence of satis is the sati memorial stones. These were known but only recently have they begun to be studied in some detail. The location, numbers, chronology and the statements both inscriptional and visual, of the hero-stones and the associated sati-stones have provided new insights into the history of these regions. Some of these areas were subject to raids by kingdoms in the vicinity, contesting territory. The sati-stones generally occur in the same locality as the hero-stones which commemorated death in the course of a heroic act of either defending the village or a herd of cattle during one of the frequent cattle-raids, or of killing predatory wild animals and so on. Sometimes the sati-stone and the hero-stone are on the same slab. The sati-stone has a standard set of symbols: the sun and the moon symbolizing the eternal memory of the person being commemorated; an upright, open, right arm and hand, bent at the elbow and clearly showing bangles intact (a woman's bangles being broken when she is widowed, the bangles being intact would be an indication of her continuing marital status); and a lime held in the hand to ward off evil. Sometimes there may be a small representation of an icon that indicates a religious sectarian identity, such as a lingam-yoni for a Shaiva or a conch shell for a Vaishnava. The sun and the moon were commonly used to mean eternity, as in inscriptions recording grants of land made by kings to brahmanas, which often conclude with the statement that they should last as long as the moon and sun. On occasion a sati is indicated by a single standing female figure or a couple, where generally the right arm of the woman has the same features as above.

Sati-stones like hero-stones occur more often, not in fertile agricultural areas but in ecologically marginal areas, where local conflicts and skirmishes would be frequent. These were often frontier areas between two ecological zones or areas where there was a competition for resources, or frontier zones between states whose boundaries would tend to shift at least a little and where there would be greater frequency of skirmishes. Possibly in marginal areas, the process of transition from tribe to jati may have required an underlining of the changing social code. Here the new norms would introduce a greater social hierarchy than before and the status of women would be gradually lowered. Tribal chiefs are also memorialized in hero-stones and this was part of the process of assimilation into the Sanskritic tradition. Doubtless by now, sati would also have been recognized as one among the many features associated with a kshatriya lifestyle, but resorted to only in exceptional circumstances.

Inscriptional and archaeological evidence suggests that the greater occurrence of immolation as also hero-stones commemorating cattle-raids seems to date to the end of the first and the early second millennium AD. This was a time when new areas were being opened up to settlement by caste-based society and there were encroachments on a larger scale into tribal areas. New castes emerged in this background of a changing economy, some with antecedents in the earlier pre-caste society. In the competition for status various observances of upper caste society became current. Why the immolation of widows was introduced requires explanation. Apart from other things it may relate to a deliberate subordination of women in the newly emerging society where women had earlier had a significant role. As a ritual it was the most traumatic in underlining the subordination of women. Or, it could have been a reaction against the many growing socio-religious movements, associated with the Bhakti tradition, some of which disapproved of caste differentiations and supported the continuing participation of women in social roles whether as wives or widows, and which movements were not always regarded with favour by the upper castes. Again, was the immolation of widows seen as a method of demarcating status?

It is interesting that there is little reference to the deification of the woman who becomes a sati at this time. The incentive to becoming a sati is accompanied by a list of rewards for the woman. She will dwell in heaven for as many years as there are hairs on the human body and will dwell with her husband served by apsaras. (In some Kannada texts the wife is said to be jealous of the apsaras and therefore insistent on dying with her husband!). Her act will purify not only her husband but also her parents and of course herself, of all sins. The inclusion of her parents was a shrewd move appealing to her filial emotions. The ultimate threat is that if she does not burn she will be reborn as a woman in many successive births. This was seen as threat enough to make any woman want to immolate herself ! The package of rewards is based quite clearly on the kshatriya view of the after-life. Only the hero went to Indraloka (or to the Shivaloka in some traditions), and lived eternally in heaven. The other view of after-life, as developed in the theory of karma and samsara, action and rebirth, did not necessarily apply to the hero. Heaven for the hero is a paradise land. The notion of sati therefore is tied to the heroic ideal, to claims to being kshatriya or following the model, and it is not surprising that up to this point in history it is generally not required of other castes. Brahmana women are not permitted to become satis in some texts such as the *Padma Purana*. But this was soon to change. In the early second millennium AD, the *Mitakshara*, a legal text treating of family law, argued that all women be permitted to become satis and that niyoga be prohibited.

A very different point of view emerges from another category of people and texts. The followers of the Shakta sects were opposed to the practice even as an expression of religious belief. The *Mahanirvana Tantra* states, 'A wife should not be burnt with her dead husband. Every woman is the embodiment of the goddess. That woman who in her delusion ascends the funeral pyre of her husband, shall go to hell.' This contradiction of the other ethic has its own interest as a statement of opposition, particularly as it comes from those who were initially regarded as being of lesser status but constituting the larger percentage of people. Possibly this kind of opposition nurtured the compensatory notion of a sati being converted into a goddess, a notion which seems to have gained currency in the later second millennium AD. Madri in the *Mahabharata,* for instance, is not deified. But the cult of worshipping sati-stones and deifying a sati as a goddess became more common in medieval Rajasthan.

As the idea developed it was said that the goddess entered the body of the woman when she resolved to become a sati. Deification was a compensation for what was otherwise seen by some as suicide. It acted as an incentive as well as an attempt to take the act onto another plane, where mundane considerations would not apply. But the deification was not individualized, for the women are often not worshipped as goddesses in their own name but as part of the generalized single sati goddess. There was less emphasis now on the continuity of living with the husband after death in heaven. Was this due to women, irrespective of their caste, being encouraged to become satis?

It is also worth remembering that Buddhist texts did not support sati and widows were instead offered the option of becoming nuns if they so chose. Some of the votive inscriptions at Buddhist stupas record donations by widows. The later Jaina texts conceded that in special circumstances a Jaina muni could die through a formal routine of slow starvation, sallekhana. This concession may have discouraged Jainas from opposing other forms of seeming suicide. Moreover, judging by the number of Jaina widows who became nuns, sati does not seem to have been the prevailing custom.

It has been stated that there was an extraordinarily large number of satis in south India at the time when the Vijayanagara kingdom was collapsing. In 1420, Nicolo de Conti visited Vijayanagara well before its peak period in the early sixteenth century and left an account that survives only through a series of translations. He describes the ritual of self-immolation and adds that three thousand wives and concubines of the king of Vijayanagara had pledged to burn themselves on the death of the king. We have only Conti's word for the pledge and there is no other evidence to prove that it was carried out. The number seems highly exaggerated. Duarte Barbosa and Fernao Nuniz visiting in the early sixteenth century also refer to the ritual but again in general terms. These were Europeans, largely interested in prospects for trade and establishing commercial relations with the kingdoms of the peninsula. They were visiting India for the first time and anxious to write about quaint customs, unfamiliar to their readers. The lack of familiarity encouraged these authors to exaggerate what they had seen or heard. Descriptions of sati headed the list of curiosities. This perhaps gives the impression that it was more prevalent in Vijayanagara than elsewhere. There is in fact little evidence from other sources to suggest that there was a substantial increase in self-immolation in the south at the time of the collapse of the Vijayanagara kingdom in the late sixteenth century.

State intervention to try and control incidents of widow immolation begins during the time of the Sultans and the Mughals. They could not prohibit it but indirectly attempted to reduce the numbers by insisting that it should not be forced on the woman. We are told that those wishing to become satis had to obtain a special license from the governors of the Mughal provinces. If this was actually so it might have acted as a deterrent. That the need for permission became part of the procedure seems evident from incidents occurring even among Indian communities living outside India. In 1723, the widow of an Indian merchant in Moscow asked permission to be burned alive alongside her husband on his funeral pyre. Her request was refused. Resenting the refusal, all the Indian merchants threatened to leave Russia, taking their wealth with them. Faced with this, the authorities gave in. The incident was repeated in 1767.

That families of wealthy traders took to this practice in the eighteenth century was doubtless due to their close proximity to political power and desire to emulate the ways of those in power. This was particularly the case in regions such as Rajasthan where many kingdoms derived substantial revenue from traders. Possibly this association with commercial groups encouraged the emergence of the sati temples. Sati memorials in the past were simple memorial stones, but the more recent temples are substantial monuments such as the one at Jhunjhunu. Such temples were often constructed by wealthy patrons, where the Marwari talent for finance combined with Rajput notions of honour, for the material benefit of both. The appropriation of the custom by other upper castes was known in the eighteenth century, although there was no uniformity of attitude towards it within the caste or even within the extended family. Thus, whereas one Peshwa was opposed to it, the wife of another became a sati in 1772. It would seem that by the eighteenth century the icon of sati was more a ritual object of worship rather than one of the ideal wife.

That sati became more prevalent among the upper castes is noticeable with the contrast of niyoga being more common at the lower levels of society. This makes good sense. In families where women worked alongside the men as among peasants and artisans, an extra hand was a help. Sati and niyoga are not juxtaposed in the texts but both practices are discussed and commented on right through the centuries. It seems to be the counter-posing of contradictory practices but which are in effect alternate solutions to the same problems.

The practice of immolating widows took a turn in a new direction in eastern India. The overwhelming incidence was among the brahmanas of this area and particularly in Bengal. The major cause for this unprecedented rise in widow immolation, particularly in the early nineteenth century has been attributed to the legal system relating to inheritance. In areas where the Dayabhaga system prevailed, as in eastern India, women were entitled to a share in the inheritance of immovable property on the death of their husbands. Sati became a means of removing one among the claimants to inheritance. It is interesting that when brahmana widows in some areas were permitted to become satis, was also the time when brahmana property holders increased—both in numbers as well as in the size of their holdings—owing to the land grants that they received from royalty. Thus what was in origin a custom associated with kshatriya notions of heroism and honour was now converted into a convenient way of eliminating an inheritor in the context of landed property. It has been suggested that the largest occurrence was among kulin brahmana families where the ratio of male to female seems to have been severely out of balance, requiring that the kulin male marry many wives from several families. The effect of this on the ritual of widow immolation was self-evident.

The movement for the abolition of widow self-immolation was hesitatingly taken up by the British Indian government and was supported by Ram Mohan Roy. Eventually in 1829 a law was passed prohibiting the practice in territories held by the British Indian government. The figures given for registered cases of sati in the early nineteenth century in the Bengal Presidency are quite staggering. In 1815 there were 378 cases. In 1818 the figure rose to 839 and in 1828 there were 463 cases. These figures make an interesting parallel to those of dowry deaths in recent years. If widow immolation is to be seen as significant to Hindu values, then it would seem that the culture had a propensity to encouraging its women to burn themselves. A magistrate of Hooghly describes the practice in 1818 as a religious act but also a choice entertainment for the neighbourhood. In areas where the Dayabhaga did not prevail and there was also an absence of kulin custom, the figures are substantially lower. The Madras Presidency in 1818 registers about 170 cases and the Bombay Presidency over the period from 1819-1827, about 50. Here it was largely among the families of chiefs and rajas.

This sharp variation in figures suggests that the appalling frequency of widow immolation in Bengal, cannot be attributed only to the disjuncture in society caused by British colonial domination. Apart from property rights there were doubtless other reasons. Given the wide popularity of Shakta and Tantric sects in eastern India, it is possible that the deliberate subordination of upper caste widows was also a reaction to the more equitable status given to women in the teaching of these sects. The Shakta sects, more than most, emphasizing the androgynous, both in belief and deity, were opposed to the self-immolation of widows.

Viewed over time, the justification for widows becoming satis moved from the initial explanation that it was the virtuous wife following her husband into death to one that included the idea of the sati becoming a goddess. In some cases the wife followed her husband irrespective of how he died, as in the case of Madri. Here the question of honour was not centrally involved as Pandu if anything died an ignoble death, unable to contain his desire for Madri. And Madri gives this as one of the reasons why she should follow her husband into the realms of Yama Being virtuous in this situation seems theoretical since neither of Pandu's wives had conceived sons through him.

The memorial stones suggest a different situation, where the husband dies a hero's death and the self-immolation of the wife is also memorialized. It is possible that immolation could have been enforced as a requirement to enhance the glory of the hero's death. The question of honour becomes central to the explanation where there is the possible violation of the wife by the enemy. Who was perceived as the enemy would vary enormously. It would range from the brigand in the forest, to the neighbouring cattle raiders, to the armies of the conquering kingdoms.

The reason in later times seems to relate to the elimination of a competitor for inheritance where both faithfulness and deification are emphasized. These situations refer to families of the upper castes commanding status and wealth. The act is supported by some persons of the upper castes, condemned by others of the same castes, but largely absent among those whose beliefs and values are said to have prevailed to a larger extent among the lower castes and persons of lesser status. The degree to which the motives conformed to the explanation given, or arose from other factors, needs to be analyzed.

This is not to deny that on some occasions it may have been an act of genuine grief and the desire to follow a husband into death. That the act of immolation is a form of sacrifice seems to be a more recent interpretation. The widow's life was not an offering or bali, since the motivation of the act in theory is that she continues to live after death with her husband in heaven. Furthermore it can only be an act of self-sacrifice if it is not enforced.

In the case of sati in Rajput society it has been argued that it involves the question of Rajput honour and is deeply ingrained in all Rajputs. It is curious that a society's honour should be dependent on women having to immolate themselves. The frequency of female infanticide in these areas today makes one suspect that it was less a matter of honour and arose from other concerns. The custom as is clear from the evidence, has not been limited to Rajputs alone in the past. The occurrence of such a custom in recent times needs to be viewed from the perspective of current claims to social class and political clout as well as to supposedly traditional ways of claiming these, apart from the fidelity of the wife in the context of competitive communities. It is also quoted as a symbol of an idealised husband-wife relationship. If so, this is an unbalanced manifestation, as has often been remarked, there is never any question of the husband immolating himself on the pyre of his wife. Nor is the immolation of the widow invariably voluntary. The widows of Bengal it is said had to be tied to the pyre and kept down by bamboo staffs.

Claiming it as a Hindu inheritance from the past is to transfer a ritual associated with a small segment of upper caste society to the entire society with the claim that it is the rite/right of the Hindu community. It was never regarded as universally applicable to all Hindus and even its limited applicability has always been controversial. Neither among kshatriyas nor among brahmanas was there a universal adherence to the custom. When it is taken up arbitrarily by some members of castes other than kshatriyas it is in the context of demonstrating status or linked to the inheritance of property. To argue that the abolition of sati is a deliberately anti-Hindu act is to replay the debate of the nineteenth century where Ram Mohan Roy had maintained correctly that it does not carry the sanction of the *Vedas* and the Sanskrit scholar Mritunjaya Vidyalankar maintained that it was not enjoined by the *shastras*. If status has to be demonstrated today there are other ways of doing it.

Sati and niyoga were both controversial but were practiced as customs although eventually by different social strata. Was niyoga the more common practice in the clan societies of the early period and did sati become more prevalent among the upper castes in the later period? Why was the brutal and gruesome act of *sati* pursued rather than the more humane and less violent niyoga? Sati is of course a more definitive control over a women's sexuality since it is a terminal condition. Frequent references are made to the female as kshetra (field or land), and the male providing the bija (seed). Land of course is owned whereas seed is free. A rise in the number of women becoming satis would suggest that it was a period of crisis for upper caste social authority, perhaps due to lower castes moving up in social ranking. This would necessitate a greater control over upper caste women. These suggestions have yet to be examined for regions where records are available. The recent social demography of these areas could be one of the parameters in such an investigation.

The extension of the symbolism of sati from the faithful wife to the goddess was not unrelated to the purposes of the social group endorsing the act. What many are now objecting to is that in today's value system, the custom becomes an act of suicide, or when enforced it becomes an act of murder, but in either case it reflects a social ethic in relation to women that is objectionable. It endorses an inconsequential existence for a woman and her subordination to the vulgarity of a public spectacle, as well as to the manipulation of those claiming to be acting in defense of traditional values.

It is not as if becoming a sati, or accepting the relationship that came with niyoga, were the only options. The majority of widows did not exercise either of these options. Their lives were dependent on how the family treated them, as they are to this day. In some cases they are the virtual matriarchal heads of a family, in others they are treated as inauspicious and reduced almost to the condition of dasis or left in widows' homes at places of pilgrimage, such as Vrindavan or Varanasi, and in yet others they lead an acceptable life as part of the family. But what happened, and we now hope it pertains only to the past, should not be forgotten as it reflects on the making of what we sometimes describe as our 'tradition'.

If sati is to be properly understood it would require a tracking down of information on widow self-immolation involving a number of sources, pertaining to a range of social groups and with reference to various regions at different points in time. Only when we examine the juxtaposition of kinship, property relations, rights of inheritance, the approach to sexuality, the ethic of the hero, attitudes to deity and adjustments to social change in the context of our history, will we begin perhaps to understand why and how women were encouraged or forced to become satis, or why there were objections to doing so. That it is important to investigate this, is because its less visible social and psychological implications have not been exposed.

19

RAPE WITHIN A CYCLE OF VIOLENCE

In 2011, the number of rapes amounted to almost one every hour, for the whole year. This is a horrendous fact and it's something that should make us all think about what we can do. We have to understand how it is that we allow this to happen, and why it happens, and what can we as citizens do to make it happen less often. We cannot prevent it altogether so at least a decrease in numbers will be an achievement.

To understand why rape is so prevalent in our society, perhaps we should discuss some of the more obvious aspects of the phenomenon—in particular two crucial aspects. : one, the creation of the general mindset in relation to women in our country, which is extremely important particularly in terms of how we use the past to create this mindset, and then in turn use it to influence the present; and the second is the present situation and what needs action.

I would like to begin with discussing the mindset. Unfortunately, it requires repeating yet again, that the attitudes of those who claim to be the leaders of our society—politicians in high office and the so-called 'god-men' are often the most influential in creating an unacceptable mindset. And what some of them have said in public and in the media, about women being raped, was I think, outrageous. This is why I think that the mindset is extremely important and needs attention, in addition to whatever we choose to do about what is currently happening. I think the statements that were made again and again were bizarre, thoughtless, jejune and frequently inane. Examples of these are that young women must be incarcerated at home after dark, girls must be forced to wear overcoats to cover themselves from head to foot, girls must not be allowed cellphones because they can then contact boys, a woman about to be raped should recite the Sarasvati mantra, and women must observe the Lakshman Rekha to avoid trouble—and of course we all know who marks the Lakshman Rekha. The most disgusting was the statement that, a raped woman is like a 'zinda lash', a living corpse. Little in all of this was said about the kind of men that rape women, and how they can be stopped from doing this? It is almost as if the men are invisible and rape somehow happens on its own. These attitudes assume that rape is inevitable if women are liberated. So the best way to avoid rape is to oppress women. This is the prevalent view in a society that is conditioned by the belief that men make the rules and women cannot question them. There may be something ridiculous about this lopsided view of society, yet it is the mindset of many.

How the mindset spills out into action was recently demonstrated in the riots of Muzaffarnagar. Ostensibly the call to rioting and violence was to object to 'love jihad', the fear that Hindu young women were falling into the clutches of and marrying Muslim young men. The other slogan was 'bahu-beti-bachau', but in the process of protecting the bahu and the beti, raping women was considered perfectly in order. Raping women is the age-old method of certain kinds of men asserting power over women, especially if the women belong to a community that they wish to humiliate. In communal conflicts it is resorted to as a weapon and a trophy of victory. Inevitably the easiest targets in situations of civil disturbance are Dalit women and those of the minority communities,since they have the least protection from the agencies of law and order, and belong to the subordinated sections of society.

It is nevertheless crucial to the discussion on how we visualize the kind of society that we want. The oppression of women has been characteristic, let me add, of most pre-modern societies the world over. As far as the past is concerned this is not an unusual situation. But we now claim to be a contemporary, modern society. We are in a position today to understand why this mindset came about and to change it in favour of a society governed by the rights that we think are essential. So let me revert to the mindset. What goes into the making of a mindset? We refer to cultural traditions from the past. Do we even examine the implications and nuances of what we assume these traditions to be? Let's just look at some of them in relation to attitudes to women, or of why they came into existence because of how society was constituted at a particular time. Or whether, given that social norms now endorse the equality of men and women, should we not change the mindset to accord with the new social requirements? If the norms of a tradition no longer hold, the question to be debated is why this is so, and if the norms need to be changed then this should be advocated, even if it means the earlier ones being jettisoned.

We are told that in the Vedic period women as a general category had a high status and were greatly respected. The *Upanishads* are quoted which refer to brilliant women philosophers such as Gargi and Maitrayi, Vedic rituals are referred to in which the patron of the ritual had to have his wife beside him otherwise the ritual would not be effective, and so on. Such actions underline status. But historians, such as Uma Chakrabarty and Kumkum Roy, have asked pertinent questions about the other women so frequently mentioned. For instance, what happened to the Vedic dasi? Why does she never come into this picture? She was the slave woman, the servant in the household, who is mentioned frequently in the *Vedas, Mahabharata* and *Ramayana,* but seldom features in our current picture of the utopian past. What was her condition? She is repeatedly listed in these texts together with the animals—cattle and horses—as chattel. They are all the property of the owner to do what he likes with them. The larger numbers of women therefore are treated as commodities. Given the references to unnamed dasis who are the mothers of brahmanas—the dasi-putra brahmanas or students such as Jabala, mentioned in the Vedic corpus—it is clear that the dasi was expected to do more than just household chores. Such activities doubtless required of a dasi should at least be acknowledged wherever they apply, when referring to the pedigree of authoritative figures. The social values of elite groups in those ancient societies and the society of today are different. In earlier times the dasis are hardly visible. Modern society demands their visibility. We today maintain that all women have equal rights among themselves and with men, but this was not the prevalent ethic of ancient times.

From the Valmiki *Ramayana* the most frequently quoted reference is to Sita and to the Lakshman *rekha*; when she inadvertently crosses it her troubles start. Because she was kidnapped, the onus is on her to prove her chastity. And this is the prototype pattern: a woman has always to prove her chastity. This Sita does by going through an agnipariksha, the fire ordeal. When she is asked to repeat the same thing a second time, consequent on some gossip about her, she decides that enough is enough. The Valmiki *Ramayana* is in origin an epic story that became a sacred book of the Vaishnavas and is a powerful text in the propagation of Rama bhakti, the worship of Rama. There are passages of exquisite poetry that give it a high literary status. But at the same time we have to keep in mind that it is a classic text of Hindu patriarchy. The man is a god and the woman has to repeatedly prove her chastity. And do we today consider what might have been the thoughts of Sita as she experiences the testing of her chastity? Have we really thought about her side of the story?

Why do we also never refer to other versions of the story? Neither the Buddhist nor the Jaina version, for example, is centrally concerned with the chastity of Sita. Over the centuries there have been many versions of what has come to be called the ramakatha. Some followed the Valmiki narrative but others differed from it, as obviously his version did not appeal to them. And in some cases they even contested it. In medieval times, in what we today disparagingly call 'feudal' society, some people seem not to have approved of the fire ordeal because there was a well-known version in which that event was altered. When the fire was blazing forth Sita was made to step aside and the chhaya Sita, a shadow Sita, entered the fire and came out unscathed. The question one has to ask is why was a chhaya Sita invented? The answer usually given is that at this time the philosophy of maya, illusion, was at its height and illusory figures were popular. But perhaps one has also to see it more realistically. Why did the shadow Sita replace the earlier version of Sita in this rendering of the story? Did some people see the fire ordeal as craven, and as Sita having to submit to injustice?

There were other popular versions of the story in which Sita asserts her rights and these versions are different from the Valmiki or the Tulasi *Ramayanas.* One of my favourite folk versions is the one in which Rama's attack on Ravana is not going too well so Sita says to Rama that she will conduct the battle on his behalf and does so and is victorious against Ravana. This is an entirely different representation of Sita and would have an appeal for women who have, or would like to have, some command over their own lives. Such versions are common in the oral literature of regional languages and in folk literature and their survival attests to their popularity. Or at least that was so before the poorly constructed television version took over and ironed out the local variations, resulting in a predictable and somewhat banal uniformity. And yet despite the fact that there are differences in these versions, telling us different things about how people viewed the story, and what social and ethical values they gave to the story, we continue to generalize from the Valmiki version excluding others.

The suggestion that alternate readings be discussed, at least at University level so as to familiarize students with their heritage, are dismissed and not permitted. Delhi University did just that. As we've seen, it removed a thought-provoking and sensitively written essay by AK Ramanujam on the many versions of the *Ramayana* from its syllabus, because a handful of Hindu students said it hurt their sentiments, since they believe there can be only one *Ramayana*, that of Valmiki. More specifically related to questions of gender and religious texts, a similar group of Muslims objected to Amina Wadud giving a lecture at Madras University on questions of Islamic texts and gender, and the lecture was cancelled by the Vice-Chancellor on the request of the police. Such actions are taking 'hurt sentiments' to an extreme, where the idea of religion as the articulation of co-existing sentiments of faith, is being belittled if not insulted by its conversion into political gamesmanship. At the same time we are allowing religious institutions and political parties that claim to be defending particular religions to increasingly dictate the content of our social and civic values. And yet at the same time, these cannot be freely discussed and if need be, questioned.

The *Bhagvad Gita,* held sacred by so many, has a verse in which Krishna states that all those who worship him can through bhakti (devotion), achieve liberation from moksha (rebirth). He goes on to say that this applies even to those who are born in the womb of sin, papa-yoni. And who does he say are the people born in this womb of sin? As we have seen, these are the vaishyas, shudras and women. I suppose it is gratifying that women can also be freed from rebirth through devotion to Krishna. But the point is that all women, irrespective of their social origin, whether they are upper caste or lower caste, are said to be born in the womb of sin, implying thereby that their origin should be treated with contempt as was that of the lower caste shudras. It hurts my sentiments as a woman to be described as originating from the womb of sin, nevertheless the suppression of this verse would not assuage my feelings. On the contrary, I would argue that it should be discussed as that might give us a better understanding of the implications of this statement for women, for vaishyas and shudras, and for the society in which vaishyas, shudras and women, live. And this understanding would clarify the contribution of such statements to the creation of a mindset.

In the early centuries AD, the worship of Shakti as the goddess became popular and her popularity increased over time. However, worshiping goddesses did not appreciably change the attitude of men towards women in daily life. Some Rajput clans regarded the clan goddess, the kuladevi, as the iconic center of their identity. Yet these clans could also be among those inculcating the need for women to burn themselves should their husbands die in battle. Needless to say, it was argued that the death of the women was required to save the honour of the male kshatriya. This was a strange equation! In some ways it was a variant on Sita's fire-ordeal. The woman's chastity was ensured by her death. As we have seen, becoming a sati was gradually idealized. But interestingly, this was also a subject of debate both in the commentaries of the social codes and in other kinds of literature.

Today Sita is quoted as the role model for women. I often wonder why we don't refer to the women of the *Mahabharata* equally often. Are these women threateningly independent? The *Mahabharata* is the story of clans in conflict. And women who belong to clan society seem to be more independent than those who belong to a society where caste is entrenched. Gandhari is married to the blind Dhritarashtra. So she chooses to go through life blindfolded. Iravati Karve, the sociologist, has asked the very pertinent question, why? Is it out of sympathy with her blind husband? Or out of resentment that she as a young and beautiful woman, has been tied for life to a blind man? As Kunti's husband is unable to give her children, her only recourse is to call upon various deities to do so. Draupadi is married inadvertently to five brothers but accepts the decision. Nevertheless she retains her independence for when Yudhishthira places her as a stake in the game of dice, she questions his legal right to do so. She was within her rights to question his action since he had previously staked himself and lost. Therefore did he have a legal right to stake anyone else?

All these women are interesting because in various ways they did not conform to the codes and yet they were accepted. But why do we today not refer to these women as role models? Is it because they cannot be subordinated to our contemporary denigration of women? I have often wondered that if we could gather together Valmiki's Sita with Gandhari, Kunti and Draupadi, what kind of conversation would they have had? I think it's worth considering.

However, please don't get me wrong. I am not suggesting that all women had miserable lives in the past. Not at all. Some even became queen-regents, such as Prabhavati Gupta who ruled the Vakataka kingdom, or Didda who lived through the reigns of son and grandson and then ruled herself in Kashmir negotiating feudal politics with great aplomb, or Raziya who was not as successful and fell victim to power politics. I am well aware that there are other aspects of the past that are highly commendable. But I am trying to ask why we emphasize those that are not in accordance with our present ideas of a just society.

If again we turn to the past, then in theory, laws regarding rape are stringent and protective of the woman to some degree. Punishment for rape tells us something about the categories of women that were raped and attitudes towards them. I would like to quote from Kautilya's *Arthashastra*. He recommends the compensation to be paid to the woman and the punishment of the man, in varying situations. Where the dasi is raped, or her daughter, obviously a household slave or a servant, each is entitled to demand compensation from the rapist, and this is set out. With reference to the raping and gang raping of a prostitute, the punishment suggested is a monetary fine, calculated in accordance with what she earns. The severest punishment is reserved for a man who sexually assaults a kinswoman, what we today would include in marital and domestic rape, or his guru's wife. Such a man is to be first castrated and then given the death penalty. But some sexual transgressions against lower caste women receive seemingly lighter punishment. The one who has raped a lower caste woman is to be branded by a specific, permanently visible mark on his forehead, by which people would recognize his crime. Interestingly this applies to all such rapists irrespective of whether they are juveniles or adults. Lower caste women in those days as well were raped, but the punishment is far more severe than is given in our times.

I would argue that we deliberately choose our models from the past in order that they conform to our present ideology. So if women are to be kept subordinated then we highlight this from the past and justify it as heritage. But when we thus select from the past in order to construct our heritage we should be aware of what we are selecting and why; and of what the other choices could be. And this heritage of course inevitably changes over time. This means looking analytically at our society, both the present and that of the past. We need to change it where change is required in the present, and to clean out that which is rotten. Where does one begin in trying to change the mindset? It is necessary to legislate, but above all and beyond that, to see that the legislation is implemented, for only then can it be effective.

Let's just go through the life cycle of the Indian woman. Fortunately this is not the general pattern for all. But it occurs in different regions in various degrees and if not debated more openly, it will continue to set the tone. And it has an impact on many women at many points in their life. The female foetus in some parts of the country is aborted and this is done to such a degree that the male-female ratio has gone haywire. Bonded brides have therefore to be imported from other states and are then made to double up as wives and servants in the household. Can we demand that the abortions should be allowed only when jointly decided through agreement by a group of doctors instead of a single one?

The female child has to face malnutrition in various forms. Compulsory schooling for the girl child should include a mid-day meal to be eaten on the premises. This might just take care of some of the malnutrition, although the girl child may not live to a school-going age. If the parents need the earnings of the child, they can be given a monetary compensation as a subsidy so that the girl can be educated. The child should not be removed from school. Talking about school, there is an absolutely desperate need for textbooks to be vetted. Textbooks in all subjects need to be read and cleared and this applies from Punjab to Karnataka, as those currently used, especially in many private schools, don't hesitate to describe women as inherently inferior. Such regressive views have no place in textbooks.

At puberty the girl is got ready for marriage. The Age of Consent Bill is observed only in some places. There is a law against dowry but it is seldom implemented. Fines are always negotiable. But if those who burn brides are sent to prison, then the law might be taken more seriously. Putting wives through fire has continued since ancient times, from Sita to sati to dowry deaths. It is a curious aspect of our social culture. Dowry is also entwined with the laws of inheritance as they are to some extent counterparts. In a society such as ours where rights over property are central to claiming status and freedom, respect for women will emerge only when they are given rights to property. Therefore, the laws against dowry will have to be interfaced with laws of inheritance, where wives and daughters are inheritors. If dowry were to be terminated and women were to get equal rights of inheritance, they and their husbands would ensure that this right was exercised. Having obtained the inheritance she could retain it in her own name and some degree of economic backing would make her less vulnerable. Had the same option been given to women with reference to dowry fewer women may have been burnt over the list of objects they brought as dowry. Civil laws and especially rights of women have to be secular and uniform, if women are to get social justice across the board. Exercising the law is as important as having it. Most religious codes in India are not supportive of equal rights to women; and where they may be, are seldom implemented as such.

There are at least two disruptive features that are creating an immense social turmoil. These have to be handled with sensitivity but with great firmness. One is the crisis in the functioning of caste. Throughout its history, controlling women has been a patriarchal method of controlling society. To retain the stability of the caste, it is crucial that the marriage of the woman is according to caste rules. And the easiest way of doing this is to clamp down on the woman. And if you read in the Manu *Dharmashastra* the eight legal and acceptable forms of marriage, in each case it is the woman who is to be either gifted, or exchanged, or abducted. The loosening of this control over the marriage in some castes is creating an immense problem for patriarchy. Caste rules relating to whom one can or cannot marry, are given preference in all communities, be they Hindu, Muslim, Sikh, or Christian. And indeed the category of Dalit is also common to all religions of India. Because of caste rules, the subordination of women becomes universally applicable in Indian society and across the board. There may be a few exceptions, such as among some communities that have observed matrilineal forms or among certain Schedule Tribes that do not observe caste.

When women choose to marry outside their caste, it is seen as an attempt to break the stability of the caste. And in this circumstance, informal organizations like the khap panchayats prefer to murder the woman as a solution. One reason for the desperate wish to keep castes intact is because castes have now also become vote banks and therefore caste becomes the base for political power and all the advantages that come with it. But both the identity and the ranking of jatis as caste, have not necessarily been either permanent or unchanging in history. Castes have had crises and have changed in composition and in status, hence the repeated reference in the Sanskrit texts to the fear of mixed castes—the varnasankara, or the sankirnajati, or of the Kaliyuga when caste codes are turned upside down and rules dispensed with. Obviously this happened enough times for it to be seen as the worst possible social disaster from the perspective of the authors of these texts. So the claim that the purity and status of the caste are being preserved in these draconian actions of the present day, is actually determined not by a wish to conform to a heritage from the past but by a concession to the politics of the present. To state that a woman embodies the honour of a man or his caste and therefore needs to be killed, is merely a way of frightening women and of justifying violence against them. Surely a man can defend his own honour? If the honour of a man requires protection through the death of a woman, then it is but a mask to reiterate his control over her sexuality, over her rights to property and over her life itself.

The other factor that has disrupted society is the rapid neo-liberalization of the economy where it is creating valueless consumer targets, leading to frustration among those who either cannot afford these goods or are unemployed. These become the meaningless symbols of affluence as is illustrated by many TV advertisements. The inability to grasp this new life-style increases the frustration that is then vented in other forms such as killing Dalits or raping women. Dalits and women by claiming their rights as citizens are seen as those who are over turning the old order in which they were subordinate beings, therefore they become the targets of contemporary violence. This becomes a way of asserting power among those for whom social violence is a way of expressing frustration. And it occurs both in rural and urban areas.

Cleaning this rot then has to be an immediate agenda. Demands have been made to combat rape by sensitizing the police and by setting up fast track courts. The time limit for the decisions of the courts must be insisted upon to prevent them from going on endlessly, as is common in this country. But equally importantly there has to be a consistent effort to change the mindset of Indian society to bring about equal respect and equal rights for women; and not only as laws, but more importantly in their practice. This is a larger and more complex programme of organization and activity; without exaggeration it is a mammoth task and I am not sure how one can begin to effectively address it. Ultimately it will have to be sorted out. And it would be so much better all round, if it comes without the clobbering of women and Dalits in the violence that is increasingly common these days.

We have a rational and workable Constitution, but which we do not implement fully. The obstacles it seems to me are caste codes, religious codes and the requirements of political, electoral aspirations. We could, for a start, begin to create an awareness of the rights that we already have by way of the Constitution and demand the implementation of these rights wherever possible. This can only be a prelude to other rights that should follow. Indian society today, it seems to me, is being mangled by the identity politics of caste and religious communities, by the construction of what we believe are hallowed, sacred traditions that cannot be changed, and by the new forms of obstructionism that call themselves 'hurt sentiments'. All these should be questioned and halted, since they are essentially forms of political mobilization to enable some groups to come to power and to prevent what is needed for us to move towards an egalitarian and just society. They are not the structures of a stable society. Their success comes from the decreasing number of people willing to read and think independently and to be actively involved in questioning what happens around them. Those that claim their sentiments to be hurt invariably accompany these claims with threats of violence or even actual violence and these are used to blackmail society into greater and greater fear and silence. The increasing frequency of the concessions that we make to the 'hurt sentiments' of this and that group can be disastrous for our future. The fear of free expression is the death knell of a democratic society. We are now witnessing the continuous stream of banning books, banning films, threatening intellectuals, killing those who expose corruption, and threatening people who speak up openly and say they want a debate on viable subjects of concern to society.

Seeing the condition of political parties at the moment and their distance from social ethics, with a couple of exceptions, it is unlikely that we can depend on them alone to bring about the change that we may want. The change has to come through a concerted effort of citizens. That this can be done has been demonstrated in the protests of young women and men against rape in the recent past all over the country. And in a sense what one is concerned about is the future of precisely this younger generation. What kind of society are they going to be living in? It is heartening that such sustained spontaneous, unorganized protests against violence and social injustice were possible. As a pointer to future action one can only welcome this.

EPILOGUE

Nations need identities. These are created from perceptions of how societies have evolved. In this, history plays a central role. Insisting on reliable history is therefore crucial to more than just a pedagogic cause. Delicate relationships between the past and present or an exacting understanding of the past, call for careful analyses.

The essays included here have put together thoughts on the interplay of the past and the present where the present interprets the past in ways that seek legitimacy for actions in the present, and the interpretation of the past may well be determined by the requirements of the present. I have argued that this is not the function of historical writing. Nevertheless, the legitimacy of history is often sought for political ideologies and matters concerning contemporary society. However much the past may be viewed from our times, as it inevitably is up to a point, the awareness of what such a view implies should not be ignored. I have tried to illustrate the problems that arise when the past is treated as the extension (backwards) of the present, and have suggested that we understand each in its own inevitably different contexts. This becomes problematic in some situations, such as in the search for a national identity that draws on the past although motivated by the present. As for whose past it draws on for such an identity, this has perforce to be inclusive of all citizens and cannot limit itself to a single community, no matter how dominant such a community may be.

The perception of the past can also be tied into the requirements of the present, as is evident by the way colonial scholarship constructed the Indian past. Nationalist historical writing challenged this construction, but perhaps not sufficiently. Instead, in the important formulation of Indian cultural and historical identity it drew on the colonial construction of the centrality of religious communities. Nationalist historians by and large, did endorse liberal values and some saw the importance of recognizing what they described as secular values, referring to the co-existence of religions. There was at the time the anticipation of creating a society subsequent to and different from, the colonial experience. Today we ask ourselves whether we chose the appropriate identity and succeeded in creating the nation we had set out to do three generations ago?

On 15th August 1947, when I made my short speech in school, I quoted—as did many others—a verse from William Wordsworth: 'Bliss was it in that dawn to be alive, But to be young was very Heaven!' In more recent years many of us have recalled the line from Faiz Ahmed Faiz, who speaks of Partition as 'not being the dawn that we had hoped for'. That disappointment lingers somewhat. We had anticipated the transformation of a colonial society into a secular democracy, characterized by a relatively equitable distribution of wealth and basic entitlements as well as access to social justice for all citizens. If this vision had been pursued into reality, over a period of two-thirds of a century, then surely it would have been sufficient to transform the erstwhile colony—to an appreciable degree—into the kind of society for which we had hoped.

I have tried in these essays to suggest a few reasons why some of our aspirations in creating a contemporary culture and drawing on the past, did not meet with fruition, but which nevertheless have not been entirely thwarted. I have restricted myself to the subject with which I have some familiarity, namely, the early past, previously referred to as 'ancient India' and sharply differentiated from medieval India. I give equal weightage to the medieval past, but since my familiarity with it is limited, it has featured marginally in these essays. My focus has been on the question of contemporary identities—the choice of an identity and the political use of identities—and the links of these with the past. I have written about only one aspect of why this has been problematic, where the past has been evoked to justify the actions of the present. If all this has come across as overly pessimistic I would like to correct that impression. If the public perception of the past has remained substantially unchanged or else accepts the colonial roots of its interpretation, because there are political and social pressures to keep it so, or even to reiterate misconceptions, there have at the same time been worthy attempts by historians and social scientists to question not only the colonial construction of the past but also the continuation of this colonial perspective through communal interpretations of history. The new studies provide insightful ways of comprehending the past, as also its relation to the present. They have been and are, part of the widespread discussion and debate on interpreting history. The response to this effort of the last fifty years although it has radically changed thinking about the past among those who research it and teach it, has not had the same impact in the public sphere. It has however, been effective in focusing on parameters other than those dictated by colonial views and in subsequent communal perspectives. It has also come closer than ever before to what may be called the realities of the past, revealing patterns of culture and the forms and degrees of interaction between communities of various kinds. This enables us to better understand the social and emotional ways of behavior among such groups of people in the past and this has an impact on how communities perceive each other today. Tolerance or intolerance, conflict or harmony, are not innate to certain categories of people as is sometimes believed, but result from particular ways of thinking and acting, encouraged by those who use these methods to control society and politics.

The anticipation of relevance continues as also the conviction that the past can be used to understand the present, rather than merely to justify the politics of conflict, where revenge is sought for what are projected as atrocities of a thousand years ago. Such an understanding directs attention to confrontation and accommodation, as also the hierarchies of power and subordination, as they have existed in the past and as they do so now. A historical perspective forces home the realization that change has been a constant factor in the past and if appropriately directed can bring about a different present. We are still currently faced with an array of choices but there should be no illusions about the fact that each choice points to a different future. Other choices might have presaged a better future.

The degree of tolerance may have been a shade more in the past as identities were perhaps not so sharply demarcated and had fuzzy edges. But sharp demarcations were not absent, as for example between the so-called pure brahmana and the impure untouchable. The oppression of the latter was sought to be justified by calling them polluted and with this excuse using them as a permanent labour source. Between the two extremes, there were a variety of others and their relationships involving lineage, occupation and belief systems. Caste hierarchy was observed to a greater or lesser extent in all religious identities, surfacing particularly when a marriage had to be arranged and patriarchy asserted. The two necessary foundations of a modern society—equal rights of all citizens and secularism—are now confronting this hierarchy.

Those that had earlier claimed an entitlement to superior status and treated the social and economic inferiority of the lower castes as the necessary counterweight to this status are hesitant to accept or might even resent the democratic processes. The counterweights of inequality were multiple, among them caste society versus those outside the pale such as Dalits and tribals, and male superiority over women embedded in patriarchy, as prevalent in most places barring a small number. Pre-modern societies were partial to the idiom of religion that went beyond the needs of the individual and permeated many aspects of life. Social protest therefore sometimes took the form of new religious sects with more liberal views. These had some function in a society where religion was defined less in formal terms and more through a range of sectarian belief and practice. The idiom of religion has seldom been democratic. A hierarchy was invented and suffused its organization. The act of worship was in itself a submission to a virtually unknown authority. Democracy therefore runs into problems when society is infused with religious organizations and leaders. Secularism becomes essential to democracy. Secularism does not require the expulsion of religion, but by liberating society from the hierarchies and inequities implicit in organized, formal religion, it gives the required space to democratic functioning.

The interplay of the past and the present is noticeable in periods of transition when societies mutate from one existing form to another. We are in the midst of such a period of transition, mutating towards what we visualize as a modern society in the process of shedding its colonial past. This implies an essential change when community identities earlier believed to have been characterized by single identities whether religion, caste, language, ethnicity, or region, have to give way to the identity of citizenship that incorporates and rises above these other identities. A nation grows out of a collective of communities with multiple identities inherited from a shared past. The shared past is not a static given, but accumulates and evolves through its history. Identities have always been multiple, but the combination of the constituents and the nature of the interface of communities, followed different patterns in earlier times and the pattern changes with the move to modernization.

Such patterns draw on the different features that go into their making. Historians investigate these features through questioning the data in the shape of traces left by past societies. The questions encompass many perspectives. How does the environment help or hinder the making of a society? To what extent is a society crafted by its technological information? Who controls resources and labour? Who dominates social functions and who has to submit to this and why? In what way are the belief systems and their practices integrated into the pattern? Is the pattern reflected in the literature of the society? Are forms in art and architecture representative of the social ambitions of the communities involved? Where these variables change from time to time, there the pattern also changes.

Community identities do not arise fully formed out of nowhere: they have to be constructed and their understanding of their own history is a necessary part of this construction, sometimes even its foundation. Historical investigation can contribute to this understanding. The methods of historical investigation are not static and are improved upon with advances in knowledge. Hence the historical perception of how communities functioned in the past is assessed afresh when there are new tools for looking at existing evidence or indeed when there is new evidence. Whether a society wishes to be open to a revision of its understanding of its own past is, of course, another matter, but even resistance eventually recedes giving way to new perceptions.

The initial attempt at creating what was thought to be a modern society in India did not evolve through a period of transition as it did in Europe but came abruptly with the disjuncture of colonialism. It had potential for introducing the kind of emancipation associated with modernization. But this deeper change became stymied when a superficial imitation of the colonizer was viewed as sufficient, rather than restructuring society to accommodate change. Colonial education in any case, did not encourage understanding or changing the structure of the Indian social system in an essential way. It reinforced the colonial view of Indian society. From this perspective communities were thought of as ghettoized units identified by religion. The attempt was not to re-analyze and reformulate society but to maintain a veneer of newness, an attitude that has not been discarded. This is seen most acutely in perceptions of the core of social functioning, namely in relation to gender and to social inequality. Logic and rationality that should motivate questions of where we are at, tend to be set aside. Where logic and rationality are not the basis of an on-going process of questioning and encouraging new views of the world around us, thinking gets ossified.

Nations that have been colonies need to evaluate the colonial comprehension of both their past and their present to a far greater degree than most have tended to do. And India is no exception. The adoption of the Constitution was a good start. If it had been implemented with a healthy degree of commitment, the social and economic polity could have been for the greater good. But the initial promise met with some obvious hurdles. One was that very little attempt was made to redefine the purpose and form of the various aspects of state functioning—changing them from a colonial system to a democratic system. The bureaucratic structures have in essence remained colonial as have the attitudes that they engendered among those who controlled them. Only a minority of administrators and guardians today think of themselves as being, 'of the people'. For the majority, those whom they govern are 'the Other' and the system exists so that it can be milked. An incident occurs and we suddenly discover that we are still being governed by colonial legislation—as happened recently with the withdrawal of W. Doniger's book. Such legislation is not expected in a secular, democratic society. The most radical change was that of adult franchise. This is now battling both caste politics and the corporate financing of political parties. The media could have provided space for liberal thinking, but they have with rare exceptions, become the propagators of the conservative and the conventional, backed by a corporate takeover. The turn away from a firm commitment to a secular democracy has been with us now for a few decades. The frequency of major communal riots points to the continued use of religious identities for political mobilization.

In 1991 there was a change in direction. It took a new form that was said would ensure economic and social change for the betterment of all. The question is, did it? Various reasons point to the date of 1991 and the subsequent years. The most obvious is the change in the pattern of the economy. Economic growth came to be linked less to an independent economy and more to the global market with all the attendant problems of the change. Among these are the representatives of crony capitalism that control various agencies of economic development but the reduction of poverty is not their concern. From the 1990s corporate power and control has increased enormously and the impoverishment of the peasant has declined only in a few places and that too by a miniscule amount. Half of India's citizens remain below the poverty line. But with the focus on the economy what was not foreseen was the direction that came to be taken by changes in social attitudes and values. There has been some change, but it has not been what was promised by the liberalization of the economy. The reiteration of social conservatism as a panacea to problems and the degree to which it is accommodated is disturbing. Markets thrive on competitive activity and this in turn introduces insecurities of many kinds. The middle class has grown in numbers and so has its insecurity, which makes for a society more prone to aggression as a solution. Combining social insecurity and aggression fuels the politics of religious identities and religious fundamentalism. This is viewed as an acceptable solution. The claim to hurt religious sentiments becomes a manifestation of this.

The believed threat to what are regarded as 'traditional' systems of social functioning creates a fear of the reality of social change, so imitations of modernity suffice. This is obvious for example, from the content of the most-watched serials on TV channels and the invasion of mall culture. Activities seen as particular threats are matters relating to religion, to gender roles, and to Scheduled Castes and Scheduled Tribes (to use the colonial nomenclature, which remains unchanged). These social categories are still regarded as inherently inferior. These are all general areas in which the past did have a different perspective and pattern of behaviour, and this was challenged by the move towards a secular democracy. By examining the conditions in the past and understanding why they were the way they were, we can comprehend what needs to change in our times. What we regard as freedom of expression was permitted largely only to privileged groups in early societies, or those who were voluntarily or otherwise outside the social pale.

Some believe that a secular society means the banishing of religion. On the contrary religion in a secular society can be a source of inner strength in the private lives of many. It implies a belief in a supernatural power that is most often worshipped in the form of a deity who has the right to reward or punish in accordance with the actions of the worshipper and this explains the events in his or her life. The problem arises with the next step—when the religion is so formulated that it attracts a following, the organization of which impinges on how a contemporary democratic society should function. Religious organizations, as I have said, tend to be anti-democratic and hierarchical. All believers may be equal in the eyes of God, and on the supernatural plane, but this does not ensure equality in the here and now. A group from within the religion generally formulates a code of ethics and social laws that may or may not be in conformity with the best interests of the rest of society. This right to formulate a social code should ideally remain with the general will of the people rather than with a segment identifying with a particular religion. If religious codes prevail there will be multiple codes, some protecting and some creating social inequalities. Where the rules of social functioning, sanctified by religion and backed by the rules of caste, are intermeshed as social codes, there the confrontation with secularism becomes more complex. The propagation of a religion results in its creating institutions, meant for the betterment of society, such as schools, but also intended to draw a following as agencies of propagation. Such institutions discourage the ultimate role of rationality and logic in the knowledge on which education draws, since their premises are based on faith. A further step is when religion becomes religiosity. Here the focus is less on the teaching of the religion and more on its display, which in this situation is carried out with much fanfare and the expending of wealth. It is more a claim to status and what money can buy than a concern with belief in deity. Religiosity is generally a characteristic of situations when there is a fear that the dominant position held by the followers of a religion is beginning to decline, and therefore has to be publicized where possible.

An extreme form of religion controlling public life is of course communalism, a modern phenomenon in India. Politics and the act of governance is affected by mobilization along religious lines and by political ideology based on religious identities. Communal organizations have diverse functions. They endorse the politics of religious identities and in doing so oppose democracy by giving priority to the numerically largest religious community. This is sometimes disguised by claiming that their concern is with culture rather than religion and politics—as if culture precludes these. Yet their definition of culture is neither liberal nor inclusive. Even more devastating is their pointing to the 'enemy within' society. To subdue such an enemy requires the setting aside of democratic norms and appropriating unquestioned dictatorial powers. In India the 'enemy within' includes a range of people all said to be antagonistic to ancient traditions, although such traditions are recent inventions. This becomes evident as the roll-call of 'enemies' is added to. Foremost among them are minority communities that are demonized as being unpatriotic. This is followed by people with any kind of liberal opinion, those who are opposed to the hold of superstition on society, Marxists—actual or imagined, women who assert their equality with men, homosexuals, transgenders, and such like.

Communalism has had a long gestation period of almost a century. Much effort has gone into furthering it in the last few years in various ways. Of these the more obvious are frequent communal riots that sometimes take on the dimension of a genocide; the communalizing of those in government services, reflected in the debate as to whether they have encouraged violence and rioting; the marginalizing of liberal opinion in the media to accommodate communal views; the consistency with which sessions of Parliament are subjected to filibustering so that legislation supporting democratic and secular norms is stymied; and the regularity with which books on history and religion written from a secular perspective have been banned or sought to be banned. These are not incidental or accidental activities. In the late twentieth century, the kind of history that supported communal interpretations of the past had to confront a new history challenging communal constructions. The challenge has strengthened the new explorations in history, and despite the banning of books and the personal attacks on those pursuing these explorations, this history is now a presence to be reckoned with.

The notion of majority and minority communities is quite alien to the Indian past and was created after the British Indian Censuses when the population was counted according to religious affiliations. These were in some ways inapplicable to most people since affiliation to a formal religion such as Hinduism or Islam, was reflected largely only in the small elite groups of society, whereas the vast numbers of the others were rather vague about which religion they conformed to. In effect therefore, the actual majority community of largely the middle to lower castes was that of people who had mixed religions or who easily crossed from one to the others as and when they chose to; and the minority communities were those small elite upper-caste groups that returned themselves as followers of one of the two formal religions. Continuing with the concepts of the predetermined majority and minority communities is contrary to both democratic and to secular functioning.

When religion becomes the basis of political mobilization then it has to be properly organized for the purpose. A spectrum of militia-type organizations work towards policing society and the simplest method is through terrorizing people. We have known the Muslim National Guards of the Muslim League, the Bajrang Dal of the Sangh Parivar, the Khaqsars and the RSS both modelled on the Fascisti of Italy, and various others attached to other religious groups, such as the more recent Babbar Khalsa and the variety of senas whose name betrays their function. They determine the contents of the religious message, which is religious fundamentalism of their own making, with a heavy political content, and hold it to be in conformity with the 'tradition'. The appeal is also through the claim that they are teaching the true, supposedly indigenous history of the religion, community and country, as only they know it. The disturbing element in all this is the degree to which the more unsavoury ideas of such organizations have permeated the Indian middle-class. When the guard is down and people speak freely, it is not unusual to hear racist, sexist and communal remarks surfacing in conversations from those seemingly modern in their thinking. The combination of the three is not accidental. Such remarks are not only believed to be true, but are justified by being described as the received wisdom from ancient times.

Religion in India as I have tried to show in some of the essays has been closely tied to caste. Intolerance in the Indian past has been expressed more consistently and to a greater degree through caste than through differentiation in religion, although this changed with the redefinition of the social function of religion in the last two centuries. Religious intolerance was not excluded, neither in the pre-Islamic period nor when Islam was part of the Indian scene. But the far more severe intolerance was that of caste and the exclusion of large categories of people of all religions who were treated as outcastes and untouchables. Secularism therefore does not only concern religion but also requires the devaluation of caste. The co-existence of religions alone, even if all religions are treated as equal, is not sufficient since unequal access to rights and resources is essential to caste. There was in the past greater tolerance among the lower castes since their religious and social boundaries were blurred, as compared to the upper castes whose religious loyalties were more clearly defined. Popular religion in the past was less text-based, more oral and in some ways different in practice from that of the upper castes. Tolerance declines where lower castes get to be organized in imitation of the upper castes as is happening in many places today. It is not accidental that the destruction of the Babri Masjid in 1992, was followed by a decade that witnessed communal riots in many places, including Bombay in 1992-93, the genocide in Gujarat in 2002, having been preceded by the one in Delhi in 1984.

The 1990s also saw an attempt at a form of affirmative action on the demands of the Dalit component of Indian society with the implementation of the report of the Mandal Commission. But even with the best will in the world this is only a partial and temporary solution. The problem requires a different and permanent solution that can be put into action alongside reservations to ease out the latter eventually. Without that there will continue to be resentment among the upper castes when a Dalit group does well and lifts itself out of its previous oppression. There is also some resentment but of a different kind among those Dalits who have not had the opportunity to qualify for the benefits of reservations, or Dalits of non-Hindu religions who should, but do not get the same benefits.

The quotas in education were increased at the tertiary level without the necessary infrastructure of teachers and libraries. This has created immense problems for a system that cannot cope with sudden large increases. The end result is likely to be a lowering in standards all round, unless far greater attention is given to radically improve primary and secondary education since that is the foundation for the tertiary and provide teachers and libraries for all levels. This means open access for every child to quality schooling, but every government since Independence has done relatively little for school education and has enlarged the more glamorous tertiary education and IITs and IIMs. The middle class looks after its own interests and the rest have to fend for themselves. Or could it be that parties in power are somewhat fearful of an educated electorate?

The more permanent solution is of course to build towards equal opportunities for all citizens and provide the basic essentials of such citizenship—by providing free and equal access to water from wells and public supplies without the stigma of causing pollution; through education, providing primary and secondary education in well-managed schools located in less privileged areas of villages and towns instead of in the upper-caste sections; through health centres and generic medicines; by increasing employment; by breaking down the ghettoization of castes in villages and small towns; by giving access to police protection, and by making justice available to all citizens easily and speedily. These are the minimum requirements of a democratic system. We have postponed providing these requirements by doling out snippets here and there, such as quotas in education and government jobs and temporary employment schemes. However much the policy of reservation may have helped for the moment, it is not for all time. It is likely to collapse when a range of caste groups—high and low—demand reservations. It seems paradoxical for instance, that some Rajputs and some other groups who have throughout their history claimed upper caste status are now wanting to be listed as low caste in order to avail of benefits intended for those of low status. Reservation becomes a handy excuse for not improving the workplace and merely blaming inefficiency on the quota system. The many pitfalls would have been avoided had there been reservations for economically underprivileged people, cutting across stratifications of caste and religion. And this simple change can even now be effected.

As for the Scheduled Tribes, little has been done administratively to draw them into a shared history, or to understand what their pattern of living is about, or to meaningfully improve their quality of life. The contestation with the state in parts of northeastern India goes back half a century. In central India they are pawns in a game that involves a triangular contest between the state, the Naxals and the corporates, each with their own agenda. The common intention seems to be the exploitation of the tribal societies and their resources. Inevitably a few tribal leaders are now also joining in and playing out their own politics. There is little of the ethics of secular democracy in this four-cornered combat.

Attitudes towards what are called 'tribal societies' require rethinking if the situation is not to be potentially explosive. Colonial thinking made a distinction between two groups: the civilized were literate, had a formal religion and lived within territorial boundaries and were superior; the primitive had none of these features, were scattered in the Indian forests and were inferior. Another layer of prejudice came with caste Hindus projecting themselves as members of the superior Aryan race with the rest being inferior. The Aryan race, and its counterpart—the Dravidian race—may be historically non-existent as races, but discrimination is deeply embedded in many Indians. Descriptions of many forest dwelling tribes in Sanskrit texts emphasize their alienness and physical differences. Misunderstanding the past can lead to dangerous attitudes in the present. Not using racial categories, which are anyway defunct, would be a change for the better. What makes these attitudes potentially explosive is that since caste and formal religions are traditionally absent in tribal societies they tend to be more liberated than caste societies. Formal religion has come to them through Christian missionary enterprise which, given the lack of standards in most state schools, often makes those from Christian mission schools somewhat better educated than, say, a student from a village government school in a non-tribal area. Upon moving to cities for employment they are viewed as culturally and physically different, as competitors, and are subjected to racial prejudice. In the race for votes, which is seen as a game of numbers, attempts are being made to 'convert' some tribal groups into Hindus. Since conversion was not associated with Hinduism, the problem being that of assigning the appropriate caste, the conversions of recent times are based on new ways of including those who were erstwhile regarded as mleccha.

Even if these communities represent a different way of life from the caste Hindu or the Muslim, they are nevertheless, equal citizens. Such a right would be for them a change from their earlier contact with mainstream society, via the exploitation of the landowner and the trader, a historical experience that has not been eroded from their lives. And now there is the threat from those that wish to mine their lands. When the corporates move into mining their hills and buying up their lands for a pittance, no tribal is ever asked to explain his grievance before a TV camera, so that the middle-class might just catch a glimpse of what he is experiencing. When the court of law declares pre-marital sex to be immoral and bans it what understanding will there be of the tribal institution of the ghotul, where among some tribal societies young men and women spend time together and discover whom they want to marry. Mainstream feminist movements perhaps need more familiarity with such societies, if only to ascertain how their women perceive themselves, and whether they have greater freedom than most women in caste-bound societies.

A concern with a different dimension is that of changing the Indian mindset in the matter of treating women as equal citizens. This has just about begun at levels other than those of a section of the elite. Again, it is not snippets of concessions via various Bills that will be the movers and shakers of this change. It will have to be a fundamental change in the laws of the land. Additionally, the hierarchy enshrined in caste and extended to gender might explain the existing mindset.

Patriarchy is dependent on caste that allows a control over women through rules of marriage and defines a social code in which women have a distinctly subordinate status. We are witnessing extreme expressions of this control as for example in the activities of the khap panchayats where the men of the caste determine what a woman can or cannot do. This goes against the tenets of a democratic society. And in all castes the major control is exercised through determining who can marry whom. The control is tightened by the fact that women cannot inherit property or wealth from the family, leave alone daughters inheriting equal shares with sons. This leaves the daughter, wife, widow, dependent on father, husband, son, as is stipulated in the code of Manu. She has no economic base to fall back on. The contradiction lies in the fact that in India today, and in theory, a woman can be educated for any profession she chooses and marry a man of her choice. This happens among a very small percentage of women but is not the general pattern. Such changes do take a long time to become established in a society, but they can be helped along by legislation and by the enforcing of such legislation. Disallowing any kind of ban from any source on inter-caste marriages, and stringently opposing dowry by replacing it with a law of equal inheritance for all children, would go a long way towards hastening the freedom of women to lead freer lives. This does mean changes in family structures, although such changes have been known in various parts of India in the past where customary law was entirely the opposite of the Code of Manu. Where we have precedents for alternate systems that gave certain privileges to women, these should at least be brought to the forefront.

The problem in part lies with our insistence that we know what our tradition is and must act according to it. But before we quote tradition we should ask the question as to whose tradition we are observing—which caste, which class, which religious sect, which region. However much we may try and universalize past observances, there were also well-defined and accepted variants. In drawing on tradition we should respect and understand the variants, otherwise we are merely inventing a new and rather emaciated 'tradition' and insisting on its antiquity. Many groups of Indians living outside India are doing this and claiming to be more Hindu or Sikh or Muslim than those living in India.

Those that attack liberal thinking insist on their particular reading of a text or its interpretations in such a determined way that scholars who disagree with them—and most do—are targeted on the internet. This is done through lengthy 'exposures' of their supposed ignorance. They are described with a battery of vituperative expletives as being not only incompetent but also anti-Hindu or -Muslim or -Sikh—whichever religion applies. This is frequently accompanied by threats of violence and physical assault. Some of us have been living with this since the 1990s. It simmers or boils up as the occasion demands, but one is assured of an immediate abusive reaction to anything that one mentions in lectures or writes about in publications.

The repetition of the same hollow arguments makes all this predictably boring. There are some subjects that they cannot shake off. The hardy perennials like 'the Aryans' are brought up whether one has spoken about them or not. Arguing with people who make it a point of not reading what one writes makes it difficult to even get a discussion going.

One's objection is not to what is supposed to be criticism and the pathetic level of the criticism, but the fact that this kind of thinking among some groups of NRIs is being imitated by the more vacuous sections of the middle-class for whom the NRI pattern of living is what they take as their role model. Much of the criticism stems from the idea that those who make rational enquiries of the past are in effect offending religious sensibilities. This offense is not met with debate but with threats. What they are unaware of is that this has not been the rule even in the intellectual culture of early India and what they take to be their tradition. The accepted procedure for arguing was stating the views of the proponent, then responding to them, subsequent to which there could be degrees of agreement or disagreement. Every argument was met with a counter-argument, not with abuse and threats. It was an intellectual culture where debate and discussion reached sophisticated heights. By comparison, it does seem utterly petty to come down to personal abuse.

And in this day and age to go through the legal procedure of seeking to ban a book is a job for the unemployed to pass time. Banning a book ensures a striking increase in its readership, an increase registered both on the internet and in the boom of pirated publications of the book available with every street vendor. A wide readership is after all what most authors would be happy with. Those who do not read demand the banning of books. Those who read publish their counter arguments so that the debate can continue. The argument is that no one has the right to raise awkward questions about religion and if this is done then those who follow that religion have the right to silence the person. There is no question of responding to what is described as an offensive argument by producing arguments to counter it. One only has to think of the array of books that have been unilaterally banned in recent times. We shall soon compete with the Papal Index.

We assume that our current definition of 'tradition' has been the accepted one for all time. Often enough we are unable to recognize that what we refer to as heritage and tradition is actually of recent vintage. Every generation invents its traditions and claims them as ancient. That which we do not accept today, we describe as 'feudal' or 'medieval', that makes them an inevitable heritage from the past. We can blame it on the past. This may be so up to a point, but it is more a refusal to come to terms with the negative aspects of the present day that we have not been able to expunge. The claim, and the authority that such a claim brings, bestows respectability on the crudest of customs. The subordination of women cannot be dismissed merely by calling it a 'feudal' attitude as it is the reality of contemporary Indian life, and a reflection of how we accommodate such attitudes by glossing them as traditional. The texts of the past make it evident that pre-modern India allowed the exploration of ideas and activities within broader limits than are often taken as the norm today, in some spheres of life.

British Victorian attitudes for example, were not what commanded the sexual mores of Indian society.

Heritage is again something that we select from the past to suit our present needs. Platitudes abound, repeating what was said a century ago, with little attempt to inquire whether in the light of new knowledge they still hold. India continues to be described as a civilization conditioned by tolerance and non-violence, despite the existence of untouchability almost throughout its history, and the regular and unending campaigns between its many kingdoms. The Mauryan king Ashoka is today the icon of a ruler who upheld the values of non-violence and religious tolerance, and his propagation of the mutual respect of all sects is often equated with secularism. These we are told continued even after his demise. Yet the irony is that he is remembered in Brahmanical sources as only a name in a lengthy list of rulers of early India, with nothing said about his policies. This was largely because he was a patron of the heterodoxy—in this case Buddhism—and it is the Buddhist sources that describe him as a much respected patron. But Buddhism was silenced in India by the late first millennium. Even if Ashoka's policies were indirectly known in the first millennium AD, as some scholars have recently argued, he was relatively unknown in the second millennium AD. Historical records of pre-modern India had their ideological loyalties. Thus, Brahmanical representations of the past avoided mention of those who were patrons of what the brahmanas regarded as the heterodoxy, and the Buddhists gave space to their own patrons. So for a substantial part of Indian history Ashoka was ignored. In fact he was rediscovered in the nineteenth century with the decipherment of the brahmi script that resulted in a reading of his edicts. His then iconic status was such that it became a virtual rite of passage for historians of ancient India to write a monograph on Ashoka—myself not excluded!

The other iconic figure for similar reasons is the Mughal emperor, Akbar. He again spoke of the co-existence of religions rather than of religion being one among other categories of statecraft. But such an idea would have been alien to state systems of pre-modern times. The period of Islamic rule is popularly described—in conformity with Hindutva views on history—as a period of foreign rule. This is a truly a-historical statement considering that: the later Mughals had more than a casual Rajput ancestry; immigrants from neighbouring countries in medieval times settled permanently in India; the civil and military administrative structure was manned by the 'indigenous' peoples both Hindu and Muslim; the vast majority of Muslims were local converts; and above all, economic wealth was ploughed back into land and enterprise in India. This is virtually the reverse of the experience of colonialism in India. In historical terms British colonialism was the only period of foreign rule, since the British did not live in India and took its wealth back to Britain to finance other activities, leaving the colony economically impoverished.

I have touched on two kinds of pasts. One is the past that has passed into the historical landscape and which has been drawn upon in highly selective ways, to validate the present. The other is the recent past, the almost-present, which has done the selecting from the earlier past and positioned it in the present. Both processes have been attempts at forging new identities associated with contemporary times. To make the connection I have discussed a few features linked to the interface of the past and the present. The ongoing changes in the present are moving us through a transition. We have the choice of appropriating the pattern of the predetermined modernity, but if we choose differently we may attain a modernity of a different kind, which draws on secular humanism. We do have a choice and we can still make it.

The implication of the past as present requires recognition of the integration of the one with the other, but also the distinctive difference in the societies of earlier times and of our times. Cultural sensitivity lies in tracing the integration, but also in being aware of the discontinuities. Only then can the present seek legitimacy from the past.

If I have focused on the more unseemly ways in which the past has been used I have done so to indicate its dangers and to reiterate that there is another more creative and nurturing alternative. Where this is apparent, the picture is not bleak. My purpose in referring to some problems of the present is also to make the point that if the past helps us to understand the present as it inevitably does, then such an understanding of the present should help us contemplate the future.

NOTES TO THE CHAPTERS

Various versions of these essays have been published previously so their original place of publication and date are given here. However, each has been revised and updated for this book.

Interpretations of Early Indian History: Based on talks given at many places.

Historical Perspectives of Nation-Building: The essay in its original form was first presented at a seminar on 'Nation-Building, Development Process and Communication: A Search for India's Renaissance' New Delhi December 1988, and published in *Mainstream* in January 1989.

Of Histories and Identities: This essay is based on the Neelam Tiruchelavam Lecture delivered in Colombo in 2010.

In Defence of History: This essay is based on a lecture given at Thiruvananthapuram on 2 March 2002 when historians were being systematically attacked by the then government.

Writing History Textbooks: A Memoir: Based on an article published in *The History Workshop Journal*, 2009

Glimpses of a Possible History from Below: Early India: A version was published in the January 1984 issue of *Seminar* under the title, 'Continuous Beginnings'. This essay was based on my Presidential Address to the Indian History Congress held at Burdwan in 1983.

Communalism: A Historical Perspective: The ideas in this essay were first put forth in an article I wrote for *Seminar* in January 1987 entitled 'Historical Realities'.

Religion and the Secularizing of Indian Society: This essay is based on a talk given at Columbia University, March 2007.

Syndicated Hinduism: This essay was originally published as 'Syndicated Moksha' in *Seminar* in 1985. It was revised for publication in G.D. Sontheimer and H. Kulke (eds.), *Hinduism Reconsidered*, Delhi 1997.

Which of us are Aryans?: This essay was first published in *Seminar* in December 1989.

Dating the Epics: This essay, which was first published in *Seminar* in January 1976.

The Epic of the Bharatas: This essay first appeared in *Seminar* in April 2010.

The Ramayana Syndrome: The ideas in this essay were first expressed in an article I wrote for *Seminar* in January 1989.

In Defence of the Variant: This essay first appeared *Seminar* in January 1994.

Historical Memory without History: This essay was first published in 2007 in the *Economic and Political Weekly*.

The Many Narratives of Somanatha: A version of this essay was delivered as the Umashankar Joshi Memorial Lecture, in Ahmedabad, on 29 December 2012.

Women in the Indian Past: This essay is based on a talk given in Chennai 2012 for the Indian Women's Association and on an essay published in Devaki Jain (ed.) *Indian Women*, Delhi 2014

Becoming a *Sati*—The Problematic Widow: An earlier version of this essay was published in *Seminar*, February 1988, 'In History'.

Rape within a cycle of violence: This essay is adapted from a talk given for the Centre for Policy Analysis in New Delhi, in February 2013

BIBLIOGRAPHY

I have not included footnotes to the statements made in these essays, but the evidence used is referred to in the academic books that I have published. Those readers who would like to consult these may do so in the following of my books:

Aśoka and the Decline of the Mauryas, Oxford University Press, London/Delhi, 1961/2013

Ancient Indian Social History: Some Interpretations, Orient Longman, Delhi, 1978/2010

From Lineage to State, Oxford University Press, Delhi, 1984/2011

History and Beyond, Oxford University Press, Delhi, 2000/2012

Time as a Metaphor of History: Early India, Oxford University Press, Delhi, 1996/2011

Sakuntala: Texts, Readings, Histories, Kali for Women, Delhi, 1999/2010

Cultural Pasts, Oxford University Press, Delhi, 2000/2010

Somanatha: The Many Voices of a History, Viking/Penguin India, 2004/2008

The Aryan: Recasting Constructs, Three Essays, Delhi, 2008/2011

Readings in Early Indian History, Oxford University Press, Delhi, 2013

The Past Before Us: Historical Traditions of Early North India, Permanent Black, Ranikhet/Harvard University Press, 2013

[The first date refers to the initial date of publication and the second date to the last impression]

INDEX